When Hell Froze Over

The Secret War Between the United States and Russia in 1918

iBooks

Habent Sua Fata Libelli

iBooks

Manhanset House
Shelter Island Hts., New York 11965-0342
Tel: 212-427-7139
bricktower@aol.com • www.ibooksinc.com

Library of Congress Cataloging-in-Publication Data

When Hell Froze Over,
The Secret War Between the United States and Russia in 1918
Halliday, E. M. p. cm.

1. Non-Fiction—History—Russia, 1918 2. Non-Fiction—Military History—
World War I
Non-Fiction, I. Title.

978-1-59687-430-5, Trade Paper

February 2015

Second Printing

When Hell Froze Over

The Secret War Between the United States and Russia in 1918

E. M. HALLIDAY

AMERICAN PARTICIPATION in ARCHANGEL FORCE WINTER 1918.

CONTENTS

INTRODUCTION 9

1 TOULGAS 15

2 WHAT IT WAS ALL ABOUT 27

3 DOUGHBOYS TO THE RESCUE 45

4 THE DRIVE FOR THE TRANS-SIBERIAN 65

5 IRONSIDE TAKES OVER 87

6 ONCE MORE UNTO THE BREACH 109

7 THE WAY IT WAS 127

8 THE SNOWS OF NIJNI GORA 143

9 THE RETREAT FROM SHENKURSK 159

10 GALA ARCHANGEL 167

11 A CRUEL DILEMMA 183

12 SPRING-A LITTLE LATE THAT YEAR 199

13 THE END OF SOMETHING 221

AFTERWORD 235

NOTES 245

BIBLIOGRAPHY 253

Murmansk

of Bothnia

Kem

Archangel

Isinki

Vyborg

Petrograd

Reval

Narva

Vologda

Rybinsk

Pskov

Kostroma

Riga

Yaroslavl

River Dvina

Nizhni-Novgorod

Sviazhsk

Kazan

ilna

Moscow

Murom

Minsk

Mogilev

Tula

st-Litovsk

Gomel

Tambov

Volga

Sama

Kursk

E. M. Halliday was born and raised in Brooklyn, New York, and attended Columbia University and the University of Michigan (where he got a Ph.D. in literature with a dissertation on the novels of Ernest Hemingway).

During World War II he was an enlisted reporter for Army newspapers and a field correspondent for *Yank*, the Army magazine. From 1946 to 1962 he taught literature and history at the University of Michigan, the University of Chicago and North Carolina State. In 1951-1952 he was a Fulbright scholar in France. From 1963 to 1979 he was a senior editor with the history magazine, *American Heritage*.

The author of many magazine and journal articles, he has also written the young adult history *Russia in Revolution, John Berryman and the Thirties* (a memoir of his long friendship with the poet) and has a book on Thomas Jefferson, *Understanding Thomas Jefferson*, forthcoming from HarperCollins in the fall of 2000. He lives in New York City with a word processor and a cat.

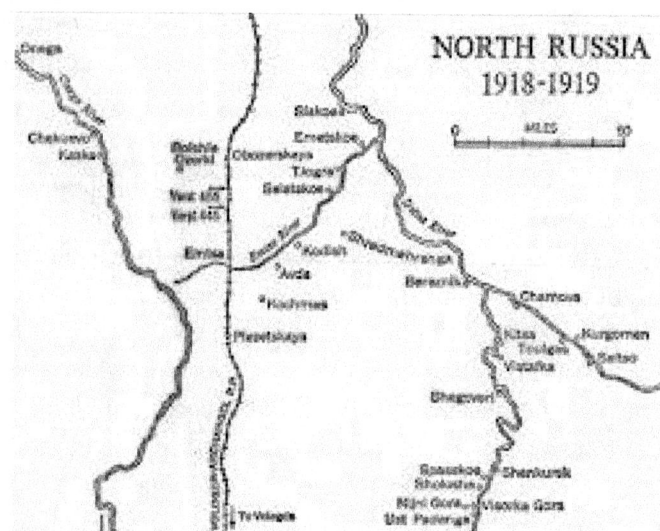

NORTH RUSSIA
1918-1919

Introduction

by E. M. Halliday

On December 31, 1991, across the enormous expanse of Russia, all flags of the Union of Soviet Socialist Republics were officially taken down. The daring experiment of ruling many millions of people in widely different societies under a communist central government, begun by the Bolshevik revolution in November, 1917, had come to an end.

One thing that was quite constant during those seventy-four years, as most Americans have been aware, was mutual suspicion and hostility between the USSR and the USA. It did fluctuate to some extent, reaching a lull during World War II as the two nations joined forces to defeat Nazi Germany, but at times rising to a terrifying pitch, with both sides threatening to use nuclear ballistic missiles capable of destroying not only each other, but in effect the entire fabric of world civilization. The world waited in awful suspense in October, 1962, when Soviet ships carrying long-range missiles for installation in Cuba were ordered by Nikita Khrushchev to turn back only after President Kennedy announced that if one missile were launched against America from Cuba, American missiles would retaliate immediately and massively against the USSR.

Many citizens of both superpowers have wondered about the basic cause of American-Russian hostility, usually concluding that it derived from the inevitable conflict between the capitalistic and Marxist economic systems, and their consequent political differences. There was truth in this; but historically there was a particular root cause that few had ever heard of.

What was Nikita Khrushchev talking about, puzzled Americans asked, when during a visit to the USA in 1959 he said: "We remember the grim days when American soldiers went to our soil, headed by their generals, to help the White Guard ... strangle the new revolution.... . Never have any of our soldiers been on American soil, but your soldiers were on Russian soil. These are the facts."

This book is an attempt to give a clear account and explanation of those facts.

The American Expedition to North Russia in 1918-1919 has been oddly neglected by professional historians, with the result that most US citizens, including even the best educated and well-read, have been unaware of its existence. Partly this has been because it got under way in the closing weeks of the Great War (now usually called World War I), and like a side show at a circus where they are already striking the tent, it drew little attention.

Besides that there was the confusion and obscurity surrounding it with regard to its purpose, especially in Washington and among the American troops who were involved: they literally had no idea what they were being sent to do. Even President Woodrow Wilson, as will be seen, was in a spin of uncertainty as to whether he should or should not authorize the expedition, and the British leadership—for it was to be an Allied operation, including British and French soldiers, but with British officers in all the top command positions-offered little clarification.

Without further enlightenment, five thousand American doughboys found themselves, early in September of 1918, after a long, slow trip from England through the icy waters of the Arctic Ocean, disembarking at the Russian port of Archangel-and more than half of them no sooner ashore than they were, with astonishment, packed off to "the front" to fight "the Bolos"-which was to say units of the Soviet Red Army. The operation thus turned out to be, willy-nilly and right from the start, and invasion of Soviet territory.

Although I believe the significance of the expedition goes far beyond its physical magnitude, I have tried to avoid building it into something bigger than it actually was. In terms of the number of soldiers engaged and the number of casualties, the campaign in North Russia was a relatively minor affair. The rate of casualties there was somewhat lower than it was for American troops in France during World War I; yet the conditions under which the fighting took place were often far more severe-they were, in fact, fantastic, with winter temperatures even at noon often thirty or forty degrees below zero.

As for the long-term impact of the invasion on Soviet-American relations it can be said that no full understanding of the

Cold War is possible without taking into account what happened in North Russia in 1918-19. It got things off to a bad start, to say the least, and-as Khruschev demonstrated forty years later-it was never forgotten by the Communists.

This book is not intended as an academic work, and such paraphernalia as appendixes and exact source references are missing. I have, however, made a continuous effort to be as accurate as possible. Readers curious about the evidence for a factual statement will usually find a clue to its source in the discursive notes, arranged by chapter numbers, at the end of the book.

As for interpretations and judgments, although no excuses are offered for those I have made, I have not tried to answer the big question: whether the Allied intervention in North Russia should never have been launched at all, or whether it should have been pursued on a large enough scale and effectively enough to overthrow the communist government. I leave it to the reader to decide.

Although it has now been forty years since the first publication of this book-under the title *The Ignorant Armies*-I still recall with thanks the help I got in my research from many sources, particularly the staff of the World War I Branch of the National Archives, and the staffs of the libraries of Duke University and North Carolina State University. I will always be grateful to the many veterans of the expedition whom I interviewed in Michigan, for sharing their memories, especially the generous contributions of the late Hugh D. McPhail and the late Harry H. Mead. (As I write this, in the year 2000, I realize with sadness that with little doubt *all* of the veterans of the combat in North Russia, both American and Soviet, are now gone-many of them for so long that the words "the late" are hardly appropriate. *Sic transit ...*)

I am happy to say, however, that my editor at Harper & Brothers, M. S. (Buzz) Wyeth, who helped me tremendously in organizing the first edition, is still very much alive and well. Nor can the constant help and encouragement from my very wonderful wife, Beverley Cline Halliday, ever be forgotten, though it has been twenty-five years since I last saw her lovely face.

E. M. Halliday, *New York, NY*

And we are here as on a darkling plain
Swept with confused alarms of struggle and flight,
Where ignorant armies clash by night.

-Matthew Arnold
"Dover Beach"

CHAPTER 1

TOULGAS

AS THE LAST SHOTS of World War I echoed into silence in France on the morning of November 11, 1918, an American army captain named Robert Boyd was leading his troops in desperate battle in the heart of North Russia nearly two thousand miles to the east. The enemy was the Red army of Soviet Russia.

Neither Boyd nor the three hundred American infantrymen under his command had heard anything about the end of the war with Germany, but there is no reason to think it would have made any difference to them at the moment. Supported by another three hundred troops, including a company of Royal Scots and a few Canadians, they were under heavy attack by more than a thousand Soviet infantry. The village of Toulgas, where the Allies were barricaded in log blockhouses and peasant dwellings, was practically surrounded: only to the east, across the two-mile width of the Dvina River, were they free of Bolshevik rifle fire. But from the river, whenever the Soviet infantry fell back into the cover of the enclosing forest, Soviet gunboats blasted the Allied position with high-explosive shells. Escape that way was out of the question; and to the north, in the direction of the Allied base nearly two hundred miles away at Archangel, the route was blocked by six hundred Russian riflemen who, circling through the forest from the south, had suddenly attacked Toulgas in the rear. There appeared to be no prospect of Allied reinforcements. To answer the Soviet heavy artillery, the Allies had only two three-inch pieces manned by fifty-seven men of the Canadian Expeditionary Force: they had soon found the Bolshevik guns beyond their range. The situation looked hopeless, and the American and British soldiers eyed their bayonets thoughtfully whenever a lull came in the onslaught. It seemed quite likely that most of them would die with bayonets in their hands.

The Russian attack from the rear had come as a complete surprise. Increased Soviet patrol activity had been noticed in the area south of Toulgas beginning on November 7, the first anniversary of the Bolshevik revolution. To the north, however, where the lines of communication led fifty miles back to the Allied supply base of Bereznik, it appeared unlikely that there was any danger. The Allies held the forest trail and the Dvina River all the way from Toulgas north to Archangel, and the movement of large forces except by these two routes was thought to be out of the question by the British general, R. G. Finlayson, who inspected the Toulgas position on November 10. Although there had been some freezing weather, the pine forests were still swampy and treacherous underfoot, and this, added to the thick underbrush, made Touglas look safe from the north.

The erratic weather-freezing by night and thawing by day-had also fooled the Americans and British into a sense of false security with regard to the Communist* artillery. Earlier in the fall British gunboats had held their own on the Dvina; but with the first deep frost they had hastily made for Archangel for fear of being frozen in. The Soviet gunboats, in like manner, had retreated up river (that is, southward) to their base at Kotlas. Now in November, however, the river had thawed sufficiently in the vicinity of Toulgas to allow navigation by the Soviet craft. Down the river, two hundred miles further north, ice jams still packed the stream, and the Allied boats were immobilized for the season. When the Soviet gunboats returned to Toulgas, therefore, they were unchallenged by Allied river craft and could sit a few miles off in the stream lofting 4.7 and 6-inch shells at will into the Toulgas defenses.

*The official name of the party was changed from Bolshevik to Communist in 1918. Since the latter designation has now become so familiar, the terms are used interchangeably in this book. Likewise, "Allies" was a term which, in strict parlance, did not include the United States; but common usage has made the distinction unnecessary here.

Captain Boyd and his men, most of whom were posted in blockhouses and billets in Toulgas itself, were unpleasantly interrupted

at breakfast on November 11, by rifle fire and shrill cries of *hourra!*
hourra! from attacking Bolshevik infantrymen, who had crept upon
the village from the south, through darkness and the heavy morning
mist. In that direction Lieutenant Harry M. Dennis was commanding
a squad of Americans in a cluster of buildings somewhat grandiosely
named Upper Toulgas, south of the main settlement by a few hundred
yards. He immediately realized that he had more on his hands than
the squad could manage, and withdrew quickly toward Boyd's position
by a wooden bridge crossing the deep, narrow stream, tributary to the
Dvina, which cut between Upper Toulgas and Toulgas. Just as Dennis
and his squad reached the central defenses, under a pelting fire from
the attacking Reds, Captain Boyd was dismayed to hear, directly from
his rear, the crash of hundreds of Soviet rifles, mingled with the vicious
chatter of machine guns. He realized that, contrary to all predictions,
the Bolsheviks had managed to move a powerful force of men through
the forest underbrush and mud, in a wide encirclement, to attack the
dozen or so buildings to the north known as Lower Toulgas. Two things
were particularly distressing about this realization. The little field
hospital of the Allied force, occupying a log hut in Lower Toulgas, had
been left with a number of Allied sick and wounded in it, virtually
unguarded; and between Lower Toulgas and the main village were
emplaced the two Canadian field pieces which constituted the only
artillery the little Allied force possessed. There was nothing to prevent
capture of the field hospital; and there were only the Canadian
artillerymen themselves, plus one American squad with a Lewis
machine gun, to prevent capture of the artillery.

At this juncture there occurred a short chain of fatal events
that largely determined the outcome of the whole battle. The
Bolsheviks attacking in the rear, under command of a giant of a man
named Melochofski, took a few crucial minutes to ransack the
buildings of Lower Toulgas, including the field hospital. Melochofski,
wearing a huge black fur hat that made him look like a very caricature
of Bolshevism, entered the hospital and ordered his soldiers to kill the
invalid British and Americans. Two things stopped him. The British
noncom medical officer had the presence of mind to realize that the
Reds were probably exhausted from their all-night trek through the
swampy forest: he hurriedly set before Melochofski the tastiest rations

available, and a large jug of rum. At this point the Allied soldiers were astonished when a young woman, wearing very much the same clothing as the Bolshevik fighters, strode into the room and announced that she would shoot the first Soviet soldier who offered to carry out Melochofski's order. This formidable female, whose face was as striking as her behavior, turned out to be the Bolshevik commander's mistress: she had chosen to follow him through mud, slush, dark of night, and rifle fire, rather than sit behind in a Soviet base up the river. Somewhat mollified by rum and love, Melochofski countermanded his order, and the lady was left to watch over the wounded while the Bolshevik leader went forth to continue the attack on Toulgas. He was to return a few hours later, mortally wounded, to die in the arms of this dauntless woman.

The ransacking of Lower Toulgas and the episode in the hospital had taken only a few minutes; but it was long enough for the Canadian artillerymen to make a vital-or lethal-adjustment. Their two field guns had been emplaced with the muzzles pointing south, ready to shoot over the heads of their companions in Toulgas at any Soviet forces attacking from that direction. Now, working in feverish haste, the Canadians dragged their guns out of the slits, swung them around 180 degrees, and loaded them with shrapnel fuse 5, a quick-bursting charge intended for work at very close range. Meanwhile they were covered by the American machine-gun squad, and by those of their own contingent who were not needed on the guns, firing and refiring their rifles as fast as they could reload.

Hundreds of Melochofski's men were now charging through the mud toward the artillery emplacement, shooting as they came. The Canadian gunners, who were old hands from the western front, touched off the first blast point-blank, and the shrapnel exploded squarely in the midst of the oncoming mass of Bolsheviks. Dismembered corpses and splattering pieces of torn flesh were blown in all directions, and the unwounded Soviet soldiers wavered. Urged on by their officers, they drove forward another few yards, only to meet head-on the second blast from the mouths of the Canadian guns. This mass slaughter was too much for the Bolsheviks, and those who could made for the protection of the forest or the buildings of Lower Toulgas; scores were left shattered and dead behind them. From the cover of the woods and buildings, however, the Soviet troops directed heavy rifle fire at the Canadian guns; and the company of Royal Scots coming out from the main defenses in Toulgas suffered severe casualties as they made their way to the support of the artillerymen.

While the surprise attack on Lower Toulgas had thus been successfully turned back, at least for the time being, Captain Boyd's infantrymen in the center village of Toulgas had experienced relatively little difficulty holding off the assault from the south. A strong log blockhouse had been built by the Americans at the north end of the wooden bridge across the stream, and the Soviet attackers were kept away from the approaches to the bridge by concentrated machine-gun fire. Apparently, moreover, the several hundred Bolsheviks attacking from the south were counting heavily on the surprise blow at the Allies' rear, and were thrown into consternation by the debacle created by the fast work of the Canadian artillery. Thus, as the shadows lengthened rapidly in the November afternoon, the desperate situation of the Allied force appeared to be temporarily stabilized. Shortly before the early subarctic nightfall, Lieutenant Dennis led a platoon of Americans out from the defenses into the edge of the forest and dislodged a string of Soviet snipers who had been causing trouble. About the same time, the Canadian gunners put a few carefully-aimed shells into the buildings of Lower Toulgas (excepting the hospital) where Bolshevik soldiers had taken cover; then, reversing their guns again, they sent two salvos whistling over Toulgas into the woods toward the south, to let both parts of the Soviet force know that the guns were intact, and ready for anything. Darkness fell on the first day of the battle of Toulgas.

Although a considerable number had been killed and wounded among the Royal Scots, Allied casualties had been light indeed compared to what the Russians had suffered. Close to a hundred Soviet soldiers lay dead on the now freezing ground, and it was certain that hundreds more had been seriously wounded. Still, there was little hope among the Allied officers of relief or escape from the Soviet encirclement. The Reds had cut the telegraph line to the city of Archangel, and the only possible communication with Allied headquarters there was by way of a small British outpost two miles across the cold Dvina on the eastern bank. But no reinforcement was expected from that quarter: Soviet gunboats could easily deny passage to the small Allied craft available.

About 11 P.M. Captain Boyd was momentarily cheered by the appearance of signal lights blinking from the British position. At the very least he anticipated a message of encouragement. "I was dumbfounded," he said later, "when the code message turned out to be a peremptory demand that I account immediately for six dozen Red Cross mufflers which had been sent to my outfit and not properly receipted for." Clearly, communication with Archangel was in sorry shape. In any case, however, Boyd knew that because of acute transportation problems, there was slim chance of help from other units of the twelve thousand Allied troops distributed sparsely across the huge expanse of the province of Archangel. Quite aside from the harassing fire of Soviet rifles, which continued to come sporadically all night from the edge of the forest, the American and British soldiers at Toulgas could find little inducement to easy sleep during the night of November 11, 1918, while all across the world millions of people were jubilantly celebrating the end of World War I.

If any of them got any sleep, it came abruptly to an end as the dim northern sun rose above the trees of the forest, across the Dvina River, the next morning. With the daylight appeared two Soviet gunboats mounting six-inch guns; and it soon became evident that others were concealed further up the river, around a bend. From these heavy guns, and from an entire battery of field howitzers which had been put ashore at Upper Toulgas and established at the rim of the forest, the Bolsheviks now began a bombardment of the Allied position unlike anything the Americans had ever seen before. Shells crashed into the village every few seconds, throwing great geysers of dirt and debris against the log walls of the houses and gouging the muddy streets with shellholes. Before long it was clear that the chosen bull's-eye of the target was the blockhouse which the Americans had constructed to guard the bridge. If the Bolsheviks could knock that out, their avenue of advance into Toulgas would be clear.

Inside the blockhouse, six doughboys under Sergeant Floyd A. Wallace waited grimly, while the Communist gunners bracketed in on their primitive fortress. For hours the Americans had almost incredible luck: shells struck all around the blockhouse, digging a veritable trench within a few yards of the building, but none hit directly. Twice, shells exploded in the middle of a huge straw pile outside the building, blasting a mass of straw and dirt into one of the loopholes of the blockhouse through which the Americans were sighting their machine guns on the bridge. They were unable to clear the hole from the inside, and Sergeant Wallace, with courage above and beyond the call of common sense, coolly ran out and removed the straw while a torrent of Soviet machine-gun slugs spattered around him. A few minutes later the same thing happened again; again Wallace calmly went outside to clear the hole. He succeeded, but this time a bullet caught him as he turned to re-enter the blockhouse, and he stumbled back inside with a serious wound.

At noon a Bolshevik shell landed squarely on the blockhouse. "It crumpled like paper," as Lieutenant John Cudahy of the American infantry company described it. Two of the men inside were killed instantly; the others were badly wounded. Except for Private Charles Bell, who elected to stick by his machine gun in the shattered remains of the blockhouse despite an ugly face gash that left him scarred for life, the injured crawled out of the wreckage and across to the house of the Toulgas parish priest, twenty yards away. The bridge was now in danger of being taken by the Soviet infantry, who had been crouching at the edge of the forest waiting for the knockout blow on the blockhouse. As they charged for the bridge, however, three Americans, carrying a Lewis gun and panniers of ammunition, rushed from a peasant dwelling across the road from the ruined blockhouse, heading for a ditch alongside the house of the priest. Falling flat every few yards, and proceeding by zigzag rushes in between, they made the cover of the ditch, set up the machine gun, and turned back the Soviet charge on the bridge with lethally accurate fire. They were happy to find themselves assisted, in this crisis, by crossfire from a second American machine gun which other doughboys had thoughtfully installed in the village church, directly across the road from the priest's house. So it was that the Bolshevik infantry found themselves repulsed in their rush on the bridge, despite the fact that the American blockhouse had been reduced to splinters.

Time and again, that November afternoon, the Soviet troops started for the crucial bridge; time and again they were driven back by American machine-gun and rifle fire, leaving a growing heap of fallen comrades in the clearing. When darkness fell, and the gunboats and Soviet field artillery relented their high-explosive pounding of Toulgas, the Allies were still in full possession of the central village, and had regained Lower Toulgas to boot. The tired Bolsheviks who had made the unsuccessful attack in the rear had shown little disposition to rush the muzzles of the Canadian three-inchers again, and skirmish patrols of Royal Scots had retaken such buildings of the lower village as still stood intact after the Canadian artillery probe earlier. The Scots found, to their utter amazement, that the British and American invalids in the little field hospital were doing very well, under the care of "Lady Olga," as the mistress of the late Melochofski had been dubbed by her new patients. As subsequent events proved, the lady's sympathy for her fellow human beings, individually or collectively, was a good deal stronger than her political persuasion: she later was sent to the Allied rear, and quite willingly served as a nurse in Allied hospitals for the duration of the campaign in North Russia. It is, regrettably, not clear what became of her when the Bolsheviks finally took over the region for good.

Although the Soviet artillery attack, which had dumped some fifteen hundred heavy shells into the Toulgas defenses on November 12 alone, eased off with nightfall, the menacing whine and thunderous detonation of the six-inchers continued at unpredictable intervals all night. When sleep came to the American and British defenders, it came from sheer exhaustion. "Men were hollow-eyed from weariness and so utterly tired that they were indifferent to the shrieking shells and all else," wrote one participant later. November 13 was much like November 12: repeated rushes on the bridge leading into town, repeatedly thrown back by withering machine-gun fire; and all the while high-explosive shells booming into Toulgas, often at the rate of one every fifteen seconds. Even for the western front, in World War I, that was considered heavy bombardment. It appeared that the end of the battle would be merely a question of time, since the Bolsheviks seemed to have an endless supply of ammunition for their guns, whereas Allied supplies, both in munitions and rations, were severely limited. (An ironic fact, grimly noted by the doughboys during the attack, was that shell fragments picked up in the village indicated their point of manufacture as the U.S.A. The huge supplies of munitions enjoyed by the Reds were derived largely from materiel shipped, on loan, to czarist Russia before the Communist revolution, while the Czar's armies were still fighting against Germany.) In this situation a council of war was held by the British and American officers, and it was decided that if indeed there was any hope at all, it lay not in defense, but in an outrageously daring counter-attack.

The young officer to whom the counter-attack was entrusted was Lieutenant John Cudahy, of Cudahy, Wisconsin, a scion of the famous meat-packing family. Thirty-one years old in 1918, he was a Harvard graduate with an LL.B. from the University of Wisconsin; he had practiced law for several years before joining the army in 1917. A sensitive man with a proud family tradition behind him, Cudahy now faced in North Russia a type of ordeal for which his civilian background had ill prepared him. The devilish bombardment and the fierce infantry struggle of the battle of Toulgas had seared his spirit with unforgettable images of horror, but he led his men into the attack with the determination that, in any event, none of them would be taken alive by the Bolsheviks.

The desperate Allied plan, formulated in the early-morning hours of November 14, was for the American infantry company to infiltrate into the fringe of the forest before daylight, and to launch a surprise assault on the Soviet force encamped in the woods on the flank of Upper Toulgas. In the pre-dawn mist the entire company gained the concealment of the dark forest without discovery. Cudahy spread his men in a wide arc, and proceeding stealthily, they managed nearly to surround a Bolshevik observation post and ammunition dump. Taking the sleepy Communists utterly unawares, the Americans killed several guards and sent the rest packing in the direction of the main Soviet bivouac. On Cudahy's orders, the doughboys made as much noise as possible in an effort to convey the idea that Allied reinforcements had just arrived. This ancient ruse succeeded beyond their wildest hopes. One of the first buildings captured turned out to be piled high with small-arms ammunition; and when this had quickly been set afire, the sound of the exploding cartridges evidently convinced the fleeing Communists that an entire Allied regiment was in pursuit. When the Americans came out of the woods to attack the log houses of Upper Toulgas, they found to their delight that the buildings had been abandoned by all but a few Soviet snipers; and these now threw down their rifles and rushed forward with shouts of "To varisch!"

This lucky turn of events was capped by a quirk of nature transforming what might have been only a temporary rout into a full-fledged retreat. The temperature had fallen sharply during the night, and now, with the thermometer close to zero, the broad waters of the Dvina began to freeze again. The Bolshevik gunboats headed upstream for Kotlas to avoid getting stuck; and without their artillery support the Red commanders decided that Toulgas was too tough a nut to crack. The remnants of the several hundred Bolsheviks who had made the enervating night march and beseiged Lower Toulgas from the north, on the first day of the battle, now had even more trouble getting back than they did making the forest circuit in the first place. Days later some of them, hopelessly lost in the trackless wastes of the great pine woods, stumbled into Russian villages behind the Allied line, starved and half crazy with cold and exhaustion. The bodies of many others, dead from wounds and freezing, were found later in the surrounding forest.

According to Bolshevik prisoners taken at the end of the battle for Toulgas, Trotsky himself directed the attack. It is not impossible, for this was during the period when the dynamic Red army commissar was traveling many hundreds of miles from day to day in his famous armored train, descending suddenly upon first one and then another of the many fronts where the Soviet armies were fighting against White Russians, Czechs, and sundry other enemies. He was said by the prisoners to have watched the battle from one of the river gunboats, and to have harangued the Bolshevik troops with an oration, celebrating the revolution's first birthday, in which he swore to drive the foreign invaders "beneath the ice of the White Sea."

If Trotsky was at Toulgas, he must have gone away thoroughly enraged with the outcome of the attack. Over three hundred of his soldiers, including several of his best commanders, were killed, and countless others wounded, while the Allies had only twenty-eight killed and about seventy wounded. What had promised to be a massacre of Americans and British had turned out to be a massacre of Bolsheviks.

Nominally, at least, they were Bolsheviks. Of the thirty-odd prisoners captured by the Americans at Toulgas, only one admitted, upon interrogation, any sympathy with the Communist cause; the rest claimed to have been forced into the Red army, or to have joined as an alternative to starvation. With due allowance for their desire to please their captors, both claims seemed to have some plausibility. A certain reluctance to fight had been observed by the Americans among many of the Soviet soldiers during the battle; and the destitute condition of most of the surrounding peasant villages suggested that food was indeed scarce in Russia. Undoubtedly one of Trotsky's shrewdest strokes was his iron insistence that the Red army came first at mealtime: the daily ration for his men in North Russia was fourteen ounces of meat, more than a pound of bread, and tea, sugar, and tobacco. The prisoners were, nevertheless, a beggarly-looking lot, dressed in nondescript peasant clothes rather than uniforms: high leather or felt boots, curled fur hats of dirty gray, shapeless *moujik* (peasant) blouses or tunics.

At the same time, the very fact that an ordinary peasant was indistinguishable from a Bolshevik soldier when neither was carrying a rifle made the Allies perhaps overly suspicious of some of the local natives. The fate of Upper Toulgas illustrates the point. Several of the peasant houses there had served as Russian sniper nests during the fighting, and the British and American officers decided that these constituted a strategic threat to the main garrison. According to rumor the householders had been altogether too hospitable to their Bolshevik guests, and with this as justification the inhabitants were given three hours to evacuate before their homes were burned to the ground.

Snow was falling as the Allied soldiers set fire to the simple log dwellings. The *moujiks* had cleared out all their valued possessions: rude furniture, piles of clothing, and crates of utensils were gathered together outside the line of houses, ready for transportation. The women and children sobbed hysterically as their homes roared into flame, while the bearded men looked on mutely, their faces masks of incomprehension and resignation. The townspeople had already endured their share of suffering during the attack: the home of the parish priest, for example, which had served the Americans as a refuge at one point in the battle, was finally struck by shells, and the priest and his two children killed. Cudahy, who surveyed the local damage after the struggle, reported that the crown of the priest's head was "cut clean as with a scalpel, exposing the naked brains."

The Battle of Armistice Day, as the Americans learned rather bitterly to refer to it, was over; and against all expectations it was a victory for the Allies. When the lines of communication back to Archangel had been reestablished, the Americans, British, and Canadians heard the big news of the armistice on the western front; and for a few days and weeks they hoped that their ordeal in North Russia was close to its end. Through all the puzzling obscurity about the reasons for their fighting the Bolsheviks, they had clung to one idea: it was supposed to have some intimate connection with the war against Germany, for which they had been cheerfully drafted a year earlier. But now? They were completely baffled.

"Week follows week," Cudahy wrote, "and November goes by, and December, and no word comes from the War Department.... No word comes and the soldier is left to think that he has been abandoned by his country and left to rot on the barren snow wastes of Arctic Russia."

What was it all about?

CHAPTER 2

WHAT IT WAS ALL ABOUT

THE BATTLE OF TOULGAS, although it occurred just as the curtain fell on the First World War, was one of the earlier episodes in the history of American warfare against the Communists in North Russia. It was not until the summer of 1919 that the survivors of the expedition got back to their homes in Michigan and Wisconsin; they had spent over six months in combat in a world nominally at peace. It is doubtful that many of them have ever again passed so strange a period of six months in all their lives.

From the outset, a curious aura of obscurity hung over the expedition to North Russia. The Great War was lurching to a close by the time the main body of American troops landed at Archangel on September 5 and 6, 1918; and this in itself tended to shove the intervention out of the headlines. Moreover, the Supreme War Council at Versailles, which authorized the Archangel expedition, had not been anxious to publicize it, since it was meant to be as far as possible a surprise maneuver. In the United States, especially, the public was remarkably ignorant about the expedition and its purposes, to some extent because of President Wilson's painful indecision as to whether American troops should be permitted to take part. When he finally authorized American participation, it was several weeks before his decision was released to the press-and even then it was not clear just what he had decided.

After the armistice, whatever was going on in North Russia was of small interest to most Americans. The war was over; millions of American doughboys were on their way home; the situation in Russia seemed hopelessly confused; and hardly anyone except the immediate families of the five thousand young men who were sent to Archangel bothered to be concerned. In any case it would have seemed unbelievable to most people that three battalions of American infantry were fighting a deadly little war against the Soviet army in the wilds of the North Russian forests, under conditions far worse than those that had confronted most American troops in France.

The camouflage which has covered the expedition in more recent years has been compounded equally of ignorance and concealment. Even some professional historians have known little about the North Russia affair, frequently confusing it with the American intervention at Vladivostok, with which it had only the most theoretical connection. (This confusion was also rampant during the campaign itself. One American officer is said to have been ordered by the War Department to report to Archangel by way of Vladivostok-which would have been the neatest trick of the war.) Efforts have also been made in some quarters to push into oblivion a chapter of United States military and diplomatic history which was far from glorious, and which became embarrassing in view of our joint effort with the Soviet Union, during World War II, to defeat Nazi Germany. It has been more convenient to perpetuate the myth that the U.S.S.R. is one major power with which the U.S.A. has never been in armed conflict.

Both aspects of the camouflage were epitomized by the experience of an enlisted U.S. army reporter for *Yank*, the service magazine, at Fort Sill, Oklahoma, in 1943. He had heard that the new post engineer, a colonel, had served in North Russia in his youth. Looking for a feature story, the reporter, whose acquaintance with the expedition was rather less than rudimentary, queried the colonel at some length in an interview. He was told that the purpose of the intervention had been to guard great stores of war materiel which had been sent to Archangel by the Allies while Russia was still fighting Germany. Asked whether there had been any fighting between American and Soviet troops, the colonel became uneasy and evasive, but finally conceded that "we did lob a few shells at them." The reporter then repaired to the post library, where the *Encyclopedia Britannica* threw no light whatsoever on the point, and the *Columbia Encyclopedia* stated flatly that "American forces did not participate in the fighting between the Allies and the Bolsheviks." Thoroughly derailed, the reporter concluded that the story was not of great interest after all, and went off to write a feature article about the WAC's. Several years later he stumbled upon the statistic that of the five thousand American soldiers who took part in the North Russia campaign, very nearly half were casualties, from one cause or another, before the expedition was over.

The decision to permit United States collaboration in the Allied intervention of Russia, which in 1958 became the subject of a five-hundred-page study by Mr. George F. Kennan,* was certainly one of the most agonizing choices ever made by President Woodrow Wilson. Briefly, the background of Wilson's ambivalence was as follows.

*The Decision to Intervene, Princeton University Press, 1958.

Less than four months after the Bolshevik revolution in Russia on November 7, 1917, Lenin and Trotsky, under pressure from a multitude of grievous problems, had officially eliminated the Russian war against Germany by the Treaty of Brest-Litovsk. Although this handed Germany about one-fourth of Russia's population and arable land, and about three-fourths of her current industrial potential in terms of coal and iron, it freed the Bolshevik leaders to concentrate on economic and political chaos at home, including an enthusiastic civil war driven against them on two sides by White Russian forces.

From the point of view of the Allies, the treaty was a disaster. Germany was clearly building up for a gigantic spring offensive on the western front, and the prospect of unleashed German divisions from the Russian front moving west to bolster that offensive caused profound anxiety in the halls of the Allied Supreme War Council at Versailles. Actually, as Winston Churchill estimated later, a million German soldiers had already been moved from east to west before the treaty was signed, thus spectacularly violating one provision of an armistice agreement reached between the Bolsheviks and the Germans in December, 1917.

The dreaded German offensive, which began promptly on March 21, 1918, was bad enough to vindicate the gloom of the most pessimistic prophets. It soon swept across France almost to the coast, and General Pershing reported to the U.S. War Department that defeat stared the Allies in the face. As yet, only one American division was at the front, but the mobilization of American fighting strength was now in full gear. Back on the Potomac, Wilson anxiously pondered the problem that agitated the Allied leaders in France: how to divert enough German strength to relieve the terrible pressure in the west.

There was plenty of ready advice from the French and British. In June, Churchill (then British Minister of Munitions) gave the Imperial War Cabinet a pithy formula for victory: "Above all things reconstitute the fighting front in the East…. If we cannot…. no end can be discerned to the war. Vain will be all the sacrifices of the peoples and the armies…. We must not take 'No' for an answer either from America or from Japan."

But to Wilson, the problem looked by no means that clear-cut. Reconstituting the eastern front unquestionably meant some kind of intervention in Russia; and the sixth of his famous fourteen points for an effective peace had demanded, unequivocally, "the evacuation of all Russian territory" by foreign forces. Moreover, being an extremely idealistic man, Wilson had felt from the first a sincere empathy for the people of Russia in their overthrow of czarist tyranny; and he was still hopeful that the Bolshevik revolution of November, 1917, might turn out in the long run to be compatible with a democratic government that would bring liberty and justice to every Russian citizen. To the first All-Russian Congress of Soviets, which met in Moscow in March, 1918, Wilson had sent a warm message declaring that the United States "will avail itself of every opportunity to secure for Russia once more complete sovereignty and independence in her own affairs…. The whole heart of the people of the United States is with the people of Russia in the attempt to free themselves forever from autocratic government and become masters of their own fate."

Military pressures, however, could not be denied. By April some fifty thousand German troops were in Finland, apparently threatening to invade Russia (despite the Treaty of Brest-Litovsk) in the very area considered by the British as the best place to begin the crucial reconstruction of the eastern front. This was at Murmansk, a recently developed ice-free port on the Arctic Ocean straight north of Petrograd, and connected with that city by a new railroad. Together the railroad and the port formed Russia's only open route to the rest of the world, by sea, during the winter months. It was also believed that the Germans were considering Murmansk as an ideal spot for a new submarine base from which to harass Allied shipping in northern waters, and that they had an eye on millions of dollars' worth of Allied war materiel supposedly stored in warehouses and dumps at Archangel.

So important to Russia was the Murmansk-Archangel area that Lenin and Trostsky even seemed willing to invite Allied aid in holding it against the Germans, and for months Allied diplomats hoped that the desired intervention might take place with the blessing of the two Russian leaders. In retrospect, however, it is clear that the Communists had no intention of allowing the Allies more than a toe in the door. What they were after was survival for the Soviet government, and a proletarian revolution for the rest of the world. If they could play off against each other the chief capitalistic combatants in the world struggle, and at the same time lessen a threat to Soviet rule in Russia, they would tolerate whatever seemed to be required. At the moment, limited intervention by the Allies at Murmansk seemed to be required, and Britain and France were only too anxious to co-operate.

For these reasons British and French warships entered the Murmansk harbor in April, 1918, and a few troops were landed. In May these vessels were followed by the United States cruiser *Olympia*, rather reluctantly dispatched by President Wilson to demonstrate Allied unity. (It was the same ship from whose venerable bridge Commodore Dewey had made the celebrated remark, "You may fire when you are ready, Gridley," in Manila Bay on May 1, 1898.) But as the spring wore on, the Bolshevik and the Allied conceptions of this intervention and its aims steadily diverged. For the Allies, the overriding purpose was the re-creation of the eastern front against Germany; for the Soviets, the purpose was self-preservation. And self-preservation meant for them concomitant goals quite contrary to those of the Allies: the *avoidance* of renewed conflict with Germany, and at the same time the avoidance of any large-scale interference from Allied forces.

An open split was inevitable, and as it developed it assumed a curious form. Under the impressive shadow of the Allied naval guns in the harbor, the Murmansk Regional Soviet leaned more and more toward the view taken by the Allies, so that by June, when the first large contingent of British troops was landed, these local representatives of Lenin and Trotsky were decidedly at odds with their masters. They constituted, in fact, a splinter government; and this the Bolshevik leaders were not hesitant to point out. Lenin telegraphed the Murmansk Soviet on June 25 and 26: "[England's] direct intention is … overthrowing the Workmen's and Peasants' power … If you still refuse to understand Soviet policy equally hostile to the English and to the Germans, blame it on yourself." To this the head of the Murmansk Soviet replied, in what must have been one of the more petulant telegrams ever sent Lenin by a Communist underling: "It is all very well for you to talk that way, sitting there in Moscow." Moscow thereupon declared the leaders of the Murmansk Soviet to be outlaws and enemies of the proletariat. This did not prevent them from concluding a formal agreement with the Allies, on July 6, 1918, authorizing Allied intervention in accordance with the announced aim of resurrecting the eastern front against Germany.

In Washington, Wilson had been sweating out the situation almost literally: it was a very hot July. (He himself wrote that he had been "sweating blood" over the problem.) Gradually, he had been pushed toward approving of Allied intervention in Russia; but his inclination to resist was such that a veritable minuet of vacillation had ensued.

The problem was complicated by the fact that, quite aside from intervention at the northern ports of Murmansk and Archangel, there appeared to be good reason, from the point of view of American interests, for intervention at Vladivostok, two thousand miles across Siberia on the Pacific coast. The important factor there was some disturbing activity on the part of the Japanese: they had landed an undetermined number of troops, and showed signs of being more concerned with their own territorial expansion in Siberia and Manchuria than with the war aims of the Allies.

Simultaneously there existed another reason impelling Wilson toward intervention in the Far East. Over forty thousand Czechoslovakian soldiers, most of them once a unit of the Imperial

Russian Army fighting against Germany, were strung out along the great Trans-Siberian Railroad in a state of frustrated suspense. They had begun to move eastward toward Vladivostok in March, 1918, with the idea of shipping from there to the western front, to renew the struggle. At first the Soviet authorities had agreed to this plan; but they insisted on certain stipulations, including the virtual disarming of the Czech corps before entrainment. The Czechs proved exceedingly reluctant to give up their arms, and a number of violent clashes between them and Soviet authorities resulted ultimately in a general Czech uprising against the Bolsheviks, at the end of May. By late June they were in control of long segments of the railroad, including the eastern terminal at Vladivostok; but their units had been split into two groups disconnected from each other by Bolshevik forces. Wilson felt that his own intense sympathy for the heroic efforts of the Czech corps reflected that of the American people as a whole, and he saw in the Czech predicament a final justification for intervention in Russia. American troops could legitimately enter Siberia to help the Czechs consolidate their lines of communication and, presumably, to help them ship from Vladivostok back to the western front to resume the war against Germany.

The decision on North Russia was more difficult for Wilson, but certainly was eased by his commitment to intervention in Siberia. Intervention was intervention, and if large numbers of American troops were to be landed in Vladivostok, it seemed consistent to allow them also to land at Murmansk or Archangel. As a result of the agreement between the Murmansk Soviet and the Allies on July 6, Wilson was able to believe that some part of the Russian people were not averse to Allied intervention in North Russia. Moreover, he had recently been assured that General Foch, top Allied commander in Europe, approved the diversion of some American troops from France to Murmansk and Archangel from a purely military standpoint. There also had been talk of transporting at least part of the Czech corps to France by way of Archangel instead of Vladivostok; and this would of course be facilitated if the port were in Allied hands.

An additional factor in Wilson's decision about North Russia was the advice of his diplomatic representatives. Although probably few Presidents have habitually paid less attention to the recommendations of their ambassadors, Wilson must have given some weight to the fact that David R. Francis, United States ambassador to Russia, was an ardent advocate of intervention. Since this gentleman was to play an important role in the sequence of events, in the late summer and early fall of 1918, that led to the death of young Americans on Russian soil, his background and character deserve notice.

Francis was not only our last ambassador to czarist Russia, but in a sense our first to the Soviet Union-if allowance is made for the fact that the United States did not officially recognize the Soviet regime until 1933. A former mayor of St. Louis, governor of Missouri, Secretary of the Interior (under Cleveland), and wealthy businessman, he went as ambassador to Russia in 1916, at the age of sixty-five. He and his staff were Petrograd during the "ten days that shook the world" in November, 1917, observing the Communist, revolution from the safety of the American embassy. In February, 1918, he removed the embassy staff to the old town of Vologda, about 250 miles north of Moscow, there to await developments in the confused relations between the new Soviet government and his own.

The representatives of England, France, and Italy followed him to Vologda, and in a battered but respectable building which had been a kind of country club Francis held forth as dean of the diplomatic corps throughout the spring and early summer. Joseph Noulens, the French ambassador, has left a droll if slightly malicious sketch of Francis at this period, presiding over meetings of his colleagues "without ceasing for an instant to masticate his chewing gum." As Noulens recalled it, Francis would frequently demonstrate his "ballistic prowess" by spitting unerringly into a cuspidor placed seven or eight feet away, the jet passing in front of the Italian ambassador who, despite the impeccability of the American's trajectory, hastily drew in his legs each time.

With his personal background as a rugged American individualist, Francis could hardly have been expected, in his late sixties, to take a favorable view of the Communist revolution. His communiques to the Department of State as well as his memoirs bear witness to the profound contempt which he increasingly felt for the Bolsheviks and their theory of government. As the year 1918 grew older, he more frequently referred to Bolshevism as "a foul monster," or employed some other pungent epithet not calculated to please anyone of the Communist persuasion. By July he was optimistically convinced that the Soviet government was, to all intents and purposes, "a corpse." What was to prove important for the fate of the American troops consigned to North Russia was the slant this conviction gave to Francis' view of Allied intervention, plus a certain truculence which was not the least salient trait in a predominantly egoistic character. From late spring of 1918 onward, the ambassador consistently urged Allied intervention at Archangel; and his tendency was to view it as a belligerent enterprise. He was persuaded, that is to say, that intervention ought to be in considerable force, and might well involve deep military penetration into Russian territory, co-operation with the Czech corps against the Red army, and even, with luck, a hastening of burial ceremonies for the Soviet regime itself. As future events at Archangel were to demonstrate, he never relinquished this view, but rather became steadily more confirmed and more vehement in its promotion.

Ironically enough, Ambassador Francis took his stand on intervention at Archangel directly against the advice of a subordinate diplomatic officer who was stationed there, and who might have been presumed to know something about relevant conditions. This was Felix Cole, the American consul at the northern port. A native of St. Louis, and a Harvard graduate, Cole went to Russia in 1913 and worked for a time in the automobile business; later he was connected with a publishing concern in Petrograd. Several years of residence brought him competence in the Russian language, as well as a Russian wife. With Russia's involvement in World War I, Cole offered his abilities to the U.S. Foreign Service; and from the summer of 1917 he had been in office at Archangel.

By the spring of 1918, with Allied intervention already accomplished at Murmansk and vigorously urged by Ambassador Francis for Archangel, Cole decided that he must express to his government his own view of the probable consequences, based on what he had learned about Russia. He therefore dispatched, on June 1, a long letter to the Secretary of State. It is a lucid and eloquent document, and although some of its starling foresight will only appear as we follow the actual developments of the North Russia campaign, it needs only to be quoted to show how sharply Cole's view of intervention in Russia differed from that of Francis:

> Sir: I have the honor to request your attention to the following considerations regarding intervention in Russia by the Allies.... . Intervention will begin on a small scale but with each step forward will grow in scope and in its demands for ships, men, money and materials.
>
> To hold Archangel a part of the Archangel-Vologda Railroad must be held. As the River Dvina diverges to the east from the railroad line a part of the river must be held.... . If the munitions evacuated toward the interior from Archangel are to be salved by force the railroad to and beyond Vologda must be held and the river to and beyond Kotlas. This means not the mere occupation of Archangel, but an expedition into the interior of Russia.... . Intervention can not reckon on active support from Russians. All the fight is out of Russia.... .
>
> The Socialist Revolutionists ... who now advocate intervention are discredited officeholders seeking to regain power. They were only able to "lead" the people when they advocated peace (no more fighting), anti-imperialism (an excuse to desert from the front), and socialism (an excuse to raise wages indefinitely or to steal land or property belonging to others-such is the ignorant peasant's understanding of it). The very men who now pray for our bayonets to restore them to power are the ones who did more than even the Bolsheviks to ruin the Russian front and the Allies' common cause in Russia.... .
>
> The Socialist Revolutionist ... "intellectuals" will never rule Russia. Their place is around the steaming samovar, not in the halls of government. Their invitation to enter Russia is not an invitation from the Russian people.... .
>
> Every foreign invasion that has gone deep into Russia has been swallowed up.... . If we intervene, going farther into Russia as we succeed, we shall be swallowed up.... .

Cole's letter was sent by ship, and took until July 19 to reach Washington-too late. Ambassador Francis, who received a copy at Vologda much earlier, might have wired Cole's misgivings to Washington; but of course nearly everything the consul at Archangel said irritated Francis, whose heart was set on early and violent intervention. So Cole's prophetic analysis was shoved aside, to find its place in history only when the abortive Allied invasion of Russia had long since been abandoned, and the chroniclers had begun to compile the official records of that ominous introduction to American-Soviet relations.

Meanwhile, in Washington, Wilson had finally taken the fatal step. On July 17, 1918, he officially put his stamp of consent on armed intervention in which Americans would share: three battalions of infantry and three companies of engineers were to be committed to the North Russia expedition. The night before Wilson reached his decision (to make a point of historical curiosity), Czar Nicholas II and his family had been shot by Bolsheviks in a cellar in Ekaterinburg, Russia. This had nothing to do with Wilson's action. But the highly disturbed state of the President's mind, with respect especially to the venture in North Russia, was strikingly revealed in an *aide-memoire* of the same date, July 17, setting forth America's official view of intervention in Russia.

"Military intervention there," Wilson wrote, "would add to the present sad confusion in Russia rather than cure it ... would be of no advantage in the prosecution of our main design, to win the war against Germany." The government of the United States, he went on, "cannot, therefore, take part in such intervention or sanction it in principle ... Military action is admissible in Russia, as the Government of the United States sees the circumstances, only to help the Czecho-Slovaks consolidate their forces and get into successful cooperation with their Slavic kinsmen and to steady any efforts at self-government or self-defense in which the Russians themselves may be willing to accept assistance. Whether from Vladivostok or from Murmansk and Archangel, the only legitimate object for which American or Allied troops can be employed ... is to guard military stores which may subsequently be needed by Russian forces and to render such aid as may be acceptable to the Russians in the organization of their own self-defense. The United States Government is not in a position, and has no expectation of being in a position, to take part in organized intervention in adequate force from either Vladivostok or Murmansk and Archangel ... it will feel at liberty to use the few troops it can spare only for the purposes here stated... ."

Several things are remarkable about this important document, which Wilson is said to have typed out himself without staff consultation or assistance. First of all, with respect to North Russia, it at least gave the appearance of denying the validity of what was, from the British and French point of view, the chief goal of the expedition to the northern ports: the re-establishment of a second front against Germany. Secondly, by some strange mental process approaching George Orwell's double-think, it denied that the landing of American troops in Russia (which Wilson had just authorized) would constitute, as a matter of fact, "military intervention." Thirdly, it nevertheless insisted that "military action" in Siberia was "admissible" to help the Czechs "consolidate their forces"; but it left uncertain just what the Czechs were expected to do *after* they had consolidated their forces. (In actuality, they were by this time in full-blown warfare against the Bolsheviks.) Finally, the document definitely seemed to anticipate conflict between the aims of the United States in Russia and those of the British and French, and to disassociate the United States government from action beyond the ambiguous yet insistent limitations set in advance by Wilson.

But despite the many explicit peculiarities of this *aide-memoire*, its most remarkable over-all feature lay in what it omitted entirely. Nowhere does Wilson openly recognize what was in truth the cardinal fact about the situation in Russia in the summer of 1918: that a vicious civil war was in progress between the Soviet forces and various White Russian groups, in addition to the Czechs. It would seem that the aftermath of the Bolshevik revolution had proved so distressing and baffling to Wilson that now he preferred almost to ignore it, or to pretend it did not exist, than to face up to the hard realities it imposed on American and Allied foreign policy. Mr. Kennan suggests that what was in Wilson's mind, when he avoided reference to the struggle with the Bolsheviks, was the fond hope that the mere arrival of American, Japanese, British, and French forces in Russia might touch off a "spontaneous, democratic action" which in the long run would bring the right kind of government to the Russian people without American troops having done anything that could be construed as interference in the internal political affairs of the country. In all of modern history there may never have been a fonder hope, more thoroughly doomed to disappointment.

As far as Murmansk and Archangel were concerned, it is hard to see how Wilson could have deceived himself into thinking that his conditions for American participation would really be honored by England and France, whose diplomatic representatives soon received copies of the July 17 *aide-memoire*. He knew, for one thing, that the Supreme War Council had decided on British command for the North Russia expedition, so that the five thousand troops making up the American contingent would be directly under British rather than American generals. What is more significant, he knew that the British view of the mission in North Russia was far different from his own pacific image thereof; in fact it drastically violated the terms he had laid down, just as much, and in the same way, as did Ambassador Francis' view. As early as July 3, Wilson had received through the Supreme War Council a British analysis of why the northern ports must be occupied; prominent among the reasons was the need for "bridgeheads into Russia from the north from which forces can eventually advance rapidly to the center of Russia."

Behind this demand lay two motives entertained by many of the French statesmen as well as the British. One of them was officially admitted; the other was officially concealed, although it was widely known to exist. The first was the desire to strike down through North Russia from Archangel to the Trans-Siberian Railroad, four hundred miles southward, and there effect a junction with the Czechs, who in the meantime were to have fought their way westward along that railroad until they reached at least as far as the city of Viatka. This would have posed a new and formidable Allied threat to Germany in the east. The second motive was the hope that this maneuver, or military events subsequent to it, might happily coincide with a complete overthrow of the Communist government, thus removing a nasty threat to world security and to civilization. Like Ambassador Francis, many prominent Allied leaders regarded the demise of the Soviet regime, in the midsummer of 1918, as not only highly desirable, but in all probability easy to bring about, since the Communist leaders were plagued by the most formidable economic, political, and military problems imaginable.

Quite obviously, none of this fitted in at all with Wilson's official statement of American policy in Russia. Yet even as he pronounced that policy he set in motion wheels that in less than two months were to bring American soldiers into deadly combat with the Soviet army when, under British orders, they proceeded to carry out the British-French plan for the intervention in North Russia. It was as strange and tragic a conglomeration of cross-purposes as twentieth-century diplomacy was ever to witness, and it may fairly be said to have set the pattern for forty years of troubled American-Soviet relations.

By the end of July, the stage was completely set for intervention at Archangel. Ambassador Francis, together with his staff and the diplomatic corps of Great Britain and France, had succeeded in outwitting the Soviet leaders, who had been trying to lure them back to Moscow. Instead, the special trains reserved for the Allied diplomats headed north from Vologda, directly to Archangel, on July 25. The northern port, however, was still in Bolshevik hands, and the representatives of the Allies therefore sailed, after some bickering with the Soviet authorities, for Kandalaksha, at the western end of the White Sea, which was held by the British. The Allied diplomats were well aware that an anti-Bolshevik *coup d'etat*, masterminded by British secret-service men, was about to take place at Archangel, and, as Francis wryly put it, "we felt that we would not want to be there when it occurred." They were to return to Archangel, as it happened, in less than two weeks.

At Murmansk, meanwhile, the actual execution of the invasion at Archangel had been entrusted to Major General F. C. Poole, of the British army. Although he so far had only fifteen hundred troops at his disposal, Poole decided to go ahead with the venture without waiting for reinforcements. A fleet of about a dozen vessels, including transports, cargo ships, and three warships, therefore sailed for Archangel on July 31, arriving at the outer harbor defenses of the city on August 1. These consisted mainly of a couple of batteries of six-inch guns on the island of Mudyug, about fifteen miles north of Archangel, on the outlying edge of the delta formed by the Dvina River's entrance into the White Sea. Under bombardment from the guns of the British light cruiser *Attentive*, and a few seaplanes launched from the deck of the British carrier *Nairana*, the Bolshevik batteries soon surrendered, having preserved their honor by landing one shell on the forward smokestack of the *Attentive*.

Efforts by Communist commanders to prevent further progress of the Allied convoy by sinking ships in the channel proved unsuccessful, and by late afternoon of August 2 the British and French vessels were entering the harbor of Archangel. In the meantime the anti-Bolshevik *coup d'etat* prearranged through British agents had been enormously successful in the city, so that when General Poole landed he found it under the control of a purportedly democratic, pro-Allied government.

Throughout this episode Consul Felix Cole, although he must have witnessed the Allied landing with decidedly mixed feelings, played the role of diplomatic representative in classic style. He had steadily pretended ignorance of Allied intentions during the days preceding the attack, assuring the local Red commander that he found the possibility of war between America and Russia inconceivable. On August 1, with news of the Allied armada's approach agitating the entire town, he stayed discreetly inside the consulate building. This, however, did not prevent him from being arrested by some men in uniform who claimed to be from Communist headquarters. They appeared suddenly at the consulate at 11 P.M., and Cole barely had time to burn the secret diplomatic codes before he was taken away. It turned out that his captors were actually adventurers whose object was a Bolshevik safe containing over four million rubles; they had wanted him for a possible hostage. Their scheme miscarried, however, and with the installation of the new government Cole was released.

The Bolsheviks had been frightened by the British seaplanes into believing that the invasion was on a very large scale, and had hastily departed for points south by the morning of August 2, making the local revolution against their regime a relatively easy and bloodless affair. The uprising was efficiently planned and executed by one G. E. Chaplin-no comedian, but a former czarist naval officer who had been in Archangel for some time masquerading as a British officer having something to do with the diplomatic corps. The leader of the new government, also by Allied prearrangement, was N. V. Chaikovsky, an old-time Russian revolutionary of the socialist stamp who had spent many years in exile, including several in Independence, Kansas, where he had unsuccessfully tried to establish a new religious cult.

A considerable portion of Archangel's hundred thousand inhabitants, as it turned out later, were Bolshevik in sentiment; but the city also contained thousands of rabid anti-Bolsheviks, and when the Allied leaders disembarked they were greeted by huge crowds of waving and cheering people. "The people simply went wild with joy to an extent almost beyond imagination," reported an American naval captain who came along with General Poole's staff. Felix Cole, however, noted significantly that the laboring class was "patently absent" from the crowds that met the newcomers.

No doubt the civilian jubilation contributed something to the boldness with which Poole proceeded to pursue the retreating Reds. It must be noted, however, that in any case he was an enthusiastic advocate of the British plan to drive down through Russia to the Trans-Siberian Railroad, to meet the Czech troops from Siberia. In addition, he was described by a fellow general as "one of the most confirmed optimists it has ever been my fortune to meet"; and he apparently considered the Red army to be no army at all, but a rabble of starving peasants and czarist deserters, herded unwillingly into battle by a parcel of maniacal revolutionaries who probably were in the pay of the Germans. He expected them to fly like quail before the onslaught of British, French, and American arms; and he expected the people of North Russia, whom he assumed to be mostly avid haters of the Bolshevik upstarts, to rally patriotically to the Allied caused by the thousand. Both of these expectations proved to be remarkably ill-founded; but Poole's opening gambit was premised on them, and the rest of the campaign took shape from his impetuous start.

While it was to be a little over a month before the contingent of five thousand American soldiers reached the docks of Archangel, it appears that the first fighting men of the Allied expedition to go into action against the Bolsheviks on land were, oddly enough, American sailors. Fifty of them, detached from the U.S. cruiser *Olympia*, had come along with Poole's forces in search of adventure after several months of boredom in Murmansk. They went ashore on the morning of August 3, just when the Bolsheviks who had retreated a few miles south of the city were beginning to show some signs of resistance. But counter-attack was soon discouraged by the British seaplanes, which flew down the railroad bombing and strafing the Soviet rear guard, while the *Attentive*, having moved a short way up the broad mouth of the Dvina, assisted with a few shells from her guns.

The bluejackets, however, were in no mood to be cheated of a chance at combat. Twenty-five of them, under command of a naval ensign, undertook an exploration of the railroad yards at Bakaritza, across the river from Archangel proper. The Bolsheviks had hastily put out of commission most of the locomotives that they were unable to take with them, but the sailors found one in reasonable working order. It was an old wood burner with a funnel-shaped smokestack, like most of the engines on the Archangel-Vologda line; but it moved. Hitching on a couple of flatcars, and mounting machine guns on the cars, they all piled aboard with their rifles, and were soon racing south down the railroad, hoping for a glimpse of the retreating Reds.

With the old locomotive burning wood at a furious rate, it was not long before they had the satisfaction of exchanging a few pot shots with the tail of the Soviet column, rattling southward behind another old engine at nearly the same speed. The young American crusaders covered about thirty miles down the line before a hotbox stopped them and gave the Bolsheviks a chance to burn a bridge against further pursuit. If the sailors had begun to imagine a quick and glorious trip to Vologda, or even Moscow, they were now painfully disillusioned: the Bolsheviks turned out to have plenty of guns and ammunition, and no reluctance whatever to use them against American commandos. A brisk rifle and machine-gun skirmish near the bridge resulted in a stalemate, with the naval ensign suffering a leg wound and thus presumably losing the first American blood ever shed in armed conflict with the Soviet army. The Bolsheviks showed no disposition to retreat further, and the sailors began to wonder with considerable interest how long it would be before some of General Poole's British or French soldiers arrived to support them.

Thus began America's first combat with Russia. It was less than three weeks after President Wilson had taken the final step to approve American participation in intervention. But the reality already was removed, by an infinitude that neither time nor distance could measure, from his vision of a friendly intervention that somehow would avoid intrusion in the internal affairs of Russia, and offer, as he put it, "only such aid as shall be acceptable to the Russian people in their endeavor to regain control of their own affairs, their own territory, and their own destiny."

CHAPTER 3

DOUGHBOYS TO THE RESCUE

IT IS VIRTUALLY A truism of military life, respectfully regarded by the United States Army, that the unexpected is what will probably happen. But the unexpected seldom bears as little resemblance to what might reasonably be anticipated as it did in the case of the 339th Infantry Regiment, recruited at Fort Custer, Michigan, in 1918. Made up almost entirely of Middle Western draftees, with reserve officers and "ninety-day-wonders" from the officer training camps in command of all the companies, the regiment trained with considerable enthusiasm for participation in the war against the hated Hun. When they embarked for England in the summer of 1918 as part of the 85th Division, it was with eager if somewhat nervous visions of chasing Germans across the fields of Flanders and France, somehow making the world "safe for democracy" as they went. Before the summer was over they were lost in the gloomy wastes of North Russia, fighting a strange enemy called "the Bolsheviks" for reasons that, to almost all of them, were totally obscure.

Early in August a rumor floated around the camp at Stoney Castle, England, where the regiment was awaiting orders for France, that something had gone awry. Lieutenant Harry H. Mead, of Company A, had bumped into an old college friend in London, Lowell Thomas. Thomas, who was just in from Paris as a war correspondent, had offered the tantalizing hint, picked up in the environs of the Supreme War Council, that the 339th was headed for "guard duty" somewhere in Russia. Before long the rumor got ominously concrete support. The Enfield rifles with which the Americans had trained were taken from them and replaced by long, old-fashioned-looking pieces that had been manufactured in the U.S. for export to the Imperial Russian Army. It was never made quite clear to the doughboys why this exchange was necessary, although the popular theory was that a large stock of ammunition for the Russian rifles would be ready and waiting in Russia. It is safe to say, in any case, that most of the infantrymen felt an unpleasant sense of insecurity with these strange weapons in their hands; and it was hardly eased when they found that the bolt actions often jammed, and that the range scales were calculated in Russian paces instead of yards. Many of them never got a chance to target these rifles before being obliged to fire them in defense of their lives against the Red Army.

The new weapons were accompanied by new winter outfits, British type, with long sheepskin-lined overcoats, fur hats, and Shackleton boots-specially designed by the famous Arctic explorer. The cold-weather clothing, of course, was stowed away for later use-much later, presumably. This was to cause some regret in the early fall, when many of the Yanks discovered that even in September the North Russian nights are far from warm. On top of everything else it was known that the regiment had been issued a thousand pairs of skis and five thousand pairs of snowshoes. Since a large part of the 339th consisted of Detroit and Milwaukee clerks, mechanics, and factory workers who barely knew one end of a ski from the other, the news of this exotic shipment caused some consternation in the ranks, although it undoubtedly imbued the regimental atmosphere with a certain sporting quality. There were even those who voiced the opinion that the 339th was heading for a lark.

By the last week in August all preparations had allegedly been made, and orders had been received to set sail for Murmansk. One battalion of the 310th Engineers, the 337th Field Hospital, and the 337th Ambulance Company were ordered to North Russia as service troops for the three combat battalions of the 339th Infantry Regiment. The total contingent numbered about forty-five hundred men, all under the command of Colonel George E. Stewart; another five hundred, also drawn from the 85th Division, were to come about a fortnight later as replacements. The troops boarded the British transports *Tydeus, Nagoya,* and *Somali,* at Newcastle-on-Tyne on August 27, heading up toward the Arctic Circle with appropriate zigzags for the confusion of lurking German submarines. For three days nothing much happened. The weather got noticeably colder, and some of the soldiers wished they had been allowed to wear overcoats, instead of stuffing them into the hold in barracks bags. On one of the ships the cook ran out of yeast, and there was grumbling about the lack of bread until someone in the galley remembered that potato stock could be used for leavening.

On the fourth day, influenza broke out viciously on both the *Nagoya* and the *Somali*. By the fifth day, every available bed in the sick bays was occupied, and hundreds of men were violently ill. "Congestion was so bad," reported one soldier, "that men with a temperature of only 101deg or 102deg were not put into the hospital but lay in their hammocks or on the decks." Meanwhile, to the consternation of the medical officers, it was found that someone had completely forgotten to put the usual supply of medicines aboard at Newcastle-on-Tyne. By the eighth day out, the slim quantities which a few of the officers happened to have in their personal possession were all gone, and there was nothing to do but sweat it out.

At this painful juncture Colonel Stewart received a surprising radiogram from Archangel. Instead of going first to Murmansk, ordered General Poole, the three troopships were to proceed directly to Archangel. Reason: British and French soldiers, and some American sailors, were in danger of annihilation from Bolshevik counterattacks, deep in the Russian interior. The immediate reaction of Colonel Stewart and his staff to this communication is not on record; but it may be assumed that there was a reasonable degree of shock. The mild theme of "guard duty in Russia" had begun to take on sinister overtones.

Since Stewart's orders from Washington specified only that he should report to General Poole, he promptly headed for Archangel despite the sorry condition of some five hundred of his troops. The three ships moved through the gray and gloomy mouth of the Dvina River on the cloudy morning of September 4,* and by late that afternoon were tied up at the quays of the curious northern port. Inquiries were made about hospitalization for the men down with influenza: General Poole's medical staff replied that no extra hospital facilities were ready. For two days and nights the sick soldiers remained on the troopships, while the American medical detachment frantically made emergency arrangements for their care somewhere ashore.

*Two days earlier Major General William S. Graves arrived at Vladivostok with the first contingent of what was eventually to be a force of nine thousand Americans intervening in Siberia. Unlike the Archangel intervention, this led to no organized combat with the Soviet army.

For the four thousand Americans who had so far escaped the flu, there was very little waiting. The 3rd Battalion of the 339th Infantry was ordered to pack full field equipment (minus overcoats), and to disembark on September 5 ready for immediate movement to the fighting front. Some of the men were in the first stages of influenza, and carried their heavy packs and rifles with difficulty; but they were no sooner off the ship than they were herded into a couple of troop trains-boxcars, that is-waiting on sidings in the dingy freight yard. It was chilly, and a steady rain dripped out of the lead-colored sky. The two antiquated locomotives worked up steam and pulled slowly out onto the tracks, moving straight south from the outskirts of Archangel into the forest of pines that hemmed the railroad on both sides. The 3d Battalion was on its way to battle with scarcely more than a glance at the strange metropolis that was to be the expedition's base of operations for the next nine months. Some of its members were soon to lie buried beneath Russian sod without seeing anything of it but the wharves and the seventeenth-century cathedral, near the waterfront, whose five high domes dominated Archangel. On one of the cathedral's outside walls, an enormous fresco in full color represented the Last Judgment.

The 2nd Battalion, meanwhile, had been marched off the troopships and ordered to a duty somewhat more in line with what had been looked for: patrolling the city itself. The 1st Battalion, however, was still aboard ship on the evening of September 5, having watched the 3rd disembark and entrain with a certain degree of envy. At least they were off ship and going into some kind of action. It was thus with a species of relief that the men of the 1st Battalion heard, before turning in for the night, that the next day they too would be on their way to the fighting front. They were a little surprised to learn, however, that the front they were destined for was by no means the same one, on the railroad, to which their friends in the 3rd Battalion had been dispatched. They were to proceed, instead, by river barges up the broad Dvina, to a point separated from the railroad by seventy-five or eighty miles of swamp, tundra, and forest. In full field array (again, however, minus overcoats), they were loaded onto a string of barges on the evening of September 6, and the slow and tedious trip up the river began. By this time the men were beginning to look back on the troopships almost with nostalgia. The barges, it seems, had been used for hauling coal, cattle, flax, and various other produce over a period of many years, and had gathered, as one soldier wrote, "an unbelievable amount of filth and dirt." Furthermore the holds, where the soldiers slept, were leaky. Dozens of new cases of influenza developed every day of the five-day trip, and several men died before the battalion put into shore at the town of Bereznik, 130 miles upstream, which had been chosen to become an advance base.

Now, less than a week after arriving in North Russia, the American contingent had already been deployed in a way that darkly foreshadowed the shape of the entire campaign. The 339th Infantry had been split into combat units cut off from each other by many miles of practically impassable terrain. The combat troops were connected to the main base at Archangel by severely attenuated supply lines, especially on the river: for quick communication on that front a single telegraph wire, frequently out of order, led back to General Poole's headquarters in the city. British officers were in top command everywhere; and from the beginning Colonel Stewart, nominal CO of the 339th, nearly disappeared from view as far as his men were concerned.

All of this was the more or less inevitable consequence of events that had occurred between August 2, when Poole's meager invasion force landed at Archangel, and September 4, when the American soldiers steamed into the harbor. Despite his lack of manpower, the "confirmed optimist" who had been placed in top command of the Allied forces in North Russia was ruddily determined to launch a thoroughly aggressive campaign. "I am quite cheerfully taking great risks," he cabled the War Office on August 12.

There is no indication that Poole ever understood the severe restrictions President Wilson had stipulated for the conduct of Allied intervention. Heartily pleased with the dash and spirit of the sailors from the *Olympia*, who had led the way down the railroad in pursuit of the Reds, he dispatched a company of French poilus to their aid as soon as the French had disembarked, during the first week of August.

They were part of the 21st Colonial Battalion, which had been trained for combat in the tropics. Muttering the special brand of profanity which is one of the notable by-products of French military life, they moved obediently but rather reluctantly into action. Already they had seen too much of the war, and they had little gusto for this strange affair in the North Russian forests under British command and against an enemy who had not yet been clearly identified. They arrived down the railroad, where the American sailors had been in dubious battle against far superior Bolshevik forces, soon enough to prevent a rout.

A look at his maps told General Poole that, aside from the railroad, there was only one means of penetration into Russia that might implement his bristling ambition to reach the Trans-Siberian Railroad and join forces with the Czech brigades coming (theoretically) from Siberia. Archangel Province was an area considerably larger than Texas, and much colder. Its 330,000 square miles consisted mostly of tundra and thick fir forests interspersed with huge swamps and bogs: wandering through this vast inhospitality, six large rivers flowed north to empty ice water into the White Sea. Along these rivers and their tributaries, the sparse peasant population of North Russia lived in primitive villages and towns. During the short arctic summers they doggedly worked the fertile land along the river banks, for crops to carry them through the ferocious arctic winters. In spring, summer, and fall, the only easy means of transportation across Archangel Province were the rivers, on the one hand, and the Archangel-Vologda Railroad, cutting straight south through the forests and swamps, on the other. For Poole's belligerent purposes, the great Dvina River, flowing northwest to Archangel, was clearly the only important complement to the railroad: navigable by fairly large boats and barges as far as Kotlas, nearly four hundred miles southeast, it was met there by another branch of the Trans-Siberian Railroad leading down to Viatka, two hundred miles further. It was at Viatka that Poole envisaged himself triumphantly greeting the leaders of the anti-Bolshevik Czechoslovakian troops, and reclaiming Russia for the Allied cause against Germany.

In retrospect it is difficult to regard General Poole's plan as anything but wildly quixotic. He was an experienced field officer-service in South Africa and in France; D.S.O., etc.-and although his staff was equipped neither with reliable detail maps nor other adequate intelligence of the geography involved in the campaign he had planned, he must have understood the general character of the natural obstacles he confronted. There was also reason to assume that he understood the essential points of the political situation, since he was supposed to be more or less expertly informed on Russian matters. In view of all this it is astonishing that he imagined it would be possible for his little expedition to succeed where Napoleon had failed-to march through the interior of Russia, fighting all the way, and achieve the objective before the dreaded Russian snows immobilized the entire venture. Nearly six hundred miles of rugged terrain separated Archangel from Viatka, and the first hard freeze could be expected before November.

Possibly Poole was carried away by the ease with which he took the city of Archangel, and by the apparent fright of the Communists as they fled southward along both avenues of escape, the railroad and the Dvina. At any rate he not only sent his French infantry down the railroad in the wake of the American bluejackets, but hurriedly organized a river force of British soldiers and sent them upstream in barges behind a couple of British gunboats. Most of these soldiers wore wound stripes from the western front, and were listed by the British army as "Category C-3"-that is, fit only for limited operations such as guard duty. This reflects the fact that in the British War Office there was some confusion as to whether the North Russia affair was to unfold according to the warlike vision of General Poole and Ambassador Francis, or according to the peaceful vision of President Wilson. It also explains why, when he received a regiment of able-bodied Americans as reinforcements, Poole saw to it that they were distributed among all the most dangerous spots, instead of being used as one unit. In the meantime his small detachment of second-hand soldiers did their best to carry out his aggressive orders as they proceeded up the Dvina. By the end of August they had run into severe Bolshevik opposition, and were sorely in need of the American aid that came a few days later.

While the 1st and 3rd Battalions were moving into positions as pawns on General Poole's fantastic North Russian chessboard, the

2nd Battalion was back at Archangel getting acquainted with the local urban scene. It was one that struck the boys from Michigan and Wisconsin as remarkably odd. Archangel in 1918 was a city of incongruities. There were substantial homes and public buildings, electric lights, and trolley cars-and boardwalks, mud streets, and open sewers that stank for blocks. In 1918, as today, the city was primarily a seaport, laid out in a crescent shape to conform to the shoreline of the Dvina's mouth, with the main thoroughfare-Troitsky Prospect-running parallel to the waterfront. It was, in fact, "mostly waterfront," as a member of the expedition recalled it later. "Hulks of boats and masts and cordage and docks and warehouses in the front, with muddy streets. Behind, many buildings, gray-weathered ones and white-painted ones topped with many chimneys, and towering here and there a smoke stack or graceful spire or dome with minarets." Above all, and visible from many miles away, towered the great cathedral, its blue-green domes spangled with golden stars. The square, massive public buildings-schools, government offices, the Archangel provincial capitol-were of brick or stone; most of the other structures in the city were of logs, occasionally covered with clapboards. At the southern horn of the city's crescent was Smolny, a warehouse district facing the rail yards at Bakaritza, across the broad and muddy Dvina. At the northern horn sat Solombala, an industrial suburb with "sawmills, shipyards, hospitals, seminary, and a hard reputation." Colonel Stewart found comfortable headquarters in a building formerly used as a technical institute, near the center of town, while the 2nd Battalion was installed at Smolny, the regimental supply company at Bakaritza, and the headquarters company at Solombala. The city was thus thoroughly covered by American troops in case of trouble; and trouble was not the last thing they expected.

It came immediately, in the form of a curtain raiser on the tragi-comic drama of Russian intrigue and politics which was to bemuse and stultify Archangel for an entire year before the struggle against Communism in North Russia was over. The clue to understanding this otherwise baffling series of events was the fact that the anti-Bolshevik forces in North Russia, as everywhere else, were by no means united at any level even barely below the surface. As we have seen, simultaneously with General Poole's landing at Archangel at the beginning of August, 1918, a group of Russian socialists, led by N. V. Chaikovsky, had proclaimed the formation of the "Supreme Administration of the Northern Region," a provisional government which was to exercise authority until the great day when the Communists would be defeated and the true revolution would be re-established. For Chaikovsky's group, the true revolution was, of course, that of March, 1917, which had set up a democratic regime under Kerensky. This had lasted only until November 7 of the same year, when the Bolsheviks took over Russia.

Chaikovsky, whose years in Kansas had failed to bring him down very close to earth, exhibited from the beginning a startling lack of realism. He resolutely refused to recognize that without intervention of the Allied forces his "Supreme Administration" could never have taken office at all, and he proceeded to issue complicated decrees to the people of Archangel as if General Poole was there merely as his guest, and the Bolsheviks were a million miles away. Moreover, he ignored the fact that the Russian officers who had brought off the insurrection against the Bolsheviks in Archangel, Commander Chaplin and his friends, were anything but enthusiastic about socialism and were actually, most of them, monarchists.

It would be hard to say who reacted less favorably to Chaikovsky's lofty statesmanship, Poole or Chaplin. If there was one area where Poole's famous optimism deserted him it was in anything smacking of left-wing politics; and Chaplin at the moment was interested chiefly in getting on with military action against the Bolsheviks to the south of the city without interference from men whom he regarded as theoretical dreamers. There were frequent clashes of authority from the start, for example a great bicker between Chaikovsky and Poole as to whether the red flag of the Social Democratic revolution should be permitted to wave beside the Russian national tricolor on the government buildings. Chaikovsky and his ministers thought it should, whereas Poole (and Chaplin too, for that matter) responded to the red flag like a bull to a matador's cape. The British general soon sent Chaikovsky a letter, couched in terms of elaborate diplomatic politeness, which so transparently veiled its peremptory nature as to be almost ridiculous: "... I have the honor to inform you that the city of Archangel as well as the whole province are at present undermartial law … I have given orders to the military not to permit any display of red flags in Archangel. I have the honor to beg you to comply with my orders. I remain your faithful servant." Cole, the American consul, was of the opinion that Poole's intransigence about the red flag alienated the factory workers of Archangel, and made them more susceptible to the Bolshevik propaganda line that the Allied intervention was imperialist interference. Poole also turned a very tough face to the inhabitants with regard to pro-Bolshevik propaganda, posting a notice that anyone convicted of spreading false rumors "calculated to provoke unrest or disturbance among the troops and population favorably disposed towards the Allies" would suffer the death penalty.

The clash between the British military and Chaikovsky's Socialist government continued throughout August, providing a scenario that in other circumstances might have made an excellent Gilbert-and-Sullivan opera. Chaikovsky, although piously proclaiming a return of "freedom of the press," tried to squeeze out of circulation an Archangel anti-socialist newspaper by cutting off its supply of newsprint; Poole promptly ordered that the supply should be resumed "upon the Commander-in-Chief's request." Poole asked for military courts for the trial of suspected Bolsheviks; Chaikovsky ordered military courts staffed by Russian officers, whereupon Poole insisted that the courts include representatives of the British, French, and American armies. To implement one of his pet projects, Poole authorized the recruitment of Russian volunteers in the "Slavo-British Legion" to fight the Reds in British uniforms, under British command; and the French hastily matched this by setting up a recruiting office for the French Foreign Legion. From the point of view of many White Russians this looked like an effort to prevent them from forming their own anti-Bolshevik army, and they complained bitterly to that effect.

Chaplin, exceedingly annoyed by all of this, and especially by what he considered Chaikovsky's bumbling futility, decided by the first week in September that he had had enough, and proceeded to take action on his own. Whatever else may be said of him, Chaplin was bold, dashing, and a born conspirator. In his middle thirties, handsomely dark, of slight but very lithe build, he presented a fittingly dramatic contrast to the aged Chaikovsky with his white beard, pale blue eyes, and vague, utopian air. Chaplin's maneuver had a beautiful simplicity: at midnight of September 5 he ordered out a detachment of Russian troops and had them surround the building where the ministers of the Supreme Administration shared a large apartment. Then an officer went in and arrested them. They were conducted, or abducted, to the steamer *Archangel Michael*, which promptly set forth and took them to Solovetsky Island, a day's journey out into the White Sea, where they were to be politely incarcerated in an old monastery. The question of General Poole's part in this remarkable stroke of politics is still a matter of dispute, but it appears that connivance is the best construction that can legitimately be put upon it. For one thing, the headquarters of British military intelligence was directly across the street from the building where Chaikovsky and his ministers lived; for another, Allied military patrols were notably absent from the neighborhood when Chaplin and his guards arrived. Poole had been informed that something was in the wind, and this absence of vigil suggests at least a comfortable complacency.

At any rate there is no indication that Poole lost any sleep on the night of September 5, or that he failed to eat breakfast the next morning upon being informed of Chaplin's *coup d'etat*. On the contrary, he blandly joined Chaplin and the Allied diplomatic representatives for a review of the newly-arrived American troops and received their salute before he bothered to tell the American ambassador what had happened. The American, French, and Italian ambassadors, and the British commissioner, it will be remembered, had passed through Archangel late in July, and had returned in August to establish their offices in the city. The elderly Francis, although he was in bad health, had taken an active interest in the affairs of the Russian government under Chaikovsky, and on the whole leaned toward that side in the series of conflicts with the British military. When the 2nd Battalion of the 339th Infantry had passed in review at ten o'clock on the morning of September 6, General Poole, standing beside Francis on the steps of the capitol building, turned and remarked, "There was a revolution here last night."

Francis, who when taken by surprise was inclined to eschew the language of diplomacy, answered: "The hell you say! Who pulled it off?" On being told that Chaplin had done it, Francis waved the Russian commander over to his side for verification. Chaplin evidently was feeling quite pleased with himself, and cheerfully admitted his part in the night's work. "The ministers were in General Poole's way," he explained in his excellent English, adding, "I see no use for any government here anyway."* As Francis recalled it later, his reply to Chaplin was: "I think this is the most flagrant usurpation of power I ever knew, and don't you circulate that proclamation that General Poole tells me you have written until I can see it, and show it to my colleagues."

*According to Chaplin's published memoirs, however, his real object in deposing Chaikovsky's government was to set up a Russian authority in Archangel which would not be easily pushed around either by Poole or by the Allied ambassadors.

It turned out, however, that many copies of Chaplin's proclamation, announcing the demise of Chaikovsky's government, had already been circulated, and the news had rapidly spread through Archangel and its suburbs. Unfortunately it was widely interpreted as a power move, with Allied support, to do away with democratic government and perhaps restore the monarchy; and this impression was actively pushed by two of Chaikovsky's ministers who, having escaped Chaplin by not being at home when the raid was made, promptly put out their own proclamation denouncing the *coup d'etat*. They even claimed that the Grand Duke Michael, brother of the murdered Czar, had arrived in Archangel and was ready to take over. (The Grand Duke had, in fact, been shot in Ekaterinburg on June 12, several weeks before the Czar and his immediate family were killed.) Since General Poole's management of affairs in the city had by now considerably cooled the enthusiasm shown by the middle-class inhabitants when he arrived, and since the laboring class had been suspicious of Allied intentions right from the start, things now began to assume an ugly look. Thousands of workmen and peasants from the outlying districts moved into the city, some of them armed, and an outbreak of civil war behind the Allied lines appeared to be a distinct possibility.

The American military role in this curious affair was ironic: quite by accident it gave the impression of American backing for the *coup d'etat*, and seriously damaged the otherwise favorable reaction of the Russian population to the arrival of United States troops a couple of days earlier. The simple fact that Chaplin's audacious *Putsch* was carried out so soon after the Americans tied up at the docks of Archangel gave color to the rumor that it was committed with American approval, and the parade of United States infantry at the very hour when news of Chaikovsky's abduction was flying through the city added, from the point of view of a majority of the citizens, insult to injury. With this was soon compounded a bizarre mistake that seemed to verify the theory of American power behind Chaplin; for when the city trolley motormen went on strike (along with most of the other metropolitan workers)in protest against the kidnapping of the government, someone on Poole's staff decided that the Americans could handle the emergency. Without consulting Colonel Stewart, an American major then complied with a telephone request from British headquarters by sending United States soldiers to operate the cars, together with guards for each trolley stop to prevent overcrowding or rioting: no fares were to be collected. Thus it was that within a few hours after the *coup d'etat*, motormen and conductors, sometime public servants in Detroit and Hamtramck, were running public transportation in Archangel, dressed in United States army uniforms instead of their immemorial blue. While they showed no hesitation about taking advantage of the free rides, the citizens of Archangel looked upon this service as strikebreaking, and consequently as aid to the anti-government (and allegedly monarchist) group who had started all the trouble.

At this point Ambassador Francis made up his mind to take action. As dean of the Allied diplomatic corps and official representative of the foreign nation best liked by most Russians in Archangel, he wielded a good deal of local prestige; even General Poole treated him with respect. Calling the British general and the other diplomats to his apartment at noon, Francis again deplored the abduction of Chaikovsky and his ministers, and suggested that Chaplin be arrested. Poole objected strenuously to this, saying that Chaplin was the only Allied hope of organizing a White Russian army against the Bolsheviks. He did, however, agree to the reinstallation of the kidnaped ministers, and a wireless message was accordingly sent out ordering their return as soon as they should arrive at Solovetsky Island. Meanwhile Chaplin was thoroughly scolded by Francis in the presence of the Allied diplomats, and an Allied proclamation was authorized announcing the imminent return of the Supreme Administration. Chaplin, as might have been expected, was not very docile on this occasion, replying to Francis that he was a Russian officer on Russian soil, and not an underling of President Wilson. Nevertheless, he took the precaution of temporarily moving his quarters to a British ship in Archangel harbor when the kidnaped ministers were returned to power: they could not touch him there.

By the morning of Saturday, September 7, the citizens of Archangel found telegraph poles and walls adorned with three proclamations: one from Chaplin, announcing the removal of the government; a second from two unremoved members of that government denouncing Chaplin; and a third from the Allied ambassadors reassuring the people that all was well. As Francis remarked, in one of his better understatements, "To say that the populace was confused inadequately expresses the condition of their minds."

The members of the 2nd Battalion, 339th Infantry, meanwhile, went about their somewhat puzzling duties with a very obscure notion as to just what was going on. It may well be that none of them was more confused than their regimental commanding officer, whose feelings must have resembled those of someone who has stumbled backstage during a rehearsal of the *Yeomen of the Guard* put on by a mental institution. Colonel Stewart was to be the target of intense criticism before the campaign in North Russia was well under way, but it must be admitted that whatever his failings, he received a most unpropitious introduction to his office and its responsibilities when he debarked at Archangel. He had been given no detailed instructions from the War Department about the purpose or limitations of the expedition. There is no evidence, for instance, that he had seen the terms of President Wilson's *aide-memoire*, which prohibited anything, for American troops, except guarding military stores and helping the Russians organize "their own self-defense." He had been told simply to report to Poole; and Poole had rushed more than half his regiment down the railroad and up the river to the fighting fronts before Stewart had the opportunity to consult with Ambassador Francis or anyone else.

The real irony of the American situation in North Russia in the fall of 1918, however, was that Ambassador Francis, for all his good intentions, his devotion to President Wilson, and his tireless concentration on his duties, took a view of Allied intervention that was just as contrary to Wilson's intentions as that of General Poole. There is thus a wryly comic aspect to the conversation, reported by Francis in his memoirs, which occurred when Stewart came to see the ambassador shortly after the arrival of the 339th Infantry. After pointing out that he was the official interpreter of United States policy in Russia, Francis said, "If I should tell you not to obey one of General Poole's orders what would you do?" Stewart answered, "I would obey you." What Francis undoubtedly had in mind was his friction with Poole over relations with Chaikovsky's government. If, instead, he had been thinking of the glaring contradiction between Poole's military actions against the Bolsheviks and President Wilson's insistence on peaceful intervention, the whole shape of Allied action at Archangel might have been different-possibly with far-reaching results in terms of later relations between the government of the Soviet Union and that of the United States. But Francis had long since been committed to Poole's bellicose campaign plans, and was enthusiastic about American participation in the attempt to fight down to the Trans-Siberian Railroad and join the Czechs. Even more than Poole, in fact, he was fervently anti-Communist, and made no bones about his hope that the Allied intervention would bring about a complete overthrow of the Bolshevik regime.

Apparently it never convincingly occurred to Francis that in permitting the use of American troops for an offensive action deep into the Russian interior he was violating the United States policy which, as he himself insisted, he was in Russia to interpret. It is true that he was not well-most of the time he was in Archangel he was confined to his apartment, and much of it he spent in bed-and there are some other extenuating circumstances. His communication with the State Department was badly hampered by fearful congestion of the cable lines, garbled messages, and the fact that from late in July until August 9 he was on the move from Vologda, to Archangel, to Kandalaksha and Murmansk, and finally back to Archangel. It appears that he did not see the State Department's summary of Wilson's *aide memoire*, which was dispatched on August 3, until August 22. By that time Poole had already committed troops, including the bluejackets from the *Olympia*, to his fantastic scheme of penetration to the Trans-Siberian; and we have seen that most of the American infantrymen who arrived on September 4 were instantly sent after them. (It seems, incidentally, that Francis did not discover until September 7, the day after the Chaplin *coup d'etat*, that two battalions of the 339th Infantry had already gone off to the fighting fronts; but there is no reason to think he would have objected had he been consulted.) Finally, there was the simple fact that General Poole had been designated Allied commander in chief of the expedition-yet, as Francis showed in the Chaplin episode, he was by no means afraid to challenge Poole, and considered that in the final analysis the position of American ambassador gave him the right to countermand orders from Poole to the ranking American military officer.

After all excuses have been considered, however, the key factor in Francis' failure to keep American soldiers from fighting, killing, and being killed by Soviet soldiers remains his unflagging conviction that Bolshevism must be destroyed. His feeling about this was so intense that it conditioned his interpretation of the instructions he received from the State Department, sometimes to the point of gross distortion. When he had studied the summary of Wilson's *aide-memoire*, for instance, he wired the Department that although it was "mystifying on first reading," it appeared "admirably adapted to Russian situation.... I shall endeavor to follow policy outlined when American troops arrive." It soon became clear, however, that as Francis saw things that policy had the elasticity of a balloon: it could be stretched to cover Poole's drive down to Kotlas and Vologda, or even farther.

What did he see in Wilson's statement that warranted such an interpretation? The answer seems to be indicated in a letter from the ambassador to the Secretary of State dated August 27-not received in Washington until October 15, after a considerable number of Americans had already been killed and wounded in North Russia. "In default of instructions to the contrary," Francis wrote with amazing aplomb, "I shall ... encourage American troops ... to proceed to such points in the interior as Kotlas, Sukhona, and Vologda, as at those places, as well as in Petrograd and Moscow, are stored war supplies which the Soviet government, in violation of its promises and agreements, transferred from Archangel. Furthermore, I shall encourage American troops to obey the commands of General Poole in his effort to effect a junction with the Czecho-Slovaks and to relieve them from the menace which surrounds them; that menace is nominally Bolshevik but is virtually inspired and directed by Germany."*

*This was one of the most persistent delusions shared by General Poole and Ambassador Francis. Poole told the ambassador, for example, that the Bolsheviks opposing his troops must be "under German instruction" because they knew how to shoot machine guns. No Germans were in the Archangel area.

In other words, Francis was ready to equate Wilson's injunction "to guard military stores" with plunging through four or five hundred miles of Russian forest and tundra to the Trans-Siberian Railroad, fighting the Soviet army at every step; and possibly even driving on to Moscow and Petrograd, since there were military stores there too! He was also ready to equate Wilson's "render such protection and help as is possible to the Czecho-Slovaks against the armed Austrian and German prisoners who are attacking them" (they were, actually, fighting the Bolsheviks) with the same ambitious drive for the Trans-Siberian. It seems safe to conjecture that President Wilson never read the ambassador's letter, and that he would have been appalled had he done so.

In justice to Francis it must be observed that the Department of State did not acquit itself very brilliantly, either, in the diplomatic muddle surrounding the first combat skirmishes between the Red army and the United States army, on those fateful fall days in North Russia. Indeed, the government record of cable communications between the Department and Ambassador Francis during the month of September gives somewhat the impression of two deaf persons carrying on a conversation while their hearing aids operate only intermittently. Secretary of State Lansing had received a message from Francis as early as September 2 making it perfectly clear that General Poole was by no means limiting his military activities to the vicinity of the city of Archangel; in fact Francis somewhat exaggerated, estimating that Poole's troops had gone two hundred miles up the Dvina toward Kotlas before the end of August. It was also made clear that this had not been any mere pleasure excursion. Poole, Francis added, was "awaiting reinforcements before attempting further advance." On September 11, Secretary Lansing was informed by the Ambassador that "Americans constitute decided majority of Allied forces under Poole ... one battalion sent on railroad toward Vologda, one on Dvina toward Kotlas."

Nevertheless, on September 13 the Secretary of State wired this surprising juxtaposition of remarks to Francis: "Department approves your action fully. Determine your future course by careful compliance with policy communicated to you in Department's No. 253, September 9." No. 253, it turns out, was largely another paraphrase of Wilson's *aide-memoire*-one even more outspoken, if anything, about limiting the uses to which American troops might be put: "The Government of the United States ... has no reasonable expectation of being in a position to take part in organized intervention in adequate forces from either Vladivostok or Murmansk and Archangel. It feels that it ought to add also that it will use the few troops it can spare only for the purposes herein stated and shall feel obliged to withdraw these forces if the plans in whose execution it is now intended they should cooperate should develop into others inconsistent with the policy to which the Government of the United States feels constrained to restrict itself." It might seem reasonable to suppose that in the light of this severe admonition Ambassador Francis would have hastened to confer with Poole about the recall of American troops from the fighting fronts. It must be confessed, however, that if he wanted justification for not doing so, he had to look no further than the remainder of the Department's message of September 13: "You appreciate of course that in military matters Colonel Stewart is under the command of General Poole." Thus a thick haze of ambiguity settled over the line of communication between Washington and Archangel, and if Ambassador Francis by this time had reached the conviction that the Department of State really wanted him to do just what he was doing, regardless of what it *said*, he is perhaps not to be condemned too harshly.

By the last week in September, to judge from the cable record, Francis had embraced this conviction to the point of bemusement. For on September 26 Secretary Lansing sent to Archangel by far the most explicit, disillusioned, and realistic memorandum on the North Russian situation that had yet emanated from the United States government. If Francis had taken it literally, General Poole's offensive into the Russian interior would immediately have been brought to a halt, since his combat forces were now largely composed of members of the 339th Infantry. Lansing's message was perfectly clear: "... we shall insist with the other governments, so far as our cooperation is concerned, that all military effort in northern Russia be given up except guarding of the ports themselves and as much of the country round about them as may develop threatening conditions.... You are advised that no more American troops will be sent to the northern ports.... All that some in authority expected to happen upon the sending of Allied and American troops to the northern ports has failed of realization. This Government can not cooperate in an effort to establish lines of operation and defense through from Siberia to Archangel."

But when Ambassador Francis read this, a day or so later, he seems to have reacted much like a motorist in a speed zone where he knows the law is never enforced. He had just talked to Poole's chief of staff and learned that the still-optimistic general expected to capture Kotlas "within ten days," and Francis was in no mood to interfere. On the contrary, when on October 10 he heard someone newly-arrived from Petrograd give "a horrible account of Bolshevik cruelties," the fiery old ambassador promptly wired Washington: "... the only way to end this disgrace to civilization is for the Allies immediately to take Petrograd and Moscow by sending sufficient troops therefore to Murmansk and Archangel without delay; 50,000 would serve but 100,000 would be ample." For this belligerent and possibly farsighted suggestion the ambassador got no encouragement from the United States government; but neither, evidently, was he reprimanded.

The bewildered Colonel Stewart, meanwhile, received a wire from General March, the U.S. Chief of Staff, ordering him to make a copy of Lansing's September 26 message to Ambassador Francis, "and conform strictly with the policy there laid down." Stewart knew perfectly well that at that moment Poole was about to use American soldiers in the forefront of a fresh attack against the Bolsheviks. But there seemed to be little he could do about it beyond ordering his typist to set in capital letters, when he copied the State Department message: "WE SHALL INSIST ... THAT ALL MILITARY EFFORT IN NORTHERN RUSSIA BE GIVEN UP EXCEPT THE GUARDING OF THE PORTS THEMSELVES AND AS MUCH COUNTRY ROUND ABOUT THEM AS MAY DEVELOP THREATENING CONDITIONS."

CHAPTER 4

THE DRIVE FOR THE TRANS-SIBERIAN

WHILE EVENTS IN THE city of Archangel were unfolding with all the *eclat* of home-made comic opera, including a large number of missed cues, the green combat troops of the 339th Infantry were undertaking roles in a drama that promised to move closer to tragedy.

All night long on September 5-6 the men of the 3rd Battalion, crowded like cattle in the old Russian boxcars, slept fitfully while the two troop trains chugged jerkily southward. Sometime during the small hours of the morning they pulled into a siding at a primitive station where a northbound train had been waiting to pass. Some of the Americans roused themselves and peered across, by the light of flaring torches on the station platform, at the other train. It was loaded with Bolshevik prisoners captured that day in a fight at the tip of the railroad front; they seemed to be under guard of a few American sailors. This, then, was the enemy; and the doughboys looked the prisoners over with intense curiosity. They saw exhausted, bearded faces, torn and dirty coats and peasant blouses, and an assortment of caps, boots, and breeches that failed to give any clear idea of a uniform. "Bolo wild men," some American said. This piece of folk etymology stuck, and forever after the Bolsheviks were "Bolos" to the men of the 339th.

By morning the Americans had reached the town of Obozerskaya, eighty miles south of Archangel, which had been captured only the previous day. A principal stopping place between Archangel and Vologda, and the intersection of the railway with one of the more passable trails cutting east and west through the pine forest and swamp-land, Obozerskaya was clearly of strategic importance to the Allies. General Poole had decided to make it a base of supplies and communications for the railroad front, and had deployed his French infantry around it in fairly strong positions from which, with some difficulty, they had been able to hold off the Soviet troops to the south. Here the Americans piled out of their boxcars, stretched cramped muscles, and marched in an orderly column toward the French dugouts. Major Young, commander of the 3rd Battalion, then halted his soldiers and had his bugler blow officers' call for a conference on what to do next.

The major, whose only previous acquaintance with combat zones had been in the pages of army manuals, was determined to do things in regulation fashion. At this moment, however, an excited and gesticulating French officer appeared from one of the dugouts, speaking his native tongue with great rapidity and pointing to certain large holes in the ground nearby. The British staff officer who had accompanied the Americans from Archangel explained to Major Young what the Frenchman was saying: the holes had been caused by Soviet shells, and there was no reason to think that new holes might not appear momentarily. "Then," as one American put it afterward, "we realized we were in the fighting zone." The major shouted orders, and the doughboys hastily dispersed into the surrounding woods. A drizzling rain was coming down through the trees, and the ground turned out to be exceedingly soggy; at some of the outposts that were established the mud and water were more than shin deep. Major Young, however, possibly after checking his field manual, ordered that the Americans were not to copy the French, who had made themselves reasonably comfortable by building fires for drying socks and raising spirits. This was war, and comfort was not to be expected.

The next few days saw intense activity as the Americans prepared themselves for battle. New dugouts were built, and an outpost trench, strictly western-front style, was dug at the farthest point of advance down the railroad. Signal-corps men busily laid out field-telephone lines; a detachment of engineers even cleared a rudimentary landing field at Obozerskaya for the few creaky airplanes, retired from service in France, which the British had brought along to give the expedition a modern look. Luckily, during these activities, the Soviet artillery was quiet and the only casualty was an American soldier shot in the leg by one of his comrades who, on sentry duty the first night, nervously fired his rifle without waiting for an answer to his cry of "Halt!" Meanwhile negotiations were carried out with the local Russian peasantry for officers' billets, supply transportation by "droshky" pony cart, and volunteers for the Slavo-British Legion. The American impression was that although these dealings were accepted stolidly, none of them moved the peasants to great enthusiasm, especially the solicitations to join up and fight the Bolsheviks. General Poole's notion that thousands of patriotic Russians would rally to the struggle against Communism was already beginning to look rather dubious.

The first skirmishes with Soviet troops were tentative and exploratory. Evidently the Bolshevik leaders were uncertain of the Allied strength now ranged against them, and for a while they tended to give ground without much resistance. Two platoons of Company M thus enjoyed the excitement of easy victory on September 11, when they ran into a like number of Red Guards on the railroad at Verst 466 and drove them south to Verst 464. (Distances along the railway were indicated by markers a verst-about two-thirds of a mile-apart, and numbered consecutively from Vologda to Archangel.) This was the occasion of the Americans' first experience at the receiving end of an artillery bombardment. Patrolling along the rails, they had sighted in the distance something which a British officer insisted must be a sawmill smokestack. But the "smokestack" suddenly emitted a flash, followed by a whining, whistling noise as a shell sailed overhead to burst in the rear of the startled Americans. The Bolsheviks, like the British, possessed one armored train, equipped with one fairly heavy gun, and this was the source of the unpleasant surprise.

The Reds also had two or three airplanes which flew sporadically over the Allied lines on reconnaissance, now and then dropping small bombs. One of them got into trouble over Verst 464 on the evening of September 15 and had to make a crash landing. Here Major Young distinguished himself by deciding that the plane was an Allied craft and rushing forward to greet its occupants with the eager cry, "Don't fire! We are Americans!" (This soon became a sardonic watchword with the men of the outfit.) The Bolsheviks in the disabled plane promptly replied with a machine gun, and Major Young dived into the underbrush with such conviction that his watching men were sure he had been hit by a slug. The Russians then scrambled out of their plane and off into the woods while the doughboys, as one of them put it, "ran up and pulled the moss off their battalion commander."

This was amusing enough; but on the following day the Bolsheviks struck with their first counterattack since the arrival of the Americans. Although not a large operation, this was featured by a disturbing portent of the kind of thing likely to happen in the unfamiliar Russian woods and swamps. Two platoons of Company I, under Lieutenant Gordon B. Reese, somehow got separated from the rest of the battalion and soon ran completely out of ammunition. Reese then demonstrated a tough Yankee spirit by ordering a bayonet charge instead of retreat or surrender. The Bolsheviks had not expected this, and themselves retreated in dismay before the yelling *Amerikanskis*, who were then able to work back to the main body of the battalion. Two members of Company I, however, and one of Company I, were found dead in the woods after the fight was over. It was not yet two weeks since they had marched off the troop ship at Archangel. They were buried beneath wooden crosses at Obozerskaya, two boys from Detroit and one from Pittsburgh who had come a long way to die, for reasons that were by no means clear.

At any rate one thing was by now brutally clear to the men of the 3rd Battalion: they were committed to battle, and there was little prospect that the situation would get any easier as they went along. The British officer in command of Allied troops on the railway front thoroughly understood General Poole's purpose and conveyed it to the Americans in unequivocal terms: "All patrols must be aggressive, and it must be impressed on all ranks that we are fighting an offensive war, and not a defensive one." Possibly it was the grotesque gap between this order and President Wilson's policy of peaceful intervention in North Russia that was responsible for the odd behavior of the American commanding officer when he visited the railway front the day after the first American casualties. He had not yet been officially posted on that policy, but many American officials in Archangel knew of it, and he must have been generally aware of the chasm between American theory and British practice.

According to a military intelligence report, Stewart "seemed to be in very much of a hurry" during his visit, and "discussed matters with his officers in a preoccupied sort of way." The three soldiers killed in combat were about to be buried with appropriate ceremony, since their death had seemed significant to the rest of the battalion; but, the report went on, "Colonel Stewart, though cognizant of the situation, left before the men were buried and instead of adding dignity to the ceremony as his presence would have done, a contrary impression was created and a feeling of hurt caused so far as the men were concerned. They expected their Colonel to be present at the ceremony of burial of his first three men killed in action, which he could have done by remaining five minutes additional... ." It is understandable that the sight of dead Americans being lowered into Russian ground was not one that appealed to the commanding officer who was supposed to have kept them from such a doom. But Stewart, hopelessly puzzled by the tangle of cross-purposes among General Poole, Ambassador Francis, the State Department, and the War Department, had already begun to practice the only solution he usually would be capable of: looking the other way. To the men of the 339th Infantry it was a solution that spelled negligence, whatever its causes; and there is no fault harder for soldiers to forgive in their commanding officer.

Back in Archangel, General Poole had now decided to make a concerted drive for the Trans-Siberian Railroad along both the Archangel-Vologda tracks and the Dvina River. (It was this decision that caused Ambassador Francis to wire the State Department that the capture of Kotlas was expected "within ten days.") Poole's chief of staff, General R. G. Finlayson, turned up at Obozerskaya on September 28, and explained to the Allied officers that the first objective was to be the town of Plesetskaya, a Bolshevik supply base of some importance, fifty miles down the railroad. Finlayson, it seems, wanted action and wanted it fast. His orders were that the advance was to commence that very night, and that Colonel Sutherland, the British officer in command at Obozerskaya, should proceed to work out his strategy immediately.

Sutherland, who already was viewed with some suspicion by the American officers under him because of his offhand and rather contemptuous manner, devised a plan of classical simplicity-at least on paper. A French infantry company, with artillery support, would push straight down the railroad, while two columns of Americans would circle through the forest to launch co-ordinated assaults from two places on the eastern flank, thus taking the Communists on the railroad by disastrous surprise. Unfortunately, however, Sutherland's intelligence officers had not bothered to reconnoiter the swampy forest in the area involved, relying instead on outdated foresters' maps and information gleaned from local woodcutters. According to Captain Joel Moore, an American who commanded one of the flanking columns, Colonel Sutherland's cheery reply to remonstrances over the lack of reconnaissance was "You Americans can do it somehow, you know."

The attack was scheduled for dawn on September 29. At five o'clock of the preceding afternoon the American flanking detachments headed into the woods. The larger of the two, consisting of a company and a half of the 3rd Battalion, was supposed to follow a blazed trail eastward through the forest to a broad, north-south cutting, allegedly laid out for wagons in the time of Peter the Great. Proceeding southward down this venerable thoroughfare, they then would cut back into the woods opposite Verst 455, camp overnight, and strike the Soviet position from its right and slightly to the rear, at 6 A.M. It all sounded beautiful and easy.

None of the members of the party, however, had been over the ground. Darkness engulfed the forest long before they reached Peter the Great's wagon trail, and the going was far slower than had been anticipated. "Could not see the man ahead of you," Captain Moore noted later. "Ears told you he was tripping over fallen timber or sloshing in knee-deep bog hole. Hard breathing told the story of exertion." A stream, barely indicated on the map the leaders were following, turned out to be waist deep, with no fords discoverable. Wet to their belts, the column emerged temporarily from the woods, after hours of stumbling through the thick underbrush, into a great bog-totally ignored on their map. Blundering and falling in the sticky ooze, part of the detachment got separated from the rest. The marsh, instead of turning again into solid ground, opened out into what appeared, by the pale starlight, to be a shallow lake. Hours behind schedule, the

American officers agreed in desperation that the flanking attack must already be considered a failure, and decided that only a retreat by the blazed forest trail made any sense. Two noncommissioned officers who had been Michigan woodsmen, in somewhat earlier and happier days, managed to scout the way back through the marsh to the trail, where the lost segment of the column had been waiting. Soggy and cold, in a state of exhausted chagrin, the whole detachment dragged back to the Allied position on the railroad. By now it was early Sunday morning, September 29. On the way, with daylight breaking, they heard the Allied artillery open the attack, and knew that their French infantry comrades must be poised for the assault, expecting the flanking support which now had evaporated. For, as it later developed, the other flanking column never reached its objective either, but got utterly lost in the woods for twenty-four hours.

The French, however, did fairly well almost entirely on their own. At Verst 458 they captured a railroad bridge, driving the Bolsheviks back before they could blow it up to prevent Allied rail advance, and held it valiantly, although the Soviet troops counter-attacked in force. Some American support was given by a handful of men from the 3rd Battalion's headquarters company, who had been hastily and incompletely trained to use trench mortars just since their arrival in Russia; but these brave amateurs soon found themselves out of mortar ammunition, and forced to defend themselves with rifles and hand grenades. Both they and the French were now under heavy attack; and a volunteer platoon of Captain Moore's tired company, who had been trying to dry out their soaked clothing around fires a few hundred yards to the rear, pulled themselves together and rushed down to the bridge with machine guns and rifles.

The bridge was held; but at this juncture a piece of battle irony occurred for which the Americans were never able to forgive their British commander. Ensconced in his railroad-car headquarters several miles up the track toward Archangel, Colonel Sutherland misconstrued a telephoned report of the action and, evidently thinking the Bolsheviks had retaken the bridge, ordered his artillery to shell it forthwith. Eight Americans were wounded, two of them mortally, by shrapnel from the Allied guns before the mistake was rectified. An American soldier who was acting as orderly in

Sutherland's headquarters reported afterward that the British colonel, having been informed of his error, telephoned "for another quart of whisky" before calling his artillery commander to order an increase of range. This vivid detail deeply impressed the soldiers of the 3rd Battalion, and true or not, it pushed to a critical point the already sour relations between the British field officers and the Americans under them.

Even the successful holding of the bridge at Verst 458 was in spite of Colonel Sutherland, for after the unfortunate shelling episode he ordered the doughboys and poilus to retire. This they were most loath to do, and the American commander at field headquarters, Major J. Brooks Nichols, quickly requested a countermanding order. Nichols had arrived at the scene of his first battle altogether *in medias res*; for only on September 28 had it been decided that he was a better choice to command the fighting 3rd Battalion than Major Young, dubious hero of the encounter with the downed Soviet airplane. Nichols remained on the railroad front for the rest of the campaign and won a solid popularity with his countrymen-soldiers. A reserve officer, he exhibited such military timber that the British awarded him the D.S.O.-high honor for a man whose most desperate feat in civilian life was, as a fellow officer put it, "to mashie-nib out of a double-bunkered trap on the Detroit Country Club golf course."

Notwithstanding a considerable cost in killed and wounded, and some very gallant fighting, nightfall of September 29 found the French and Americans a bare two miles closer to their objective than they started. The combination of Sutherland's blundering and far stiffer Soviet resistance than had been expected now made Plesetskaya appear a long way over the horizon; as for Vologda, the city on the Trans-Siberian which General Poole still aimed to take before snow came, it was beginning to shift, in the minds of the men actually at the front, into the hazy realm of never-never land. Back in Archangel, however, cheerfully studying his maps, Poole refused to falter: the push to join the Czechs was to carry on.

Despite the paucity of his troops the British general had not changed his strategy of a dual advance, one major force moving against the Bolsheviks along the railroad, and a second up the Dvina River toward Kotlas. It will be remembered that the 1st Battalion of the 339th

Infantry had been "rushed" (in barges towed against the current) to Bereznik, a town up the river chosen as a supply base for the drive to Kotlas. It was a place of somewhat more impressive accommodations than most of the villages along the Dvina, for it had served the late Czar as the site of a hunting lodge. After a couple of days in which to recover from the trip and bury two more victims of influenza, most of the battalion pressed on to the village of Chamova, about thirty miles away. (Two platoons of Company A, under Captain Odjard, were left behind, and were soon to be deep in adventures of their own.) In this vicinity Poole's Royal Scots had been having great trouble with large Soviet scouting parties as well as with heavy (if usually inaccurate) bombardment from Soviet gunboats. The Dvina at this point, some 150 miles southeast of Archangel, is well over a mile wide, meandering through low, marshy country, with many small islands splitting the muddy stream. The advance company reached Chamova in the early-morning darkness of September 17, and had barely settled down for some sleep when the sound of rifle fire on the riverbank roused them. A small detachment of Royal Scots had gone down to meet, as they thought, an Allied supply boat from Bereznik. Actually it was a Bolshevik gunboat which opened fire immediately, killing two of the Scots. The Americans, coming fast out of their bedrolls, sprayed the craft with rifle bullets, and it put out into the stream only to cross over to a nearby island and moor. While some of the men of the 1st Battalion were considering an amphibious action by means of rowboats, a British gunboat suddenly appeared around a bend in the river. It threw a shell neatly amidships in the Soviet boat, setting it afire and disappointing the doughboys, who had rather relished the idea of capturing it intact.

Their lust for battle was satisfied soon enough. Pushing about thirty miles along the soggy bank of the Dvina on a two-day march, they found the Bolsheviks firmly established at the village of Seltso and evincing no sign of further retreat. Unfortunately the ground around the village resembled in no way the solid terrain of Fort Custer, Michigan, where the men of the 3rd Battalion had practiced assault actions. Between the Americans and the drab huddle of log buildings was over a mile of wide, open swamp; the only way to get there, it appeared, was to wade. On the afternoon of September 19 Company D, under Captain Coleman, did wade (in ordinary army shoes, puttees, and breeches) until they were within fifteen hundred yards of the village.

Then a hail of rifle and machine-gun fire stopped them, and there was nothing to do but bog down, literally, in the swamp. B and C Companies came up from the rear, but in view of the enemy fire remained along the edges of the woods bordering the swamp. "None of the officers in command of this movement," wrote a battalion chronicler afterward, "knew anything of the geography nor much of anything else regarding this position, so the men were compelled to dig in as best they could in the mud and water to await orders from Colonel Corbley, who had not come up."

Corbley, it developed, had been pinned down by Soviet artillery fire (much of it from improvised gunboats) in another village a few miles downstream; and a battery of White Russian guns, which had been promised as support for the American infantry attack, had also been unable to get into battle position in time. Darkness came, and the Soviet guns now turned their attention to the marsh and the nearby woods, searching haphazardly for the American bivouacs. But the sky was heavily overcast, and the impossibility of observation made the fire ineffective-except psychologically. It was the first time the men of the 1st Battalion had been under an artillery barrage, and the local conditions were not conducive to taking this jarring novelty with insouciance. It was cold, and rain had begun to fall. Crouched miserably in the ooze of the swamp or the drippings fringes of the adjacent forest, without overcoats and without food, the Americans waited apprehensively for dawn. Their dreams of combat had never taken just this shape; and if this was "guard duty at Archangel" most of them had already had their fill of it.

Early the next morning a platoon leader took a patrol through the woods to see if there was any likelihood of another approach to the village. They had not gone far before a blast of machine-gun fire proved that the Bolsheviks had outposts well placed around their perimeter. The patrol hastily withdrew, discovering when they had returned to their original position that one noncom was no longer with them. A search party crept back through the dripping underbrush-but not a single trace was ever found of Corporal Herbert Schroeder, of Detroit, Michigan.

All day the battalion remained in assault position in front of the little Russian village, unable to launch a moving attack. B

Company tried to go ahead, about noon, but ran into such withering fire from Bolshevik rifles and machine guns that they fell back with three men killed and eight wounded. Just when it all looked hopeless good fortune came in the shape of the battery of White Russian field pieces, whose horses finally had struggled close enough, along the miry road paralleling the river, to bracket in on Seltso. The Russian officer in command of the battery knew his business, and laid a fifteen-minute barrage so accurately into the village defenses that 5 P.M., when the 1st Battalion of the 339th clambered out of the mud and charged forward, the Communists had already decided to clear out. Into the battered and bedraggled village rushed the Americans, finding to their incredulous relief that the rear guard of the enemy had just departed at the other end of town. It seemed like a miracle, one of them remembered later, and the doughboys, "with white, strained faces, in contrast with their muck-daubed uniforms, shook hands prayerfully as they discussed how a determined defense could have murdered them all in making that frontal attack across a swamp."

The rest of the Seltso story is a little lesson in military irony, resulting in turn from bad strategy. Field conditions were such that General Poole's drive for the Trans-Siberian seemed even more phantasmal on the Dvina than over on the Archangel-Vologda Railroad, a hundred miles of swampy forest away, where the 3rd Battalion was burying its first dead during the same week that Seltso was captured. Valiantly trying to realize Poole's megalomaniacal plan, the inexperienced Americans soon found that they were over-extended at Seltso, at least for the moment. Supplies were not reaching them, and the White Russian artillery had again been unable to pull through the mud to a position from which the light field pieces could follow the Communists, now withdrawn several miles upstream. Some of the Soviet gunboats, on the other hand, mounted six-and nine-inch guns that carried far enough to make Seltso a delightful target with no fear of Allied artillery reprisal. In view of these depressing facts Major Corbley, CO of the 1st Battalion, ordered a withdrawal; and on the very morning following the taking of the village the exasperated doughboys slogged back across the swamp and down the river road to a safer position. It all was beginning to look like a game of winner take nothing.

The British command, nevertheless, had made no change in strategy or objective: Kotlas, over three hundred miles southeast on the

Dvina, was still to be captured with as little delay as possible. A British
gunboat moved upstream past Seltso, and with this jot of naval support
Company B marched out again to attack the Bolsheviks. They headed
for a settlement called Pouchuga, where the enemy was reported to have
made a halt. It had now been raining steadily for a week, and the mud
was endless. The Americans were still without overcoats and-even
worse-without tobacco. A supply convoy of Russian pony carts did catch
up with them, however, when morale had sunk to its lowest so far; each
man got one pack of cigarettes. "They stunk, as anyone who smoked
British issue cigarettes can tell you," Captain Boyd, of Company B, later
recalled; but he remembered the moment as one of the best of the
campaign even though all of his soldiers were cold, tired, wet and
discouraged. "You could see man after man light his cigarette, take a
long draw, and relax in unadulterated enjoyment. Ten minutes later they
were a different outfit ... Lucy Page Gaston and the Anti-Cigarette
League please note."

Company B's attack on Pouchuga, even with the help of tobacco,
proved to be abortive. Captain Boyd soon realized that his force was
tremendously outnumbered, and he was not disposed to waste American
lives in an assault almost certain to fail. Half of the company managed
to withdraw northward without trouble, but Boyd himself, leading two
platoons, was cut off by a Soviet flanking party. He took his men across
a swamp onto a semi-island at the edge of the Dvina, and there they hid
in the underbrush while the Bolsheviks ransacked the woods along the
bank, close enough to afford the Americans a short course in Slavic
profanity.

The Soviet searchers finally gave up, and Boyd and his men got
back to terra firma and a safe retreat to Seltso. His party was in miserable
condition, however. Many feet were painfully swollen from days and
nights in water-soaked shoes; everyone was chilled and wet, and several
were injured. Corporal J. C. Downs, one of whose eyes had been shot
out in the skirmishing, had gone for days without medical treatment,
but had remained incredibly cheerful-one of the bravest men, Boyd
thought, that he had ever seen anywhere.

* * *

But official second-guessing now seemed to direct the destiny of the 1st Battalion. Poole's staff officers back in Archangel had become aware that the Dvina was not the only important river in Archangel Province. Its largest tributary, the Vaga, a narrower but much swifter stream, flowed north into the Dvina at a point near Bereznik, the Dvina supply base; and in two respects the Vaga appeared to deserve more attention than it had yet received. It offered the Bolsheviks an obvious route for a wedge between the railroad and the Dvina, which might easily cut off the troops in the Seltso area from the rear; and on its high, sandy bank sat Shenkursk, the second largest city of the province. A Russian summer resort of some popularity, Shenkursk had brick buildings, schools, fine churches, a monastery, sawmills, army barracks, and a population of several thousand. Its possession was important, not only strategically, but in terms of prestige; and General Poole had now discovered that prestige for the Allies was not an automatic consequence of their having arrived in Russia and begun to fight the Bolsheviks.

It is puzzling that the Soviet leaders did not attempt to hold Shenkursk against the invaders. Possibly it seemed to them such an obvious military objective that they simply assumed most of Poole's river force would be sent against it. What actually happened was that barely more than two platoons of Company A, left in Bereznik when the rest of the battalion went on up the Dvina, were ordered to "take" the town. Leading this less than overwhelming force, Captain Otto Odjard and Lieutenant Harry M. Mead boarded a river steamer on September 16, and the next day took possession of Shenkursk without firing a shot. According to the citizens, who turned out in large numbers to greet the newcomers, the Bolshevik garrison had fled in disorder upon the news of the American approach.

Company A of the 339th Infantry was later to have more battle casualties than any other in the regiment; but for a brief interlude it looked as if they had hit it lucky. In Shenkursk they were quartered in comfortable barracks, their field rations of hardtack and "bully beef" were marvelously supplemented by fresh meat and eggs, and, as one soldier noted wistfully, "there were even women there who wore hats and stockings, in place of boots and shawls." But they had just settled comfortably into their new surroundings when an order from Archangel burst the happy bubble of anticipation. British staff officers, the headquarters unit for the Vaga River command, were on their way to occupy Shenkursk accompanied by great quantities of supplies, some British and Russian garrison soldiers, and the inevitable corps of orderlies and batmen. Company A of the 339th was to push on immediately up the river to make contact with the enemy: for if there was one thing General Poole had no delusions about it was that the Americans under his command were his best combat troops. Those who had escaped the flu were still in excellent physical condition, and although they were inexperienced, at least they were not battle-weary like nearly all of the British and French infantrymen in North Russia.

The last week in September thus found Captain Odjard and Lieutenant Mead, their two platoons of doughboys, and a handful of White Russians from the Slavo-British Legion, steaming up the Vaga aboard an old side-wheeler appropriately named after the author of *War and Peace*: the *Tolstoy*. Although they did not know it at the time, since they had no communication with the units on the railroad and were already out of touch with the rest of the 1st Battalion, Captain Odjard's invaders were now far out in advance of any of the other Allied troops in North Russia. They had penetrated well south of Shenkursk, which was in turn about two hundred miles south of Archangel; as the crow flies they were more than halfway to the Trans-Siberian Railroad. Like Napoleon's *Grande Armee*, however, they were about to discover that Russian soldiers in retreat did not mean Russian soldiers who had given up the contest. The *Tolstoy* had arrived opposite a village called Gorka, when suddenly the ancient wood of her hull was splintered by heavy bursts of machine-gun fire from the bank. Four Americans were wounded. It was obvious immediately that the boat was not satisfactory protection and Captain Odjard made a quick decision. Heading straight for the bank the old steamer soon was in close enough for the Americans to leap into the icy water and storm ashore, spreading out into skirmish formations as they went. The Bolsheviks behind the machine guns, hardly expecting this maneuver, picked up and retreated in a hurry.

Odjard decided, however, that further progress by river boat was too dangerous, and from there on the platoons experienced the same painful marching conditions that were afflicting their comrades over on the Dvina. It was a story of soaked clothing, insufficient rations, no overcoats or tobacco, swollen feet, and discouragement. But Captain Odjard, whose Viking disposition was shortly to become a legend in the 339th Infantry, was far from daunted. By the end of the first week in October his little band was at the village of Puya, the point furthermost into the Russian interior that any element of the Allied expedition ever was to reach. A large detachment of Soviet troops here blocked their advance; and scouting reports indicated that another detachment had closed in behind them from the forest, blocking their retreat down the river. Odjard and the White Russian commander figured that by all reasonable standards they would now be expected to fight their way back toward Shenkursk; so they ordered an attack in the other direction (southward) at once. Here again, as so often in North Russia, the combination of luck and an audacity bordering on madness paid off for the Allies. With the convincing support of one 3.7 gun which had come up as part of a reinforcing detachment of White Russians, the attack was not only unbelievably successful-Odjard reported about fifty of the enemy killed, against three wounded for the Yanks-but the Bolshevik detachment cutting off the retreat route interpreted it as a prelude to heavy American reinforcements from Shenkursk, and disappeared into the depths of the forest. Thereupon the Allied force moved quickly back down the river to Rovdino, a village about thirty miles south of Shenkursk, which offered good cover and an advantageous position for holding off counter-attacks.

An analysis of the fight at Puya had revealed one cheerful fact quite obviously: although there was no lack of Bolshevik troops on this front, most of them were hopelessly untrained, and used their weapons as effectively as would be expected. Almost invariably they fired far too high. They were, in short, the epitome of what General Poole had hoped the entire Red army might turn out to be: ragged peasants with no notion of how to conduct a military operation. Unfortunately, this was by no means true everywhere in North Russia, nor was it a condition that remained long unchanged under Trotsky's driving leadership of the Bolshevik forces. But for the time being Captain Odjard's young Americans were, relatively, in the desirable military posture of crack combat troops facing green-horns-this as the surprising result of a few weeks of assault training and target shooting at Fort Custer, Michigan.

The muddy lanes and dirty log huts of Rovdino remained the advance Allied bastion on the Vaga for about two weeks, when an unexpected turn of events in Archangel profoundly changed the whole shape of the campaign. For the moment, however, we will leave Company A of the 339th in this situation in order to look briefly at two other subsidiary fronts which General Poole's plan of invasion had made necessary. Between the Dvina River and the Archangel-Vologda Railroad lay many hundreds of square miles of pine forest, tundra, and swamp through which travel was possible chiefly by foresters' trials. These were narrow, twisting, often overgrown with underbrush and trammeled by fallen logs, or intercepted by stretches of bog. The movement of artillery along them, of course, was out of the question. There was, however, one broader, firmer trail that could legitimately qualify as a road if one were disposed to define the term generously. This was the old forest highway leading from Plesetskaya, on the railway, northeast to the town of Siskoe, on the Dvina only seventy miles below Archangel. Since the Bolsheviks were firmly installed at Plesetskaya, they were in a nice position to push a flanking movement up this highway until it was far enough north to threaten both the Allied front on the railroad, to the west, and that on the Dvina, to the east. Soviet troops were already in the vicinity of Kodish and Seletskoe, on a sector of the road about halfway between Plesetskaya and Siskoe, when the Americans landed in North Russia. They were known to have severely harassed one of Poole's initial combat teams; in fact, B Force, as it was called, had not been heard from since about the end of August. It included, besides several platoons of British and French infantry, about twenty-five of the *Olympia* sailors. Orders to the 3rd Battalion of the 339th, when it arrived at Obozerskaya on September 6, were that a relief force should be sent into the forest in the general direction of Seletskoe, to see what could be found of the lost unit.

Captain Michael Donoghue, CO of Company K, accordingly moved into the woods with two platoons of infantry and a medical squad of nine men, on the afternoon of September 7. Of all the soldiers in the 339th Regiment, these felt the full strangeness of the campaign they had embarked upon sooner than any others. Two days off the troopship from England, they were already deep in the shadows of the gloomy and menacing North Russian forest with only the vaguest idea of their whereabouts and of their mission. After making about five miles, they camped for the night in a cold rain, and pressed on through the pines and underbrush early the next morning. By mid-afternoon they had covered some eighteen miles from Obozerskaya; and here they had encountered disquieting signs of recent activity. In the woods along the trail were scattered abandoned equipment, a couple of broken pony carts, and a potpourri of personal belongings. Somebody picked up a diary: it proved to be that of an American ensign who had made his last entry on August 30. Nearby, in the muddy earth, were several fresh graves.

Donoghue's rescue party was now disturbed both by uncertainty about where to go and feeling that wherever they went they might well arrive too late. Many trails criss-crossed in the forest, and at each intersection there was a guessing game: which fork should be taken? The combined woodsman's lore of all the ex-Boy-Scouts in the two platoons was hardly enough, and for five days and nights they marched and camped in the North Russian wilderness, wet to the skin, sore of foot, and baffled. As Company K official reports for that week neatly phrased it, their whereabouts was "not definitely known."

To put the matter bluntly, the searchers were now lost themselves. Looking back at these wandering American platoons from the comfortable vantage of today, one can catch a certain wry humor in the episode which was unavailable to the participants. What they did not know-there is some question whether most of them ever learned it-was that B Force, the group they were looking for, had reached the Allied lines on the railroad the day *before* Donoghue set off on the rescue mission. Why his orders were not canceled remains a military mystery. The war diary of the *Olympia* reveals that the party of American sailors, together with the French and British soldiers, had indeed run into trouble: they had fought a pitched battle with the Bolsheviks in the tangled woods on September 1 and 2. Outnumbered, and with ammunition nearly gone, they then retreated toward the railroad and arrived at a point north of Obozerskaya on September 5.

That evening the bluejackets were detailed to guard a large batch of Bolo prisoners being sent by train up to Archangel. This was of course the very train stared at by the soldiers of the 3rd Battalion (including Donoghue and his men) as they came down the line that night on their way to the front. But neither the American sailors nor soldiers understood more than half the situation, and the significance of this brief night encounter went unappreciated.

Since there had been no living sign either of the enemy or of B Force, Captain Donoghue had decided by September 12 to move southwest, in the direction of the Soviet position on the railroad, with the expectation of running into Bolsheviks before very long. At the end of the week the situation suddenly improved: contact with headquarters was re-established by signaling a British airplane which had found the Americans after considerable search. Then an American lieutenant with a machine-gun squad of twenty men appeared from Obozerskaya, bringing orders to turn around and proceed to Seletskoe, on the road leading northeast out of Plesetskaya. There a couple of hundred British and White Russian troops, sent over from the Dvina, were holding the town against a large contingent of Communists. Captain Donoghue's men arrived at the Seletskoe outposts on the morning of September 16, just in time to undergo their baptism of fire in fighting off a series of Soviet attacks that continued for two days. Allied marksmanship was nastily accurate, from the enemy's point of view, and the battle ended when some Bolshevik infantrymen decided to emulate the revolutionary tactics of the party to which they theoretically held allegiance: they assassinated their commanding officer and led an impromptu retreat to a position several miles southward, near the town of Kodish.

Unfortunately the British officer in command at Seletskoe was victimized, at this moment, by what later was described as a "highly imaginative" intelligence report. A White Russian reconnaissance patrol came in with the alarming news that the Bolshevik retreat was merely a decoy: a very heavy Soviet force was said to be circling through the forest to the rear of the Allied position at Seletskoe. The British commander promptly ordered a strategic withdrawal across the Emtsa River a short distance to the north, and when his troops had crossed over he ordered the bridge burned behind him. An American lieutenant named Ryan almost met doom in this Caesarean operation: he sat down on the bridge, greatly fatigued, as his men were preparing to destroy it, and was awakened from his sleep only when the flames were scorching skyward.

Meanwhile this wily piece of strategy was actually being duplicated, as it turned out, by the Bolsheviks, who were nervously engaged in burning another bridge a few miles to the south in anticipation of Allied pursuit. (The road, near Seletskoe, crossed and recrossed the river several times.) The ironic truth came out when a British scout, who had been so diligent in observing the Soviet maneuvers that he had been left behind when the Allies withdrew, returned to Seletskoe to report to headquarters. He found the town almost completely abandoned, most of the natives having followed the Allied troops northward with everything, as one American put it, "from the samovar to the cow." Hiking up the road to the riverbank, the puzzled cockney stood by the charred ruins of the bridge and called across to some members of Company K, who were busily digging in on the other side, "I saiy, old chaps, wot's the bloody gaime?"

The game was in fact about to become a good deal bloodier. After a detachment of the 310th Engineers had constructed a pontoon bridge back across the Emtsa the whole Allied detachment returned to Seletskoe, and there was reinforced by the other two platoons of Company K and by Company L, sent out from Obozerskaya. This reinforcement was part of General Poole's "master" plan for the drive to the Trans-Siberian: while one Allied force pushed down the railroad, and another up the Dvina, a third would capture Kodish on the forest highway and then converge with the railway force on the Soviet base at Plesetskaya. But the Kodish operation, late in September, was no more successful than those to the east and west, on the railroad and on the Dvina. Three hundred and fifty Americans crossed another bend of the Emtsa River on rafts, under Bolshevik rifle fire, and attacked, only to be frustrated by the same natural obstacle which had proved so obnoxious at Seltso and on the railroad: a Russian swamp. Lieutenant Charles F. Chappel was killed by a Soviet machine gun while leading a patrol from Company K in an effort to work around the morass; six others died with him, and twenty-four were wounded. Chappel was the first American officer to be killed in combat in North Russia. Many of the men were now suffering from exposure, with feet swollen beyond the capacity of their shoes; and under these sorry circumstances the Americans crossed back over the river, to dig in on the north bank until more reinforcements could arrive from Archangel.

The only other element to be accounted for in describing Poole's ill-fated fall drive toward the Trans-Siberian Railroad is that of the small Allied force sent far to the west, near the Onega River, to protect the supply road leading from Murmansk to Archangel. This amounted to still another "front" (making five in all), this one as isolated as any, although communications between it and staff headquarters at Archangel were theoretically better because of a telegraph line and superior trail conditions. Perhaps the most interesting thing about the Onega front was its origin: it had been established with the help of the same detachment of sailors from the *Olympia* who, less fearful than angels, had first chased the Bolsheviks down the railroad in the early days of August. Having been relieved there by the French infantry, they had been transported by steamer to the little port of Onega, on a bay of the White Sea seventy miles east of Archangel. Here they became temporarily a substantial reinforcement to a small garrison of British soldiers who had captured Onega (with practically no bloodshed) on July 31, just before the fall of Archangel to the Allies. In the middle of September, Company H of the 339th Infantry was dispatched from Archangel and took over the defense of Onega after a day's sail through the waters of Dvina Bay and Onega Bay. Two platoons were sent fifty miles up the Onega River to Chekuevo, a way station on the Murmansk-Obozerskaya-Archangel road which would become a critical point when the North Russian winter set in, and travel would no longer be possible between Murmansk and Archangel by boat.

At dawn on a wet September 24 over 300 Bolshevik troops, with several machine guns, attacked 115 Americans and 93 Russian volunteers at Chekuevo. After several hours of rather ineffective fighting in the rain, a lucky burst from a Lewis automatic killed the Bolshevik leader, one Shiskin; and taking advantage of this stroke the Americans charged forward and pursued the disorganized Reds five miles south along the river road. Their casualties had been light, and they almost enjoyed themselves as they hurried along past a great deal of clothing, rifles, and other equipment which the Bolsheviks had abandoned in their flight. The Americans returned rather complacently to their log-house billets at Chekuevo that night.

The end of September, however, brought orders from British headquarters to co-operate in the drive on Plesetskaya, about to be launched from Obozerskaya, forty miles due east of Chekuevo on the railroad. "Open the wire to Obozerskaya," read the orders, "and ascertain how far down the line our troops have reached, and then try to keep abreast of them … There is a strong enemy force at Plesetskaya on the railway and it is possible that they may retire across your front… ." As we have already seen, there was to be no difficulty about keeping "abreast" of the Allied troops on the railroad, who at this point were mostly bumbling about knee-deep in the adjacent swamps instead of moving any considerable distance down the railway. Nor did the Bolsheviks below Obozerskaya show much inclination to retreat in any direction whatsoever. The Americans of Company H, however, together with a handful of mounted Cossacks and about a hundred volunteer White Russians from the Onega countryside, dutifully attacked at daybreak on October 1, striking at the village of Kaska, a few miles south of Chekuevo.

Things went quite differently than they had in the previous week's encounter. It turned out that close to seven hundred Soviet troops were now in the area; and when the White Russians and Cossacks learned this they dissolved northward into the protection of the forest with astonishing speed. The deserted Americans, numbering just over a hundred, fought valiantly; but anything resembling a decisive attack was now impossible. When six of his men had been killed by Soviet fire, Lieutenant Clifford Phillips, the American in command of the two platoons saw the futility of the action, and ordered a withdrawal to the defenses of Chekuevo. Thus ended the drive for Plesetskaya as far as the Onega front was concerned-but as the men of Company H learned later, they had done about as well as any of their comrades, whether on the railroad, at Seletskoe and Kodish, or on the Dvina. Only on the Vaga, where Captain Odjard's gallant vanguard of Company A had met with such excellent luck, did the North Russia battle map on the first day of October show a reality that in any way matched General Poole's dream of a rapid thrust down to the Trans-Siberian Railroad; and even there the pitiful numerical scarcity of the Allied force had pretty well canceled the effect of nerve and good fortune.

At this lugubrious moment, however, something was happening in Archangel harbor that would profoundly change the entire conception and complexion of the campaign. Brigadier General Edmund Ironside was standing speculatively at the rail of the British troop carrier *Stephen* as it nosed its way in toward a Bakaritza dock. On the handsome head of this young officer was about to descend a heavy responsibility: the fate of the Allied Expedition to North Russia.

CHAPTER 5

IRONSIDE TAKES OVER

WHEN GENERAL WILLIAM EDMUND Ironside capped a long and splendid career in the service of Great Britain by ascension to the peerage in 1941, he took the title "Baron of Archangel and of Ironside." It was an interesting choice, looking back as it did to a single year in the life of a man whose entry in *Who's Who* reads like a quick trip along the British path of empire from Victoria to George VI.

A subaltern in the army in 1899, when he was not yet twenty, Ironside fought through the Boer War in South Africa and came out of it with the roots of a personal legend already sprouting romantic shoots. No doubt it was inevitable that stories would be told of such a man: six feet four inches tall, and built in magnificent proportion; handsome, intelligent, personable, and utterly devoted to the profession of soldiering. It was said that in hand-to-hand combat he had once crushed a Boer soldier to death in his tremendous arms; that later he had been sent on mysterious intelligence missions against the Germans in South Africa, mingling with them disguised as a Boer wagon driver. Receiving the Queen's medal with three clasps for his exploits, he served in the early years of the twentieth century both in Africa and India, spent two years at the Army Staff College, and by 1918 was well prepared to become one of the younger generals in the British army at the age of thirty-eight. Meanwhile he had industriously pursued his hobby of learning foreign languages in his spare time, mastering Dutch, Italian, German, Swedish, French, and (with the help of a short visit to Russia) picking up a fair knowledge of Russian.

Ironside's record in France during World War I in no way disappointed his admirers, and by 1918 he had added to his honors the D.S.O., C.M.G., K.C.B., Croix de Guerre with palms, and was an Officer of the Legion of Honor. He was in command of the 99th

Infantry Brigade in September of that year, and was enjoying himself very much. Hugely admired by his troops, who with sufficiently broad humor called him "Tiny," he was seen frequently in the front-line trenches with his walking stick and his pet bulldog. His men had done well against the Germans during the summer, and though they were now at a standstill because of heavy artillery opposition, Ironside had every hope, as he put it, of being "in at the death" in the expected Allied victory. At this very moment, however, diplomatic maneuverings, resulting from General Poole's behavior in Archangel had produced an intense flurry in the War Office in London, and with very little wavering the finger of fate swung around to point straight at Edmund Ironside.

Poole's lordly and contemptuous treatment of Chaikovsky's government, together with the kidnaping episode which had so annoyed Ambassador Francis, had given rise to complaints from the Department of State to the British government. The complaints were accompanied by a threat guaranteed to get action: "The President," Secretary of State Lansing cabled on September 12, "in the event that this reported interference is not checked, will be compelled to consider the withdrawal of the American troops from the superior command of General Poole, and the directing of Colonel Stewart to act independently in accordance with the announced policy of this Government." This made it practically certain that Poole would have to be replaced, and the War Office accordingly looked around to find a candidate. The requirements were formidable. They called for a general officer capable of commanding a polyglot army with the likelihood of friction between its national components; someone with experience in campaigning under difficult conditions; someone with a reputation for charm and tact without diminution of military firmness; preferably someone (and this sharply narrowed the possibilities) who spoke Russian. Ironside was the obvious man.

The melancholy news that he was to be taken immediately from his brigade reached Ironside on September 19. He had no idea what lay in store, since orders were simply to report to the Chief of the Imperial General Staff; but he feared it would be some kind of staff position rather than the duty he loved, commanding troops in battle. On the morning of September 20 he regretfully conducted his successor, General M'Namara, on a tour of the brigade's combat position, accompanied by the commander of the brigade's artillery support. The three officers had completed their survey and were about to leave the front line when the Germans opened up a heavy bombardment. Thus it was that Ironside's last hour on the western front was spent in a shell hole, being "plastered with mud and splinters." A lull finally came and the trio made a fast getaway, "bolting like rabbits" over the open ground to the rear to reach their horses.

In London the following evening Ironside was given the startling information that his new assignment was to be in North Russia. Nothing was said about replacing Poole: he was to go as Poole's chief of staff. The next three days were not exactly restful. There were fittings at the tailor for clothing adapted to the North Russian climate (everything Ironside wore had to be specially made because of his size); long talks at the War Office with officers who were supposed to know something about Archangel and vicinity; arrangements for passage on a troop ship; and snatches of theater-going and other appropriate pleasures with his wife, who had come down from Cambridge to see him off.

Ironside found the scene at King's Cross Railway Station, on the evening of September 25, a stirring one. It was quite cosmopolitan, with a detachment of the French Colonial Infantry in their light blue uniforms; two Canadian field artillery batteries; a group of expatriate Russian officers who had escaped the revolution, dressed in sky-blue breeches and khaki jackets adorned with big gold epaulets; "there was even," Ironside remembered afterward, "a Japanese colonel in a blue braided jacket, trailing a long sword alongside his small figure." The general was pleased to see, in the front rank of the artillerymen, a Russian-Canadian named Piskoff who had served as his groom for a couple of years in France.

The sea voyage to Archangel was not unpleasant, at least for Ironside, who as top officer aboard had no duties and a cabin all to himself. He whiled away the time browsing through Waliszewski's *History of Peter the Great*, thinking it might illuminate his new assignment somewhat. It is conceivable that Tolstoy's *War and Peace* or the memoirs of Napoleon might have been more enlightening. He chatted with some of the Russian officers and found them convinced that it would be easy to "polish off the Bolsheviks"; but Ironside was not much impressed with their military judgment since none of them had been in North Russia before; and in any case they were desk-type soldiers rather than field officers.

Sailing up the channel of the Dvina, on the last day of September, was a moving experience for all aboard. For once the weather was superb, and the brilliant sunshine lighted a wonderful medley of autumn colors in the close-growing forests on the banks, the green stands pine contrasting beautifully with the clusters of birch, locusts, and willows. The Russian officers, many of whom had not seen their native land for several years, were on the verge of hysteria. As the ship rounded a bend the five great cupolas of the Archangel cathedral reared magnificently above the forest, producing on Ironside "an unforgettable impression of Eastern splendour." The only disconcerting note, as they approached the harbor, was that none of the Russian sawmill workers along the banks returned the cheery shouts of the soldiers on the troopships, merely staring stonily or continuing their work without so much as a glance at the newcomers.

When Ironside paid his respects to General Poole the next morning, that officer was in his usual sanguine spirits. He could not think, he said, why the War Office had sent Ironside out; everything was in good shape. As a matter of fact (and this was the first Ironside knew of it) he was going to England for a month's "leave," sailing on October 14. Ironside would be acting commander in chief. This news made the young general intensely interested in the battle situation, but what little he was able to learn from Poole was not very satisfactory. He found there was no accurate map at headquarters of current troop positions, and most of the orders issued since the beginning of Poole's operations had been verbal, without written records. Nevertheless Poole was affably certain that the Allied force would soon make great progress down the railroad and up the Dvina, and participate in a general advance against Petrograd and Moscow. (It will be recalled that this was a day or two after the drive for the Trans-Siberian Railroad had broken down everywhere except on the Vaga River.) The Bolsheviks, he assured his new chief of staff, knew nothing about warfare and would soon be in a hopeless position. Ironside kept his doubts to himself and decided to visit the actual fronts at the first opportunity to see how things looked.

First, however, a few days had to be spent in Archangel meeting such dignitaries as the British charge d'affaires, Sir Francis Lindley; Ambassador Francis; Ambassador Noulens. On all of these important men Ironside made a most favorable impression. Noulens, although not ordinarily overfond of Britishers, was quite charmed by this *"magnifique geant"*; and Ambassador Francis was so struckby Ironside's godlike appearance and reputation that he went into an unaccustomed spin of euphoric enthusiasm. "General Ironsides," he cabled the Department of State, his misspelling no doubt an unconscious compliment, "is six feet four inches tall without shoes, weights 270 pounds, and is only thirty-seven years old. He is descended direct from the last Saxon king of England, was dismissed from St. Andrew's School when he was ten and one-half years old because he whipped the teacher. He was the first British officer to land in France... . He was in command of a division on the French front, when he was ordered to Russia. He relinquished his command and cleared in an aeroplane for England ... spent three days acquainting himself with Russian conditions and arrived in Archangel September 20th; he does everything that way. He speaks six languages with equal [sic] fluency-English, French, Russian, German, Italian, Swedish, and can converse although not fluently in eleven other languages." This report is, of course, replete with odd errors (there is no telling where Francis got the idea that the general had flown from France to England, or that he had arrived in Russia on September 20), but it adequately conveys the crusty old ambassador's reaction to Ironside as an almost overwhelming specimen of British upperclass manhood.

Having met the leading members of Allied officialdom and learned all he could about the military situation by talking to Poole's staff officers, Ironside started out on a tour of the more important fronts. The Allied forces were now spread out across the upper half of Archangel Province in the shape of a giant hand, the heel resting at the capital city, and each of the fingers represented by a probing column thrust into the interior. It was evident that the railway front and the two river columns (on the Dvina and the Vaga) were the most promising, if anything was to come of the drive toward junction with the Czech forces from Siberia. The new chief of staff ferried across the Dvina mouth to Bakaritza and took one of the woodburning trains down to Obozerskaya, having first stopped to pick up General Finlayson, Poole's top field officer.

It would be interesting to have a transcript of the conversation between Ironside and Finlayson as they bumped their way southward on the Archangel-Vologda railroad. They were old friends, having served together as young officers in the same artillery battery in South Africa, and there was no reason for reticence in their discussion of General Poole's invasion of Russia. Finlayson had done his best to carry out Poole's orders to push down to Viatka and Vologda, but he was far less optimistic than his commander: he had seen the actual conditions under which the small detachments of Allied troops were fighting. There was no denying that the drive for the Trans-Siberian had bogged down, and Finlayson was beginning to think about the North Russian winter, which was due to arrive in a matter of weeks. His two main columns were diverging farther and farther from each other whenever they did make progress, and problems of command, administration, and supply were altogether likely to become more acute in the near future. Finlayson himself had been kept constantly on the go, flying to the Dvina front in a seaplane, back to Archangel to consult with Poole, and steaming up and down the railway in an effort to keep things moving there.

Just south of Obozerskaya, Ironside got his first view of United States troops in action. They had been fighting, off and on, for a month, and doubtless regarded themselves now as seasoned soldiers. To the veteran British general, whose obvious youth, titanic build, and searching blue eyes had the Americans gaping, they looked distressingly inept. Squelching through the wet mud and underbrush to a defensive position alongside the tracks, Ironside found a whole company of the 3rd Battalion strung out, "peering into the forest with their arms at the ready." Observing that there was no immediate prospect of a Soviet infantry attack, the general explained to the American captain that it was unnecessary to keep all his men constantly under arms and alert; they should be resting while a few sentries stood watch. The American stared at him in amazement and then exclaimed: "What! Rest in this hellish bombardment!" "At that moment," says Ironside, "a few shells were falling wide in the forest." But although the Bolshevik artillery left the general unperturbed, he discovered on this same occasion that, with all his knowledge of exotic tongues, the American language presented difficulties beyond his comprehension. Having spoken sharply to another company commander about some point of tactics, he was astonished to have the officer from the Midwest hold out his hand with the words, "General, I'm with you." "To this day," Ironside wrote in 1953, "I am not quite certain whether he meant to say that he agreed with me, or merely had heard what I said."

On his way back to Archangel, Ironside worked over in his mind the military problem that had been dropped in his lap. His talk with Finlayson and his brief visit to the railway front had already given him a clearer view of the realities of the situation than General Poole had ever had, or ever would have. Far form speculating about reaching the Trans-Siberian before snowfall, he saw that the true task would be to establish tenable defensive positions in good time to hold them against the Bolsheviks during the winter. Shelter for his troops would clearly be one of the biggest difficulties, and he and Finlayson had agreed that a chain of log blockhouses, carefully protected by barbedwire entanglements, must be built at once. Another point was quite obvious to Ironside: since he had found sentiment in London distinctly against the commitment of any really large numbers of troops to North Russia, it was entirely likely that the upshot of the whole affair would be an Allied evacuation. The trick would be to prevent a minor-scale repetition of Gallipoli. And if the British hope of a Soviet collapse was to be assisted by military action, it would have to be White Russian forces, in the long run, who would carry it out. He decided that energetic recruitment and training of such forces must be one of his major concerns in the ensuing months. In the meantime, any progress toward union with the Czech troops on the Trans-Siberian would have to depend on the success of the Czechs.

Before going backacross the Dvina to the city, Ironside stopped at a suburb called Isaka Gora, where Commander Chaplin, mastermind of the coup against the Chaikovsky government, had been sent to cool his heels until further notice. The general had heard about the kidnaping episode, and had a feeling Chaplin was the kind of man needed to help lead a Russian army capable of fighting the Bolsheviks. He found the handsome firebrand sitting on his bed in a little village hut, singing nostalgic Russian songs and accompanying himself on the balalaika. Although the new chief of staff was not in a position to remove Chaplin from banishment, he suggested the possibility of some kind of command if and when the recruitment of large White Russian forces became a reality.

Back in Archangel, Ironside found things going not very much to his liking. The city was now in the full grip of the influenza epidemic that had come in with the American troops in September: about ten thousand people were down with it, and deaths were being reported at a rate of thirty a day. There was also considerable venereal disease. Medical facilities were in short supply. Good food, especially fresh meat and vegetables, was scarce. Ironside's immediate concern, however, was with the military situation, and he therefore had a long talk with Poole about necessary changes. Ironside felt that the operations on the Dvina and Vaga ought to be handled separately from those on the railroad and its flanks, and proposed separate commands for the two; Poole amiably assented. The whole North Russia venture had been code-named, until now, ELOPE. Ironside's study of the battle dispositions made it appear conclusively that the honeymoon was over, and from then on the two main columns were referred to simply as the Vologda Force (on the railway), and the Dvina Force.

Finlayson, Ironside felt, should command the Dvina operations, but he was in some doubt as to what to do about the railroad. Colonel Sutherland, the unpopular protagonist of the bridge-shelling episode on September 29, was due to go home to England soon, and no other British officer of sufficient experience and rank seemed to be available. Poole had nothing to offer, and when Ironside suggested asking Colonel Stewart, of the U.S. army, to take over the Vologda Force, Poole said he thought that an excellent idea. He did not tell Ironside that he had already tried, unsuccessfully, to get Stewart to do just that; and in this Poole appears to have been somewhat less than candid. It is hard to avoid the impression that he had already washed his hands of his responsibilities in North Russia, although he persisted in telling Ironside and the diplomatic corps that he would certainly return to Archangel after his trip to London. It is doubtful that he believed this himself; and he failed to convince Ambassador Francis, who wired a contrary conclusion to the State Department early in October.

When Ironside entered the massive stone building, formerly a technical institute, which the Americans had taken over as headquarters, he was unaware not only of Poole's earlier negotiations with Stewart, but also of the peculiar relationship between Stewart and

Ambassador Francis. It was the ambassador who had backed Stewart's refusal, in September, to take charge of the troops on the railway, despite insistence from the State Department that in military matters the American officer was under Poole's command. This, of course, was part of Francis' sparring tactics against the British general rather than a move toward enforcing President Wilson's restrictive policy in the use of United States troops in Russia; but recently Stewart had received an official statement of that policy, and he was by now understandably and thoroughly confused. To this it must be added that at no time in the North Russia campaign did he show any enthusiasm for leading troops in combat, or even remaining any longer than absolutely necessary in the combat areas.

Ironside had heard, however, that Stewart had won the Congressional Medal for bravery in the Philippines, and he therefore approached him with considerable hope. But before he could make his proposition, the American colonel launched into a long complaint about the trouble he was having administering his scattered troops. Ironside patiently explained the unavoidable reasons for this, stressing among other things the need to present a united Allied front to the Russians; Stewart "somewhat grudgingly agreed." But when the British general asked him to take over the Vologda Force, Stewart lapsed into a long silence which Ironside interpreted as surprise at having been asked. He then firmly refused, observing that it would be "exceeding his instructions" if he were to leave Archangel. Ironside argued for some time but got nothing for his pains except a rambling account of Stewart's army career. He therefore departed, asking the American to visit the fighting fronts often "so that his men could see that he was still in command." Although this suggestion was very feebly acted upon, it can be questioned whether at best it would have been effective. Stewart was already unpopular with the men of the 339th Infantry, and beyond that it was all too clear to them that the British were actually in command of the whole show.

Ironside settled the problem of a commander for the Vologda Force by calling on M. Noulens, the French ambassador, who recommended an officer of the French Colonial battalion named (rather surprisingly) Lucas. But now other difficulties beset the new British chief of staff. General Finlayson, having gone backup the

Dvina to his field headquarters, was exceedingly disturbed to find that the British gunboats, which had been the only fully effective counter to Bolshevik heavy artillery, had suddenly been withdrawn to Archangel. The Soviet river craft exploited this unexpected advantage assiduously, walloping a heavy bombardment into Allied positions at Seltso and vicinity that destroyed some of the newly built defenses and produced a score of casualties. These included several among the American engineer detachment sent out to help with the construction work. According to Finlayson's telegram to Ironside, no notice of the gunboat withdrawal had been given by the naval commander to the Allied ground forces: the boats simply went downstream without warning. Ironside took the telegram and headed for Poole's office; and Poole called in the British admiral to explain the business.

The ensuing argument brought the navy out on top, at least technically, for the admiral was able to produce a written order from Poole authorizing the withdrawal of the gunboats to Archangel at any time after the first of October, to insure their not getting frozen-in upstream. Poole had forgotten about it and had, as Ironside dryly phrased it, "omitted to inform the Dvina Column." Unfortunately, although there was still no ice, the water level in the river had now sunk considerably, as it was wont to do in the fall, and the admiral declared that the gunboats could not return upriver because of their draft. Suppressing his irritation at Poole's bungling as best he could, Ironside suggested sending the two Canadian field artillery batteries up the Dvina, and they were dispatched on barges shortly thereafter. Their guns were only eighteen-pounders, but they were to use them so valiantly that the record of the 16th-Canadian Field Artillery Brigade would lose none of the luster it had already acquired in France.

While Ironside was facing up to these urgent military problems, the comic-opera aspect of official life in Archangel was continuing under Chaikovsky's management with very little concession to the demands of reality. After the indignity of Chaplin's kidnaping junket, the Supreme Administration had desperately tried to regain its lost prestige in Archangel by a series of pompous promulgations and decrees, none of which had any great practical result. Meanwhile Chaikovsky was still clashing with General Poole and his staff at every turn, the Allied diplomats, led by Francis, wearily acting as referees. After a bewildering month during which Chaikovsky alternately threatened and refused to resign, the old revolutionist finally announced, on October 7, that his Supreme Administration had been replaced by an entirely new government: the "Provisional Government of the Northern Region." It was true that the personnel of this political invention was largely new-as a matter of fact three of Chaikovsky's ministers had by this time left, in disgust, for Siberia-but heading the new roster, as president, was the name of N. V. Chaikovsky.

The only important difference between the new government and the old, as things turned out, was that the new was, incredibly, even more ineffectual than the old, and more of a puppet show, pretending independence when truly it was for the most part dancing to strings pulled by the Allied military establishment. Chaikovsky's grasp on actuality seemed to become more and more tenuous as the weeks went by. He concerned himself with formulating elaborate rules for the executive sessions of the new government; he fussed over estimates of purely theoretical expenditures; he spent long hours poring over the postal-telegraph regulations, changing a word here and a phrase there. The menace of influenza in Archangel, the food shortage, the sullen faces of the unhappy populace, the streets full of marching Allied soldiers, the trains and barges coming into the city bringing wounded men from the fighting fronts-all of this drifted past Chaikovsky's visionary eyes as if in a dream. In one direction, however, he remained fairly practical: he saw to it that most of his old socialist friends got good government jobs. For one of them, a man named Martiushin, there seemed to be nothing available in Archangel, so Chaikovsky sent him on a special mission to the United States, equipped with fifty thousand rubles, to solicit sympathy for the White Russian cause.

To Chaikovsky's political vagaries General Poole added, in his last few days on the Archangel scene, a bizarre military gesture. Among the dozens of strange characters who had turned up in the city following the overthrow of the local Bolsheviks in August, there was an Armenian who called himself General Torcom. It was known that he had served as a captain in the Russian army before the Bolshevik revolution; but it was by no means clear how he had so rapidly soared in rank, or, for that matter, in whose army he was now a general. What Torcom lacked in credentials, however, he made up for in *savoir-faire*.

Apparently furnished with an endless quantity of czarist rubles, he tooka large house in Archangel and outfitted himself and his half-dozen Armenian followers in dazzling blue and red uniforms complete with high, polished boots, fancy fur hats, Turkish dirks and scimitars, and a suitable selection of chest decorations. He then proclaimed that he and his entourage constituted the "Armenian Military Mission," having arrived in Archangel after a hair-raising series of escapes from Bolsheviks who had pursued them from one end of Russia to the other. A small, bright-eyed, dapper man with a fastidiously pointed beard, he bore himself (as the French ambassador phrased it) "like a veritable chief of state," never leaving his abode without putting his bodyguard through "all the protocol of a complicated ceremony." While this behavior added color to the drab Archangel background, it was not taken seriously by anyone of importance in the city-except General Poole.

Shortly before Poole was scheduled to leave for England, Torcom announced that he had in his possession the sacred banner of the Armenian Republic, piously embroidered by young female Armenians and blessed by the Armenian patriarch, which he, Torcom, would one day carry triumphantly back to his liberated native land. He asked Poole to order a solemn formation of Allied troops in the square before the government building, where the public could witness the consecration of this hallowed cloth. The British general obligingly called out the troops on the appointed day, but not before Ambassador Noulens, sensing a fiasco, had requested that no French soldiers should take part. The formation therefore consisted only of one American company, British and White Russian troops, Poole with his staff, and "General" Torcom, gloriously arrayed, with his. There was a flourish of bugles, and all eyes turned to Torcom and the Armenian officer who was carrying the sacred flag. Torcom, striking a noble attitude, marched smartly forward-not, however, toward General Poole, who stood at attention not knowing just what to expect. To his astonishment, and to what Ambassador Noulens described as "la stupefaction generale," Torcom went straight up to Poole, saluted with great dash, and then "applied brusquely to his chest a decoration which, probably, Torcom invented himself." In the widespread embarrassment that followed (not afflicting, of course, Torcom, who was highly satisfied), the consecration of the Armenian flag was given only the most perfunctory attention, and for days gossip in Archangel social and diplomatic circles burbled with metaphors involving the old game of Pin the Tail on the Donkey.

One of Poole's last achievements in North Russia was thus to receive a spurious honor from a self-made general in the name of a country that did not even exist.* Torcom tried his blandishments later on Ironside, but with only partial success. Ironside coolly declined to be presented with "the Order of the Star of Armenia," but did arrange passage to England for Torcom, which was what the little adventurer really wanted: he by now had got into trouble with both Ambassador Noulens and with Chaikovsky, and was afraid of being arrested. To Ironside's considerable consternation, one of the first things Torcom did upon reaching London was to complain that the general had stolen from him two bears which had been intended as symbolic presents for King George and Mr. Churchill.

*Armenia had in fact been declared an "independent republic" under German auspices by the Treaty of Brest-Litovsk; but it was not this creation of the Bolsheviks that Torcom claimed to represent.

* * *

General Poole left Archangel for England on October 14, and since his parting instructions were vague, Ironside was now free to do what he thought necessary without interference from above. Although his conception of the military situation, unlike Poole's, was that inevitably it must be largely defensive, he did not feel that the Allied position on the railroad and its flanks was a very sound one. If Plesetskaya could be taken before winter set in, it would deprive the Reds of much good shelter against the cold and give it to Allied troops; it also would remove the threat of a Soviet flanking movement coming up the broad road leading from Plesetskaya to Seletskoe. Ironside therefore delayed his orders for establishing defensive lines at Kodish and on the railroad until one more attempt had been made to reach Plesetskaya before snowfall.

Things went better this time than they had at the end of September, but still not well enough to convince Ironside that the

race against winter was likely to be won in a way that would
strengthen the over-all Allied position more than weaken it. Aided
by a detachment of Royal Scots and one section of the Canadian field
artillery, sent over from the Dvina, Companies K and L of the 339th
Infantry again ferried across the Emtsa River north of Kodish, and
assaulted that village with all the energy they could muster. In a
duplication of what had happened three weeks earlier at Seltso,
Captain Donoghue's men took the town after spending a miserable
night sleeping without cover in a cold, rainy swamp. The Canadian
gunners here first showed the Americans what valuable allies they
could be: their shelling of the enemy positions was beautifully
accurate, and was without doubt largely responsible for the Reds'
abandonment of Kodish without having put up much of a struggle.

The Canadians also taught the inexperienced Americans a
somewhat grisly lesson in post-battle behavior after the town had been
occupied. Few of the boys from Detroit and vicinity had ever seen dead
men before October, 1918; they were inclined to regard with a mixture
of respect and horror the many Bolshevik corpses encountered in the
woods around Kodish. They watched with awe as the Canadians
coolly went through the dead men's pockets, appropriated money,
knives, and other booty, and tried on the better-looking leather boots
to see if they might serve victor as well as they had vanquished. Need,
however, is the mother of more than invention, and since most of the
doughboys hated the ill-fitting British hobnailed shoes which they had
been issued, it was not long before many of them, too, were looking
over enemy bodies with less pity than calculation. They were
encouraged in this battlefield pragmatism by the distressing fact that
they still were without overcoats, extra shoes, or extra socks, since
their barracks bags had been misplaced somewhere in Archangel and
had never caught up with them.

Although the offensive against the Bolsheviks was progressing
satisfactorily at Kodish, on the railroad the push for Plesetskaya
seemed unable to gather much momentum despite relatively weak
resistance. It had been decided to try once again the plan of flank
encirclement through the forest by one detachment, while another
struck straight down the tracks into the Soviet defenses. This time the
French and Americans, who had been delegated to carry out the

flanking movement, made a thorough reconnaissance of the boggy terrain which they would have to traverse; and the night march to put them in assault position consequently went off without disaster. At 5 A.M. on October 14, after a couple of hours of rest in the wet forest, they moved back toward the railroad at an angle intended to bring them in slightly to the rear of the Soviet front. The object was to blow the rails with TNT and trap the Bolshevik armored train before it could escape southward.

Unfortunately, the Reds had a high watchtower overlooking the forest at Verst 455, and the creeping Allied column was spotted, through the screen of pine trees, before it got to the rails. A skirmish detachment of Bolsheviks quickly went to meet them, and by the time the French and Americans had shot their way through, the armored train was already steaming down the tracks. The maneuver ended victoriously, however, for the Bolsheviks overestimated the size of the attacking force. Most of them piled aboard a waiting troop train and pulled out fast as they could, while the wooden cars were splintered by a sleet of bullets from French and American rifles.

At this point both sides seem to have been afflicted with morale problems. The Soviet soldiers on the railroad were mostly new recruits: young peasants forced into Bolshevik service very much against their will, and almost completely untrained. They were inclined to panic at the slightest show of aggressiveness from the Allies, and frequently had to be pushed into battle with Communist officers holding automatic rifles at their backs. The French poilus, while there was no question of their bravery, were so sorely disgusted with the North Russia campaign that any vague rumor was likely to affect their performance. During the fighting south of Verst 455, on October 16 and 17, the word went out among them that an armistice had been declared on the western front, and they promptly sat down in the woods and refused to pursue the Reds any further. "*La guerre est finie*," they explained stubbornly to the British and American officers. They were talked out of their peace strike only on the ground that they must not desert the Americans, whom they liked very much. Meanwhile it was a matter of growing agreement between the French and Americans that the British officers over them were to be described only in unprintable epithets, from Colonel Sutherland on down.

Considering the spongy state of morale on the railroad front, the lack of reinforcements, and the fact that the thermometer was already dipping nightly close to freezing, Ironside now tentatively decided that even Plesetskaya, still thirty miles distant, was an unrealistic objective. At Kodish, where the drive had been relatively successful, the Reds counterattacked heavily at the end of October, and the American troops there were forced to withdraw to the north bankof the Emtsa. Ironside consequently ordered offensive operations suspended, and both on the railroad and along the Emtsa herculean labors commenced to prepare winter defensive quarters. The heroes of these constructive efforts were the 310th Engineers, whose scattered platoons were building log blockhouses at scores of sites across the expanse of Archangel Province as November approached. The low, broad-beamed structures were modeled roughly after the native dwellings of North Russia, but more heavily built. Long, straight pine logs from the surrounding forest supplied nearly all the material needed, and many of the American engineers soon became professionally adroit with their axes and cross-cut saws. On all four sides clearings were cut, to give a field of fire easily swept by machine guns poked through openings cut for the purpose in the logs of the blockhouse; the clearings were then heavily staked out with concentric barbed wire entanglements. When and if winter attacks should come, the Americans felt they would be nearly as secure against Reds in these forts as any band of settlers ever was against Redskins. Soviet artillery was the only specter that worried them.

Back at his Archangel headquarters, chafing to get away to visit the fighting fronts, Ironside found he had inherited more than military problems from Poole. There was, for example, the question of his relationship with Chaikovsky, whom so far he had been too busy even to meet. Having concluded that the building up of a capable White Russian army must be his chief task for the winter, he went to call on the President of the Provisional Government to solicit co-operation. It surprised Ironside to be ushered into the presence of "a placid old gentleman" who seemed to be only vaguely in touch with what the British general conceived to be the real problems facing the anti-Bolshevik cause in North Russia. Chaikovsky listened in an abstracted sort of way to Ironside's analysis of what needed to be done, and then waved it all aside with the observation that any military questions should be referred to Colonel B. A. Durov, his commander in chief. Such questions were not, he implied, really very important: he knew Lenin and Trotsky and the other top Bolshevik leaders, and their regime undoubtedly was a most ephemeral thing. It was just a matter of time before the Social Revolutionaries, like himself, would reassert their democratic authority over Russia in the name of all the people. Ironside remained scrupulously polite, but went away convinced that any program to save Russia from Communism was going to get very little assistance from men with Chaspongy state of morale on the railroad frontikovsky's illusions.

He was even less impressed with Colonel Durov and his chief of staff, General Samarin, whom he next visited. He already had looked over their dossiers, which were undistinguished, and had discovered that among the ex-czarist officers in Archangel they were held in open contempt. Conversing with Durov in French, and Samarin in Russian, Ironside quickly concluded that one thing was very plain: although both of them talked agreeably of raising a large anti-Bolshevik army, they had not in fact done anything about it, nor even drawn up any specific plans. Moreover, they were full of reasons why the whole affair must be conducted slowly and with delicacy. Most of the Russian soldiers already enlisted were anxious to get home after years of service against Germany, and perhaps few of them would be willing to fight. The several hundred ex-czarist officers who were hanging idly about Archangel could not be used for the new army, which above all must be democratic. Calling for further volunteers probably would not be very effective; but on the other hand conscription was out of the question. The interview ended when Ironside, dropping diplomacy, ordered them to establish one model infantry company with no further delay: he would inspect it at the end of a week. He then went back to his headquarters and sent a telegram to the War Office asking that replacements be found for Durov and Samarin as soon as possible. The fact that he by-passed Chaikovsky was sufficient index of the degree of trust he felt he could place in the Provisional Government of North Russia.

Meeting with the Allied ambassadors in council the next day, Ironside was cordially assured of support for his plan to build up an autonomous White Russian army. To his vexation, however, he found that the British, French, and American representatives were all convinced that an armistice with Germany on the western front (which now appeared imminent) would mean "a tacit ceasefire" in North Russia, so that in their opinion little was to be feared from the Bolsheviks during the approaching winter. Ironside's idea of Soviet intentions was quite different, but the only man among the western diplomats who agreed with him was the Serbian minister, whose voice in the council was nearly inaudible.

October 29 was the date set for Ironside's review of the model infantry company, selected by Durov and Samarin from the "1st Archangel Regiment"-the fifteen hundred men who had responded to the Provisional Government's fall mobilization call. But what little training these men had received was according to Durov's conception of a truly "democratic" army; and when they were ordered to fall in for the review, the model company flatly refused. They had just held a democratic meeting and decided that now was the time to strike a blow for better treatment and "working" hours. They were not getting as good food as the British and American troops; and they had decided that saluting officers was a slavish custom which should be abandoned. Finding themselves overwhelmingly in the minority, the Russian officers of the company democratically left the barracks without attempting to restore discipline, and the fat was in the fire.

According to Ambassador Francis, Colonel Durov met this emergency by proceeding in person to the barracks, where he delivered an oration lasting two hours. It seems more likely that this was simply the impression of its length made upon the restless troops; at any rate when he had finished his harangue, Durov, bearing in mind that even mutiny must be handled democratically, invited replies from the men. A noncom spoke at length, interspersing his remarks with the question, "Am I right, comrades?" and invariably getting a shout of approval for reply. Then, as Francis reported it to the State Department, "about one thousand men attempted to speakat once." After shaking hands with one of the most clamorous soldiers and addressing him as *"Tovarisch,"* Durov then left the barracks and went off to confer with President Chaikovsky on the lamentable state of affairs in the army of the Provisional Government of the Northern Region. Meanwhile Ivan Ivanovitch Michaov, the commander of the 1st Archangel Regiment, requested relief from his command.

Ironside, who of course had been informed of the trouble at the barracks, was following a wait-and-see policy in the hope that the Russians could handle the problem themselves. But Chaikovsky, who had spent half the fall trying to block British interference in Russian affairs, now requested in great anxiety that two companies of Allied troops be sent to disarm his recalcitrant countrymen. Considering the effect this undoubtedly would have on public opinion, it was the last thing Ironside wanted to do; so instead he wired Finlayson to send down from the Dvina front two Russian colonels who had proved, under fire, that they were not easily intimidated. These officers were quickly flown to Archangel, and after a briefing with Ironside, during which he discoursed upon the futility of what he called "Tovarisch methods" of military discipline, they proceeded to the barracks, gave a few curt orders, and stood by for the result. To the surprise and relief of all concerned, including perhaps the soldiers themselves, the company fell in without a murmur, and the first abortive mutiny among the anti-Bolshevik forces in North Russia was finished. Its portent, however, was ominous.

Durov and Samarin, meanwhile, had tendered their resignations to Chaikovsky with much chagrin; and Samarin had made the absolutely classic gesture of joining, as a private, the unit of the French Foreign Legion which had recently been activated at Archangel. The spectacle of his late chief of staff being reduced overnight to the status of common soldier in a foreign army was intensely disturbing to Chaikovsky, as indeed was the entire episode, and he kept muttering to Ironside: "If we could only have let the men alone!" The whole thing, Ironside noted in his memoirs, was "Gilbertian." To match Chaikovsky's disquiet, Ambassador Noulens zoomed into a passion at the news that Samarin had elected the army of France as a refuge for his inadequacy, and the month of October thus ended with both Allied and Russian statesmen at Archangel in a mood of considerable agitation. For his part, Ironside was happy to have got rid of Durov and Samarin without having had to oust them himself.

Now came November, and with November, in North Russia, came winter. The autumn of 1918 had been relatively mild, and the rivers did not freeze solidly enough to carry sleighs until late in the month, but heavy snow fell fitfully from the first week. The days had already grown astonishingly brief, and the hazy arctic sun rolled along its short path low above the line of the forests south of Archangel. To the empty reaches of the north the spectacular lights of the aurora borealis cast their weird night refractions across the cold waters of the White Sea, which soon would be an impassable barrier of ice. Between patrols and skirmishes with Bolshevik forces, the American doughboys and engineers at their six far-flung outposts* watched the snow come down, and worked harder at completing their billets, dugouts, and blockhouses. It looked like a long, cold winter.

*A sixth front, purely defensive, had been established at Pinega, one hundred miles northeast of Archangel, about November 1.

Although hints of the coming armistice persisted, things were busy in Archangel. Ironside negotiated with Chaikovsky about permanent replacements for Durov and Samarin: two well-known Russian generals were invited to come from exile (in Italy and Sweden, respectively) and take the jobs. The influenza epidemic had subsided somewhat but adequate medical facilities were still a problem. Ironside was worried about the danger of incendiary sabotage from the city's thousands of pro-Bolshevik laborers, and checked and rechecked the condition of the fire apparatus. He had a nightmare vision of what would happen to the tenth of a million people in Archangel if the wooden city ever took flame: lack of winter cover in that climate would be utter disaster.

There were also changes in the corps of Allied officials to take note of: Rear Admiral N. A. McCully arrived as commander of U.S. naval forces in North Russia, and DeWitt Clinton Poole, after a harrowing season as American consul at Moscow, came via Finland to take over the U.S. embassy. Ambassador Francis' prostate trouble had now become acute, and it was felt that he must go to London for the required operation. The *Olympia* steamed in from Murmansk to pick him up, and on November 6 he went aboard on a stretcher carried by eight sailors. It was the last time an American ambassador would be on Russian soil until 1933.

The news of the armistice with Germany, which sparked in on the wire from Murmanskon the afternoon of November 11, set Archangel to buzzing (as Ironside observed) like a hive of bees "upset by an unwonted hammering from outside." Everyone wanted to know what the effect would be on the civil war in Russia and the responsibility of the Allied forces there. Ironside was besieged by Allied visitors asking whether the fighting was now over, and by Russian visitors asking whether they would now be abandoned to the Bolsheviks. He had little to tell them. A long message came in from London, but it turned out to be the standard congratulatory tribute from His Majesty, King George V, to his loyal troops; there was no reference to North Russia. In the absence of facts, however, the citizens of Archangel decided to exercise the will to believe, and for two weeks proceeded to celebrate as gaily as the somewhat limited resources of the town permitted. Bunting was hung out; victory dinners were hastily planned; the local archpriest announced a solemn *Te Deum* to be observed in the great cathedral; Chaikovsky made speeches; Noulens made speeches; Ironside was talked into authorizing a big military parade and three-day holiday, arranged to include the American Thanksgiving on November 28. Enterprising cooks from the American regiment even bagged a few somewhat stringy wild turkeys in the surrounding woods, to make the day gastronomically authentic. A perceptible dent was made in the huge supply of alcoholic beverages the Allies had shipped into Archangel since August.

If Ironside had entertained any of the optimistic hopes now surging through Archangel, however, they were abruptly canceled by a wire from General Finlayson, late on the day of the armistice itself. It was a terse summary of what Finlayson knew so far about the battle of Toulgas, just then reaching its height; and it made perfectly clear that as far as the Bolsheviks were concerned the armistice had no bearing on their efforts to rid Russian soil of those they regarded as foreign invaders. By November 15, of course, Ironside had the reassuring word of the surprisingly good outcome of the siege of

Toulgas: the Allied system of winter defenses, he felt, had proved itself in its first severe test. And then, on the eighteenth, he got the exhilarating news that General Poole (from whom he had not heard one word) was not coming back: Ironside was to be commander in chief, and had been made a major general.

But he was still keenly apprehensive of what the winter might bring. His little forces were committed deep in the Russian interior, and he had no authority to withdraw them except in case of absolute emergency. The White Sea was freezing. There was little if any prospect of reinforcement. The power of the North Russian civilian government was largely a fiction, and for all practical purposes the full weight of both military and civil authority now rested on Edmund Ironside.

CHAPTER 6

ONCE MORE UNTO THE BREACH

COLONEL GEORGE STEWART OF the 339th Infantry was not a popular commanding officer, but at least once during the North Russia campaign he spoke truly if somewhat cautiously for his men. On November 14, 1918, when it became evident that no immediate change in orders was forthcoming as a result of the armistice, he sent this cablegram through the proper War Department channels:

"Men of this command have performed most excellent service under the most trying climatic conditions of cold, snow, wet and miry marshes... . Allies have not been received with the hospitality the object of this expedition warranted... . The original object ... no longer exists. The winter port of Archangel will be practicable for navigation twenty to thirty days longer and then closes until June. My inference is plain. Immediate consideration requested."

The answer to this plea for withdrawal is indicated clearly enough in the combat statistics: hundreds of Americans became battle casualties in North Russia *after* the armistice. The question that plagued the American soldiers fighting for their lives in the Archangel snows that winter of 1918-19 was never, for most of the survivors, satisfactorily answered: Why?

It was indeed a delicate question for the American Department of State. Officially, the government had never admitted that units of the United States army were engaged in organized warfare with units of the Red army, and consequently it was not easy to explain why they should continue. Sidestepping was the obvious solution. On November 27 the British government was informed that since President Wilson and his Secretary of State would leave shortly for the Paris peace conference any American decision on what to do in Russia would be postponed until then.

A similar message went to DeWitt C. Poole, charge d'affaires at Archangel, but not, for some reason, until December 4. Since he was scheduled to give a speech to units of the 339th Infantry in Archangel on Thanksgiving Day, Poole was obliged to make the best of it on his own. He chose relative honesty, adorned with a few rhetorical flourishes. "You men want to know what you are doing here," he told them. "You are protecting one spot in Russia from the sanguinary bedlam of Bolshevism; you are keeping safe one spot where the real progressives of the Russian revolution may begin to lay the foundation of the great free Russian state which is to come. Don't think you are forgotten. Washington knows what you are doing, what you are up against. You may be sure that the President has thought of you and in good time will tell you and the rest of us what he expects each to do in order to hold steady the light of our forward-looking democracy."

The message that finally came in from Washington on December 5 was neither so inspiring nor so candid, nor could it usefully have been passed on to the troops. "Signing of the armistice has created no change in the situation," said Acting Secretary of State Frank Polk. "The President and Secretary of State have today [December 4] sailed for France. As already made quite clear by this Government American forces were sent to Archangel only to safeguard Russian stores and supplies and to protect the port of Archangel from attacks which were being organized or directed in whole or in part by German and Austrian prisoners of war." This stubborn preference of theory over practice was nearly matched by the British government, which advised its Archangel representative, about the same time, that "His Majesty's Government do not intend to interfere in Russian domestic affairs." To this was added, however, as a concession to what was really going on, an allusion to "certain obligations to the Czechs who are our allies and certain governments which have grown up under our protection on the White Sea, in Siberia, the Caucasus and Transcaspian."

As a matter of fact, the over-all situation in Russia early in December looked fairly hopeful from the point of view of the anti-Bolshevik cause, and this scarcely discouraged the inclination of the British, the French, and even the Americans to play for time. In the south a large Cossack army under General Denikin threatened the Bolshevik front, with powerful assistance from the French and British promised within a matter of days. The British already had an expeditionary force in Caucasia and Transcaspia; Allied squadrons patrolled the Black Sea and the Caspian as well as the Baltic; in Finland a reactionary government was making plans for a march on Petrograd. To the east, beyond the Urals, some battalions of the Czech legion had been newly consolidated with White Russian forces under the leadership of Admiral Kolchak, former commander of the Czar's Black Sea fleet. Kolchak had come into power by *coup d'etat* on November 18, and while there was much room for doubt as to how democratic his intentions might be, his military dictatorship promised an aggressive fight against the Bolsheviks that would drive through to Viatka, Kotlas, and perhaps Moscow, by spring. The Reds were, in fact, surrounded, and to the French and British it did not look like the time to be withdrawing from North Russia.

But quite aside from questions of international policy, over which of course he had no control, Ironside felt strongly that any general retreat from the front established across Archangel against the Bolsheviks might be gambling with disaster. Technically he considered it possible, but strategically it seemed like a very bad move. His intelligence reports showed clearly that the Soviet army was improving in strength, discipline, training, and equipment from week to week. Toulgas had been a near catastrophe, and there was now nothing to support the earlier notion that the Reds would suspend offensive operations when the winter weather set in. To a battalion commander who had asked withdrawal for his exhausted troops on the Dvina in October, Ironside had wired: "Any retrograde movement by you gives them [the Red army] now absolutely-lacking moral courage to continue worrying you. They will soon tire, so stick it out." Now, two months later, he no longer believed that "they will soon tire." The problem was to dig in, hang on, and live out the winter.

In this connection it is interesting to note how different a military situation may look to the commander in the field than to a statesman or staff officer in some distant war office. To Allied leaders in London and Paris, the sooner Kolchak's troops could fight through and join hands with Ironside, the better. But when Ironside contemplated the possibility, however unlikely, of battle-tired Czech and Russian legions arriving in ice-locked Archangel in the depths of the North Russian winter, he was filled with misgiving. Food and shelter for the hundred thousand inhabitants of the city and for the fifteen thousand troops under him were a sufficiently gnawing worry without the prospect of perhaps seventy thousand guests from Siberia.

As usual, however, Ironside had little time for mere worry. October and November had gone by without his ever managing to visit the Allied positions between the railroad and the Dvina, and he was a commander to whom personal contact with his combat troops meant a great deal. On December 2 he finally got away from administrative harassments, and enjoyed his first trip through the deep snow of the great fir forests in a pony sleigh. He found things in fair shape at Seletskoe and Shredmehrenga. The troops seemed to be well housed for the winter, and the state of their morale reasonably good. On the other hand he was disappointed by the attitude of the villagers he talked to along the route. They were apathetic about the fight with the Bolsheviks, and Ironside found it hard to convince them that it was not merely some private squabble between the Allies and the Communists. Chaikovsky's government, under whom they theoretically were now living, meant nothing to them, and they showed no disposition to give it their loyalty or assistance.

After a week of what amounted almost to a holiday, Ironside returned to the confusion of Archangel. One continuing problem, worked at assiduously since the fiasco of late October, was the recruitment and training of the new Russian army. Prominent in this activity was General Vladimir V. Marushevsky, who had been chief of the Russian general staff under the Kerensky government in 1917, and who had arrived in Archangel from Sweden shortly after the armistice. A man of very small stature, barely over five feet tall, Marushevsky evidently tried to make up for it by constant effusion of bustling energy. According to one of his colleagues he seldom appeared at his headquarters before noon, but when he did arrive it was invariably like a comet. By that time there was always a crowd of people waiting to see him, and he rushed through a series of hectic interviews, constantly urging his visitors to be brief, as he was exceedingly busy and could understand their needs from "half a word." He was a great disciplinarian-his political sentiments were in fact monarchist-but because of his size he sometimes had difficulty impressing the Russian soldiers under his command. "Whether he sits or stands," they used to say of him, "it's all the same." One can imagine the amusing figure he must have cut when he appeared in public beside General Ironside, who loomed above him by well over a foot.

Ironside had not yet formed a positive opinion of Marushevsky's abilities, but he was quite willing to give him a chance to show them. Consequently, when the Russian general informed him that the North Russian army was making splendid progress, Ironside suggested a parade of two companies of the 1st Archangel Regiment on December 11, prior to sending them to the railway front for completion of their training,.

As a parting gesture Marushevsky had arranged for a *Te Deum* in the Archangel cathedral; the Russian companies were to show up for that at 11 A.M. and then entrain for the front. Unhappily, when the time came the soldiers announced that they would go neither to the *Te Deum* nor to the front. Their rebellious mood stemmed partly from a recent order of Marushevsky's putting epaulets back on officers' uniforms-a hated symbol of the old regime, as far as the enlisted men were concerned. Since they already had been issued rifles and ammunition, and since they were fully in possession of the large brick building on Troitsky Prospect which was their barracks, the situation now began to look very disagreeable. There were flurries of nervous activity at the various headquarters: Marushevsky conferred with the colonel of the 1st Archangel Regiment; Ironside conferred with Ambassador Noulens (now dean of the diplomats in North Russia); a British colonel conferred with Captain Joseph Taylor of the Headquarters Company, 339th Infantry, suggesting that he prepare his men for action. A company of the Royal Marine Light Infantry was also told to stand by, and Marushevsky ordered out a detachment of Russians who were in training at a machine-gun school, together with several pieces of the school equipment. Only old Chaikovsky, who was busy drawing up a new decree reorganizing his ministry, seemed to be undisturbed, expressing to Marushevsky his confidence that all would be well.

It was now about 1:30 P.M., and rifles were being fired from the barracks windows, more or less aimlessly. By means of a loudspeaker Marushevsky ordered the mutineers to desist; but the only answer was a great deal of shouting and waving of red flags from the windows. Captain Taylor, therefore, upon a "request" from a British staff officer, hustled his doughboys down to the Russian barracks with rifles unslung, and with three trench mortars and four Lewis machine guns ready for firing. The American riflemen were scattered along Petrogradski Street wherever they could find good cover, while the mortar crews established themselves behind convenient houses. Promptly at 2 P.M. they were ordered to fire on the barracks. According to Ironside, who by this time was on the scene, the first mortar shell went over the barracks roof and landed in the courtyard, exploding squarely on top of an unlucky civilian who happened to be there at the moment. The second shell burst on the roof of the building; and what with this and the spatter of rifle and machine-gun lead against the walls, the mutinous Russians now came tumbling out onto the street with their hands in the air and frightened expressions on their faces. Their little revolution had backfired rather quickly. They were soon lined up on the parade ground under a mixed Russian and American guard, and Marushevsky sternly demanded that the ringleaders step forward. Thirteen men admitted their guilt, and in return for this candor were promptly put against a wall and shot by squads drawn from the mutinous regiment itself. During all of this the British, except for Ironside and a few other officers, had been conspicuously absent; now, much to the disgust of the Americans, the Royal Marine company hove into view, "crawling along slowly at sixty to the minute," thoroughly late for all the shooting.

Although Ironside was naturally discouraged by this first real mutiny in North Russia, he was amazed at how quickly the rebellious troops appeared to pull out of their spirit of defection. He crossed the frozen river to Bakaritza the next day and found them relaxed and cheerful, eating their dinner just before leaving in boxcars for Obozerskaya. He gave them a brief lecture on the horror of mutiny, and returned to his headquarters hopeful that service at the front might call forth their patriotic best. Before the month was out they were to have a good chance to prove themselves.

* * *

Christmas came and went without undue excitement. There was a small spate of discussion in Archangel about whether to celebrate the holiday according to the old-style Russian calendar, still adhered to by the Russian Orthodox Church, or according to the Western calendar, introduced shortly after the revolution by the Communists. Chaikovsky settled this with wisdom like Solomon's: he decreed that Christmas should be celebrated both on December 25 new style, and December 25 old style (that is, on January 7). That way everybody was satisfied, and some decided to make a good thing of it and celebrate for a whole fortnight.

Ironside, who had recently seen more than enough of celebrating in Archangel, decided to get out of town and visit Kholmogori, about forty miles up the Dvina. He had an official excuse, since it was a training center for the new Russian army; it was also a place that interested him for historical reasons. It had once been Russia's main port for ocean-going vessels; but by the time of Peter the Great the ships were larger, which resulted in the founding of Archangel with its deeper harbor. Kholmogori had thus become a kind of ghost town, but it retained a few good buildings and several churches. The general was particularly intrigued to find still standing the house in which Richard Chancellor, the famous sixteenth-century English mariner, had lived when he came to Russia to negotiate trade agreements. Ironside made a leisurely tour of the Kholmogori military installations, chatted with many of the White Russian soldiers and officers, and on Christmas day went to one of the local churches, as he put it, "to hear a bishop preach." He was disappointed in the sermon, however, for the bishop made no appeal to the people to fight Bolshevism in the name of their religion.

Christmas was also the occasion of Colonel Stewart's lone trip to the fighting fronts on the Dvina and the Vaga. His theory apparently was that the combination of Christmas packets from the Y.M.C.A. and a cheery visit from their commanding officer might do wonders for the morale of the American soldiers, which in spots was beginning to sag noticeably.

It all worked out rather badly, however. Just as he had done on the railroad front in the fall, poor Stewart managed to irritate nearly everybody. Stopping for a day or two at the larger outposts like Toulgas and the defenses around Shenkursk, the colonel delivered a set speech to the men, intended to make them accept their lot in North Russia with good grace. Since the occasion was announced with some fanfare there is reason to think that many of the men hoped Stewart might really have something to tell them. As a military intelligence report summed it up shortly afterward: "… the men expected a great deal from that visit. They were, however, much disappointed by the talk he made to them as it did not explain what they were here for, and he also said that he wanted them to understand that his work at Archangel was just as hard as theirs if not more so."

In his impromptu performances Stewart was just as gauche as he was on scheduled programs. Captain Robert Boyd, who had led the Allied troops in their staunch defense of Toulgas in November, later wrote an acid account of the colonel's visit to that stronghold.

> His advent [said Boyd] was marked principally by his losing one of his mittens, which were the ordinary issue variety. He searched everywhere, and half insinuated that Captain Dean, my adjutant, a British officer, had taken it. I could see Dean getting hot under the collar. Then he told me that my orderly must have taken it. I knew Adamson was more honest than either myself or the colonel, and that made me hot. Then he finally found the mitten where he had dropped it, on the porch, and everything was serene again.
>
> Colonel Stewart went with me up to one of the forward blockhouses, which at that time was manned by the Scots. After the stock questions of "where are you from" and "what did you do in civil life" he launched into a dissertation on the disadvantages of serving in an allied command. The Scot looked at him in surprise and said, "Why, sir, we've been very glad to serve with the Americans, sir, and especially under Lieutenant Dennis. There's an officer any man would be proud to serve under." That ended the discussion.

When Ironside got back to Archangel and considered again the question of good cover for the winter siege he knew was due from the Bolsheviks, two things bothered him. On the Vaga River, the troops stationed at Shenkursk and just south of that city were far out in advance of the rest of the Allied front, and therefore were already flanked on both sides by the enemy. This was a heritage from General Poole, who had taken Shenkursk early for prestige purposes, assuming, of course, that the Allied columns on the Dvina and on the railroad would soon move south to cover the city on the flanks. Ironside had held on there because possession of Shenkursk was of great psychological importance to Chaikovsky's government, and its citizens were largely anti-Bolshevik; but he felt that the position was a dangerous one, and he was anxious to go down and examine it himself.

For the moment, however, another problem struck him as equally urgent. On the railroad, and on its eastern flank near Kodish, Allied troops were now at a standstill. Ironside had no dreams of any continuing advance during the winter, but it seemed preposterous that his men should be forced to put up with improvised winter defenses and quarters in the middle of nowhere, when only a few miles west and south lay the substantial towns of Emtsa and Plesetskaya. If they could capture those the housing problem would be a great deal easier, the Reds would be deprived of valuable bases, and the railroad front would be much more nearly parallel with the Vaga front at Shenkursk. He thus allowed himself to consider once more the tactical blow which already had twice failed: a converging attack on Plesetskaya, straight down the railroad and angling in from the northeast on the Plesetskaya-Kodish-Seletskoe road through the forest.

His troops on this front were now battle-tried-about half of them were Americans-and their morale was good. The French, for instance, seemed to have got over their *fin de guerre* slump, and in keeping with one of his principal military theories, Ironside was anxious to give them and the Americans something soldierly to do before they grew stale from inactivity. It was true that they had been recently joined by the late mutineers of the 1st Archangel Regiment, but Ironside theorized that battle action side by side with good troops might be just what the Russians needed to complete their cure. On top of all this, he knew that the Bolsheviks were aware of his elaborate winter building activity at Verst 455 on the railroad and along the Emtsa River north of Kodish: no doubt their intelligence reports had put the Allies down as set for the winter in those positions. Complete surprise was consequently now a possibility that beckoned alluringly.

In connection with launching a surprise attack, there was one rather exciting new development. Among the officers who had organized the Archangel contingent of the French Foreign Legion was a Captain Barbateau, a French Canadian of many years' experience in the north woods. With the first fall of snow he had begun vigorously training a snowshoe detachment of Russian volunteers, and by Christmas several platoons were in such good fettle that he reported them ready for action. Since they were the only troops trained for fighting in deep snow available to the Allies, Barbateau was understandably proud of the outfit, and nobody objected when he honored his native land by dubbing them "Les Coureurs de Bois." (This sobriquet has a long history in Canada, going back to the exploits of seventeenth-century scouts and guides who first learned to negotiate the primeval forest.) Only one thing bothered him: the special snowshoes he had ordered from Canada had never arrived-it later turned out they had been sent by mistake to British troops at Murmansk-and he was forced to put up with those issued by the British at the start of the expedition. These were of the "bear-paw" type, oval hoops about eighteen inches in length, and good enough in fairly heavy, damp snow. In the winter temperatures of North Russia, however, which now were diving frequently to twenty and thirty below zero, the snow was extremely dry, light, and powdery, and even with the hoop snowshoes a heavy man could sink up to his knees. But they were far better than nothing; and everyone was eager to see what Les Coureurs could do against the Bolsheviks.

The assignment given to the snowshoe detachment was roughly the same one the Americans on the railway had flubbed so badly late in September by getting mired down in the depths of the muskeg forest. They were to swoop around through the woods and strike Emtsa, twenty miles south of Verst 455, from the east. If the Reds responded according to Allied hopes, they would be so startled by this blow that the columns pushing down the railway and down the forest road through Kodish would have relatively easy going, and Plesetskaya would fall to the Allies in time for a fine celebration on New Year's Eve.

Plans for the concerted attack were most carefully laid. Companies E and K of the 339th, plus a mortar section and machine-gun platoon, under newly-promoted Major Mike Donoghue, were to be the main attacking force on the town of Kodish, where a unit of the Sixth Red Army was quartered. A British company, liberally equipped with machine guns, would lie in wait south of Kodish to ambush the Bolsheviks as they made their exodus from the town under pressure from the Americans, while a company of the 1st Archangel Regiment would take up the pursuit and drive the remnant of the enemy down to Avda, fifteen versts south. By that time, according to the headquarters battle schedule, the Americans would be reorganized in Kodish and could come rapidly on down the forest road, through Avda, and on to Kochmas, a village another ten versts down the line. This was the program for December 30; on the thirty-first, Plesetskaya itself would be captured with the help of the railway column, which meanwhile would have taken Emtsa by nightfall on the thirtieth.

Since the surprise element was crucial, even the company commanders did not know just what was afoot until December 29; and their strict orders were that all preparations be stealthily made, so as not to arouse suspicion in any of the Bolo outposts. The Americans' position at this time was along the north bank of the Emtsa River, just north of Kodish, where they had been brought to a halt after the fighting in the fall, and where the 310th Engineers had constructed a strong line of blockhouses. Just across the snow-swept river were the outer trenches and dugouts of the 1st Petrograd Regiment, the Red army force entrusted with the defense of Kodish.

The American lieutenant in charge of the lookout post on the bank of the river was disconcerted, as the early winter darkness fell on the afternoon of December 29, to see a Bolshevik officer with a flag of truce, escorted by a squad of soldiers, making his way to the center of a wooden bridge that spanned the frozen stream. Lieutenant Lennon took a squad of his own men and advanced cautiously to the bridge to see what was up. It turned out that the Bolshevik officer had in tow a private of the Royal Scots and Private George Albers, of Company I, both of whom had been captured in the fighting in November. What was wanted, as a Russian interpreter explained, was an exchange of prisoners. Lennon said he had no authority, whereupon both the Bolshevik officer and the interpreter showed signs of irritation. If the Allied forces did not vacate the river position within two or three days, said the interpreter, the Red army was going to drive them into the waters of the White Sea, just as Comrade Trotsky had predicted. Lennon replied that this would be a good trick, since the White Sea was pretty solid at the moment. Meanwhile the two captives, under some prodding from the Bolsheviks, had announced to Lennon and his squad that life in the camp of the Soviets was not too bad. The negotiation ended with nothing accomplished, and Lennon went back to report to his superiors what had happened. Everything considered it was interpreted as a good sign: apparently the Reds were not aware of the forthcoming attack.

At midnight on the twenty-ninth, Lieutenant John Baker roused two sleepy but nervous platoons of Company E, and two of K, and led them out across the ice of the river to get into position for the assault, scheduled for 6 A.M. It was cold-twenty-odd degrees below zereo. Once across the river they had to circle widely to come in on the flank of the town of Kodish, and the thick underbrush and numerous windfalls made it very slow going in the absolute darkness. The snow, while light and dry, was three feet deep in many places and offered plenty of resistance, especially to men in long overcoats. None of this was a surprise to Baker: he had thoroughly reconnoitered the terrain, knew where he was going, and how long it would take to get there.

At 5:45 A.M. he estimated that his platoons were approximately in the assigned position, and they settled down for a brief rest. Promptly at six o'clock they heard the American trench mortars, back on the Emtsa, open up on the Bolshevik outer defenses, while the shells from the supporting section of Canadian artillery whistled overhead to drop in on Kodish itself. Baker fired a red flare from his Very pistol* to let Major Donoghue locate his position, and then moved his men forward. It all seemed to be going like clockwork: the artillery barrage rolled just ahead of them, guided by flares at prearranged intervals.

*It was a Remington. Marked with the Imperial eagle and REMINGTON ARMORY 1917 on the barrel. These rifles were manufactured for and sold to the previous Czarist government.

By this time, of course, the Reds were well aware that they were under heavy attack. A platoon of the 339th's machine-gun company had crossed the river at another place, and when Baker's troops reached the Bolshevik trenches north of the town they found them already pretty well cleaned out by the combined machine-gun and mortar fire. Any notion that Kodish was going to be easily taken was soon destroyed, however. The road leading into the town was still in enemy possession, and as Baker and his men attempted to work down it they were met by a fusillade from Soviet rifles and machine guns. They took again to the woods, and a long-drawn-out battle began. In the inky darkness of the North Russian morning, the fireworks were like nothing most of the Americans had ever witnessed before: the eerie shadows cast on the snow by the flares fired from both sides; the steady thunder of the Canadian field guns in the rear; the spurts of fire from hundreds of enemy weapons in front of them; the deafening detonations of the seven American mortars, which put over a thousand shells into the Bolshevik positions in the early hours of the fight.

But despite steady American progress into the outskirts of Kodish, and clear evidence that the Bolos were preparing to abandon the place, something was obviously wrong. Except for the highly valuable artillery support from the Canadians, Companies E and K got the distinct impression that they were capturing the Soviet position without aid from their allies. When it was all over, a good deal later, they were to find out what the trouble was: both the White Russians and the British had let them down. The commander of the detachment from the 1st Archangel Regiment offered a possibly unique excuse for his failure to move up his men: it was not, he said, "the right kind of day" for the attack. As for the British, the source of their difficulty was the commanding officer, a colonel, who failed to show up at the right time to direct the activity of the machine-gun company assigned to obstruct the Red retreat. The reason, as tersely expressed by Ironside when he reviewed the episode, was distressingly simple: "He had succumbed to the festivities of the season." (This same colonel, on an earlier inebriate occasion, was sat upon briefly by two American noncoms who mistook his prostrate form, half covered with straw, for a convenient log.)

The Americans, meanwhile, were enjoying no festival. Not only were they fighting alone, but it was apparent that the strength of the enemy had been underestimated. It was not merely a matter of numbers, although on that score the proportion was fearfully one-sided: 450 Americans actually dislodged more than 2,000 Soviet soldiers from Kodish and its surrounding defenses. What was just as noticeable was that the manner in which most of the Bolshevik troops now fought was sharply different from that of the skirmishes in the fall. Rifle fire was decidedly more accurate: evidently most of the Reds were now actually aiming before pulling the trigger. Discipline was also at a level the Yanks had not seen before. The Bolshevik soldiers fell back under the superior American fire; but they fell back in good order, and they kept shooting. The hoped-for rout did not materialize, and perhaps would not have even if the White Russians and the British had carried out their part of the attack faithfully. Trotsky's tremendous efforts at reorganizing the Red army were beginning to show results.

By late evening of December 30 the Americans were in full possession of Kodish, and two platoons, one from Company E and one from K, were half a mile south of the town, attempting to push the Bolsheviks further down the road. But now they were subjected to a disadvantage which earlier had been a problem for the Reds: Kodish was in a hollow, with hills on three sides, and it consequently was more easily attacked than defended. The Bolsheviks had previously constructed machine-gun dugouts at strong points along the road south of the town, and from these they subjected the advance American platoons to a destructive fire. There seemed to be nothing to do but dig into the snow and await further orders.

In comparison to the many frozen Bolshevik corpses the Americans had passed as they came through Kodish their casualties so far had been very light. Now, immobilized by the Soviet machine guns, they began to suffer. The officers and noncoms, moving among the men in an effort to keep up their spirits, got the worst of it: two sergeants of Company K and Lieutenant Berger of Company K and Lieutenant Berger of Company E were killed during the night. By morning many other men had been wounded. The temperature was dropping: a dozen cases of frozen hands and feet added to the troubled workof the medical squads. Meanwhile Major Donoghue had received an order from Ironside: "Hold what you have got and advance no further south; prepare defenses of Kodish." The general also wired his congratulations to the Americans: it was clear to him by now that they were the only part of the attacking forces on the Kodish front who had performed up to his expectations.

While the master plan for the capture of Plesetskaya fell far short of execution at Kodish, on the railroad it never got properly started. Here the crux was the success of the snowshoe detachment. Les Coureurs de Bois led off gallantly on December 29, aiming to swing through the woods and arrive opposite Emtsa in eighteen hours or less. But now Captain Barbateau's worries about the small British snowshoes proved to have been well founded. So high were the snowdrifts in the forest, and so dry and fluffy the snow, that the men constantly sank in much too deep for rapid travel. They were, of course, weighted down with their rifles, extra rations, and sleeping equipment. By 10 P.M. a messenger had been sent back to field headquarters on the railroad: Les Coureurs were only running about one verst an hour, and the prospect of reaching Emtsa looked dim, for they were already nearly exhausted. Colonel Lucas, French commandant on the railroad, then decided on his own authority to hold back his main attacking force while he thought things over on December 30. His cogitations were assisted, early that afternoon, by the commencement of a devilishly accurate artillery barrage from the Soviet guns located down the line in the direction of Emtsa. It was all too obvious to the Bolshevik commanders that the American assault on Kodish was planned as part of a pincer movement, and they dumped enough shells into the Allied position on the railroad front to discourage an officer with more determination than Colonel Lucas had yet shown anyone.

Seeing that there was no prospect of carrying out his part of the attack plan, Lucas sent Ironside a wire asking him to come to the front for a conference, but not specifying just what the trouble was. The general went down the railroad on New Year's Day and learned all the sorry details. He was irritated to find that Lucas had not gone over to the Kodish front to plan the co-ordinated attack in person, as he had been ordered to do. The failure of Les Coureurs de Bois was of course disappointing, but did not appear to involve any delinquency. As for the British colonel who had got drunk on the eve of the attack, Ironside quickly relieved him of his command after visiting the scene of the debauch and talking to those involved.

Fighting was still going on near Kodish, and Ironside was able to work off some of his disgust by getting into the middle of it for a few hours. He decided to spend the night in one of the American blockhouses on the Emtsa River, just north of the town. Although Kodish was in Allied hands for the moment, the Bolsheviks had not given up, and scouting patrols were slipping past to harass the river positions, crossing on the ice after the early darkness afforded them cover. Ironside had barely settled down for a drink and a chat with the American captain who was his host when a sentry called out a challenge, and everyone looked out to see what was happening. Some ghostlike figures could just be made out; they seemed to be, as the general put it, "floating in the air above the snow." Machine guns opened fire from the blockhouse, and after a few minutes no more activity could be discerned outside.

The captain then decided to sally forth and see what could be seen. He went out into the snow with Ironside close behind him. Cautiously they crossed over the clearing, through the barbed wire entanglements, and a hundred yards or so beyond. Suddenly, in the deep snow, they came upon six bodies-dead only a few minutes, but already frozen stiff. They were Soviet ski troopers, wearing white capes for camouflage. Two of them had merely been hit in the legs by machine-gun slugs: it was a convincing demonstration of what it meant to be wounded in the open when the temperature was thirty below zero.

Back in the comfortable light and warmth of the blockhouse, Ironside reflected with satisfaction that the odds in Russian winter warfare were overwhelmingly on the side of the defensive. In strongholds like the blockhouses the American engineers had built it would be possible for small Allied forces to hold off many times their number of attackers. Weapons worked well inside; outside there was constant trouble with ice-jammed parts and impossibly stiff mechanisms. Any exposure of the body meant frostbite. The barbed-wire entanglements, now almost entirely concealed in the snow, were a formidable obstacle. For the defenders only one thing seemed to present a serious problem: how, the general asked himself, could he "keep up the spirit of the men if they were never to leave the security of their blockhouses?" It was a question to which he gave much thought; and his solution, as we will see, was one not always satisfactory from the point of view of the Yankee infantryman.

It is possible that Ironside's new complacency about the advantages of the defensive had something to do with the misery suffered by Companies K and E of the 339th in attempting to hold Kodish. Apparently the general did not go forward to examine the situation of the town itself, and was unaware what an extremely vulnerable site it occupied. For days the Americans hung on grimly, undermining the log houses of the town to make dugouts to protect them against the Bolshevik artillery. One cold night, after scouts had reported an imminent Soviet attack, an American lieutenant ordered the town burned and evacuated; but he was soon superseded, and before dawn he and his men were back among the smoking, half-burned buildings, evidently doomed to hold Kodish from there to eternity. It was in fact to be February before the British command finally became convinced of something any doughboy on that front could have sworn to weeks earlier: the town of Kodish was worthless for their purposes, and was strategically untenable.

From a strictly military point of view, the operation on the Kodish front at the very end of 1918 was a puny affair (a "small offensive action," Ironside called it later). A few hundred Americans went out into the snow and the darkness and took an insignificant Russian village, held it for a while, and gave it up again to the enemy. A few dozen were wounded and frostbitten; only seven were killed outright in action. But as if the eerie northern light by which it was fought somehow had revealed truths about the battle which otherwise would have been obscure, the men who struggled in the snow at Kodish saw it as a stark epitome of the whole North Russian fiasco. The knowledge of the armistice was fresh in their minds, and it was becoming ever more clear that whatever it was they were fighting for had nothing to do with "the War." (The last mail from the States, which came in at Christmastime, asked one question: When are you coming home?) Very few of them knew enough about Communism to have any sense of dedication in shooting Communist soldiers. Far too many of the frozen enemy dead looked like the friendly Russian peasants in whose homes the Americans had sometimes been billeted to allow any sense of battle triumph, even when things were going well. The town itself was small enough, and its unfortunate strategic disposition obvious enough, so that the dullest soldier could see what, in large-scale disasters, is usually imperceptible to the private: no secret purpose was served by the operation. It was merely a blunder.

Even the brevity of the casualty list acted, in some strange way, to underscore the meaninglessness of Kodish. When thousands are lost, as at Gallipoli, a certain consolation can be found in sheer numbers, in the democracy of death. But the seven young Americans for whom the end of the year 1918 was suddenly the end of everything stood out as individuals to their comrades of Companies E and K, and their names were long remembered: Floyd Austin, Carl Berger, Bernard Crowe, Alfred Fuller, Michael Kenney, Frank Mueller, Harold Wagner. It was impossible to treat them as a mere statistic, and when the American winter position had been re-established backon the Emtsa River, it seemed that the only fitting epitaph for them was the saddest that ever can be written above the graves of fallen soldiers: They died in vain.

CHAPTER 7

THE WAY IT WAS

THE STORY OF A combat campaign is never just a story of combat. Life goes on from day to day as well as from battle to battle; and in after years when old soldiers reminisce it is often the look of the country, how the weather was, and what the natives said and did- the total aura of campaign living-that calls up memories. During the winter they spent in Archangel Province, the atmosphere of North Russian life fastened itself upon thousands of American soldiers with unforgettable poignancy.

Always, enveloping all memories, are the snow, the darkness, and the cold. From November to May the doughboys saw little if any bare ground that they had not scraped bare themselves. Often, when daylight came filtering through the pine forests, there was a fresh layer of white powder dusted over the deep drifts, and the pines and spruces wore the latest fall like garments. Chekov remarks somewhere that the best description he ever heard of snow was one given by a school girl: "The snow was white." The ineffable whiteness of the Russian winter made an impression on many Americans that was to haunt their dreams the rest of their lives.

At the same time, and paradoxically, there was the darkness. The fighting fronts were, on the average, less than three degrees of latitude below the Arctic Circle, and in December and January the soldiers were lucky if they had four hours of daylight by which to count their somewhat doubtful blessings. At that it was always a kind of half-light: the skies were generally cloudy, and the sun, when it did emerge, rose so grudgingly above the horizon that every object-a tree, a log house-cast eerie twilight shadows all day long. "Or all day short," as one veteran recalled it. "Gloomy"-that was the natural word for it; and to the distress of their officers it induced in many of the men a

corresponding state of mind. "Life became a very stale, flat, drab thing
in the vast stretches of cheerless snow reaching far across the river to
the murky, brooding skies and the encompassing sheeted forests, so
ghostly and so still, where death prowled in the shadows," John
Cudahy wrote of the winter vigil at Toulgas-and Toulgas was typical
of North Russia.

As for the cold, it was unlike anything ever before experienced
even by the boys from Michigan's upper peninsula. In the deep
midwinter it was a mild day that saw the mercury top zero. Opinions
differ as to how low it sometimes dropped-no doubt there were local
variations of severaldegrees-but there is no question that 50 below zero
was plumbed more than once, and 30 and 40 below were quite
ordinary. Fortunately, there was no lack of warm clothing for the
Allied forces. The regular issue included a sleeveless leather jerkin, a
long, heavy, sheeplined overcoat, a fur hat that could be turned far
down over the ears and neck, and very heavy gloves, or mittens with
separate trigger fingers. For warmth at night, as many as five blankets
per man were given out.

Footwear turned out to be a specialproblem. The official
British outfit, issued to the Americans as well, featured the
"Shackleton boot"-a modification of Eskimo moccasins by the famous
Antarctic explorer Sir Ernest Shackleton. These clumsy contraptions
of insulated leather and canvas were superbly warm, but their smooth,
almost heel-less soles were poorly adopted to walking on packed trails
where the snow had become hard and slippery. After a dozen or more
tumbles most of the soldiers learned to stay upright in these boots and
still move forward, but it required the development of a new gait
altogether-a kind of half-waddle, half-dance-step which soon became
known as the Shackleton Walk. ("One step forward and two steps
back-a sideslip down with a hell of a whack," was the poetic
description offered by one American.) Some men, irritated to a display
of Yankee ingenuity, managed to affix improvised cleats to the
Shackleton soles; others solved the problem by trading the offending
footwear for Russian *valenkis*, the home-made felt boots of the
peasants.

Shackleton himself, incidentally, was in Murmansk during a
good part of the North Russia campaign, attached to the staff of

General C. C. Maynard, who commanded the British troops in that sector. It was for him a military interlude between Antarctic adventures: the disastrous voyage of the *Endurance* had ended in 1916 and he was to die during the voyage of the *Quest* in 1922. Shackleton visited Archangel briefly, but his most intimate connection with the American forces there was through the notorious boots. His name was felt by most of the 339th Infantry to be part of the lexicon of mild profanity rather than of heroic polar exploration.

Merely existing in the subzero climate with some degree of comfort was one thing; working or fighting in it was another. To lose a mitten was to freeze a hand: the British fighting kit in fact included extra gauntlets strung, kiddy-style, on a kind of shoulder harness so that they could not be dropped. Great care had to be exercised in handling tools and weapons, for, as Ironside observed, "to touch metal with the bare hand was like grasping a piece of red-hot iron." In the extreme cold all types of mechanism-including the human body-behaved strangely. If too much oilwas used in a machine gun, for example, it froze. Range tables for the artillery had to be refigured, since the cold somehow cut down on the distance a shell would carry.

It was perhaps only the medical officers who had anything good to say about the effects of the North Russian climate in the dead of winter. Wounds were usually remarkably clean, and sanitation in general was greatly aided by the natural refrigeration. One American surgeon was of the opinion, moreover, that the long open-air sleigh rides many of his patients were forced to take between the fighting fronts and the rear, were "of distinct benefit." The patients themselves, on the whole, were much less enthusiastic about this arctic therapy.

Most of the time, of course, the soldiers were indoors during the coldest weather; and thanks to the construction skill of the peasants and that of the 310th Engineers, they stayed remarkably warm. Many of the structures built by the engineers, in fact, were in some points an improvement of design over the characteristic North Russian dwelling of hewn logs. Since wood was more than plentiful, it occurred to someone that double walls were the obvious answer to the insulation problem. A six-inch space left between the walls was filled with sawdust; and this proved highly successfulin blocking the frigid outdoor air.

A good many members of the 339th, however, were quartered during the winter in peasant homes. The design of these dwellings had evolved on an almost purely pragmatic basis over hundreds of years, and although they were far from luxurious, their practicality was incontestable. From an American point of view the most striking feature was the massive stove. Built of bricks before even the walls were finished, the stove was (and doubtless still is) the *focus* of the North Russian house in every sense, including of course the original Latin meaning of "hearth." It was multi-purpose, serving not only to heat the whole house, but to bake bread and cakes, to boil and fry other food, to keep the samovar hot, and to support, on its broad, flat top, the family's best bed. A great chimney rising from one end received the smoke from three or more fire boxes, and a maze of flues and air spaces inside the bulky structure insured an even distribution of heat throughout its thousands of bricks. In its smoothly cemented or enameled exterior, slots held the ends of beams for the room partitions: each room thus enjoyed the benefit of one side or corner of the stove. Nooks and alcoves around the base made comfortable spots for people to sit, when blizzards drove against the double panes of the house windows, and the mercury plunged.

The fuel economy of the North Russian stove was sufficient to have astonished Benjamin Franklin. An armful of split pine sticks, properly used, would heat the house for twenty-four hours unless the temperature was far below zero. The procedure was to remove the damper plate from the chimney base while the wood was burning to a bed of smokeless coals; then the chimney was sealed off, and the heat of the coals would slowly permeate the mass of bricks in the stove, from which it would radiate steadily throughout the house. Since ventilation in winter was provided by very small slits under the windows, many of the Americans found the atmosphere of the Russian home too snug even when the weather was most arctic. They soon discovered, for instance, that there was good reason for most of the natives going barefoot or stocking-foot when indoors: they were otherwise too warm for comfort.

Furniture was sparse. A table and a few chairs or benches were the principal items: bedsteads were conspicuously absent. Except for the place on top of the stove, which was usually reserved for grandparents and babies, the family beds were simple pallets of quilts, homespun blankets, and an occasional bearskin robe. These were rolled in the daytime and stored on a kind of shell placed up close to the ceiling; at night each person would find a good spot for his bed in a corner, or on colder nights in an alcove by the warm stove. This was doubtless one reason why the floors of the typical house were scrubbed frequently with coarse sandstone, and often were the cleanest part of the establishment. The walls and ceiling, unfortunately, being made of unpainted logs, developed multitudinous cracks after a few seasons of use, and thus were not only difficult to keep clean, but were the natural habitat of cockroaches and other types of domestic fauna.

A nineteenth-century English reformer who complained to some Russian monks about the prevalence of insects was told that the creatures served a purpose: they taught the peasants patience. The American reaction to the buggy condition of the average Russian peasant home varied from nonchalance to something bordering on horror. Lieutenant Hugh McPhail, who spent most of the cold months on the Vaga River, near Shenkursk, remembers quartering a squad of soldiers in a house which turned out to have, as it were, a living ceiling: "It was like a swarm of bees with several billion cockroaches." McPhail offered to find them another residence, but "the men said the roaches didn't bother them any, so I left them there." John Cudahy, on the other hand, wintering at Toulgas, found the vermin hard to bear, and was also intensely disturbed by the local smells: "In the dismal huts of the village," he wrote, "soldiers are packed with the crowded moujik families like herded animals, where the atmosphere is dank and pestilent with an odor like stale fish." The odor, as a matter of fact, had a perfectly legitimate origin, for the soap used by the good peasant housewives had in it a large proportion of fish oil. The black peasant bread also partook of this ingredient, and in general the fish smell was so pervasive that it had to be accepted as an inseparable element of the environment. One veteran of the North Russia campaign swears that he was distinctly uneasy for a week or two after leaving the country in the late spring of 1919, and it was only at the end of that time that he finally identified the cause: the smell was gone.

There were a few other discomforts growing out of the fact that the North Russian home was designed primarily as winter shelter. The horses and cattle were not kept in barns, but under the same roof as their masters in a stable separated from the main part of the house by a wooden wall. The stable served as a storage place for hay, grain, meat, dried fish, fish nets, and tools, and was also the location of the toilet. This opened down to the manure pile on the ground below. The waste, soon frozen, was simply allowed to accumulate all winter, and finally carried out to the fields in the spring to serve as fertilizer. It was important to do this, of course, before the big thaw came in late April.

The outside of the North Russian peasant home presented a neat but rugged appearance. Notable was the skill with which the great logs of its walls, stripped of their bark but left unpainted, had been hewn to fit together snugly. The usual method was to hollow out the side of one log to fit the curved top of the one beneath it; whatever space remained was then calked with hemp. Corner joints were a particular marvel, especially when it was remembered that nearly all the work had been done with hand-wrought axes: each joint was perfect, yet no two were alike. In the better houses the logs were also squared off on the interior side. The broad, single-ridge roofs typically had deep overhanging eaves, and construction was heavy to meet the weight of the inevitable snows. While the total effect of the weathered houses was somewhat somber, many of the peasants touched up the exterior of their homes with brightly colored designs around the doorways and up under the gables; and the window casings, usually whitewashed, also added a note of relief. The windows themselves, like the floors, were built high off the ground-about five feet was average-for snow clearance; if the house was one of the more imposing, two-story structures in the village, it was expected that only the upper story would remain clear when the January snows piled up.

Americans from Middle Western farm country were impressed by the fact that the isolated farmhouse, surrounded with cultivated fields, was never seen in North Russia. All the peasants lived in villages, however small, clustered together for mutualaid and protection. The forest, moreover, while it was the source of nearly all their building material and much of their meat, was apparently regarded as a natural phenomenon to be held severely back when civilized living was in question: the villages were treeless. "Trees and trees with never a house-and where the houses are, never a tree," one observer summed it up.

The most imposing edifice in the North Russian village was always the church. For one thing, its minarets and steeple rose high above the low peasant houses; and it was invariably painted white in contrast to the drab gray of the other buildings. To the Americans it was a symbol of the profound if somewhat primitive religiosity of the natives, the public counterpart of the icon found in one corner of the main room of every house. The Bolshevik attack on the church had not yet affected either the faith or the religious practice of these people, and the long-robed, long-bearded priest was an important functionary in every village. Since he was paid very little for his services, however, he also was a working member of the community, tilling his share of the communally owned land and taking his share of the produce. The doughboys were struck by the fact that the village priest, by no means celibate, often had a large family and had picked one of the strongest and healthiest of the local belles for his wife. This was no accident: if she died the priest was not permitted to remarry, and in North Russia a good wife was an economic necessity.

While the work activities of the men and boys nearly came to a standstill in the midwinter months, the women and girls labored hard both summer and winter. They did most of the farming during the short but intense growing season of the midnight sun; and when the snows covered the fields, and darkness descended, they spent long hours indoors, cooking, sewing, spinning, weaving crude cloth, and scrubbing things down with the pungent fish-oil soap. In general, the Americans in North Russia seem to have admired the cheerful composure of the peasant women as they went about their arduous duties, although only a small percentage of the soldiers appear to have become involved in sexual relations with them. They were, on average, not to American taste: full-faced, thick-waisted, and exceedingly broad of beam. Moreover, the strenuous warnings of the Allied command against venereal disease discouraged many of the soldiers even when they found the peasant girls willing and tolerably attractive: syphilis and gonorrhea were said to be rampant in the rural villages as well as in the city of Archangel. On the other hand, some of the Americans lived in close company with peasant families for many weeks, and something more than friendship was bound to develop from time to time. Making love on top of a stove perhaps had its peculiar appeal when the temperature was forty below zero. Even true love bloomed amid the Archangel winter, and when spring came at least eight Americans contrived to take Russian wives back to the States along with other souvenirs.

Quite aside from sex, all the evidence indicates that relations between the Americans and the North Russian peasants were generally good. Several Y.M.C.A. and Red Cross officials, the nature of whose service made them especially interested, have noted in reports and memoirs that there seemed to be an easy and natural affinity at work: in some fundamental way the average Russian and the average American seemed to be alike. This was probably true particularly in North Russia, where the peasantry had for many years enjoyed more freedom from czarist infringements and more self-government than in the heavily populated areas to the south. While they were suspicious of British intentions, and inclined to be apathetic or fatalistic with respect to the struggle between Whites and Reds, most of them accepted in good faith the American claim to be in Russia not for selfish reasons. According to one Red Cross officer, a picture of Woodrow Wilson was almost as common in North Russian homes as the ever-present icon.

It was probably the average American's ready sympathy that made him so well liked by the Russian peasants. Few of the soldiers could bear to see children stand by with hungry faces while they ate their rations, and most shared their food at one time or another. A Red Cross worker was appalled, one wintry day, to have a doughboy come to him and ask for help: he had been rather desperately trying to feed, from his personal rations, a family of twelve who were not far from starvation. Many of the 339th's mess sergeants more or less adopted a Russian orphan for regular feeding; some of them even took children, by that time cherished like their own offspring, back to the United States with them in July, 1919.

There was also the fact that most of the Americans were quite ready to accept the Russians on their own terms, without condescension. "The doughboy early learned to respect their rude homes and customs," wrote Captain Joel Moore. "He did not laugh at their oddities but spared their sensitive feelings. He shook hands a dozen times heartily, if necessary, in saying *dasvedania* [good-bye], and left the Russian secure in his own self-respect and fast friend of the American."

This was in striking contrast to the way most of the British felt toward the Russians. Ironside put his finger on the difficulty (although he did not regard it as such) when he observed of the British Tommy, "His kindly but marked contempt for all 'foreigners' provides him with an armour which is difficult to pierce." If American reports are to be believed, the favorite British epithet for the natives was "swine," and it seems likely that the "kindly" part of the contempt was lost on the average North Russian. "Generally speaking," read a guide sheet posted for the information of Allied soldiers by the British command shortly after General Poole's arrival in August, "the Russian is exactly like a child-inquisitive, easily gulled, easily offended." That they were frequently offended there is no doubt, especially when British strategy called for such maneuvers as burning whole villages into the snow to prevent their becoming cover for the enemy. On top of that, since the Provisional Government at Archangel was widely regarded as merely a puppet of the British military, efforts to build an anti-Bolshevik Russian army by means of conscription were met with less patriotic fervor than recalcitrance. One thing seemed clear to the peasants, however they felt about the Soviet regime: the British were invading their homeland, and doing it with very little regard for native feelings. In this connection, the fact that British officers obviously were in command of the expedition probably helped excuse the Americans in the eyes of the peasants. It was also clear that there was little love lost between the *Amerikanskis* and the British, thus providing a further bond between peasant and Yank.

Friction between American and British soldiers was not an uncommon thing in either world war, but in North Russia the circumstances were peculiarly unfavorable to amicable relations. From the point of view of the British Tommy, the doughboys had arrived on the scene rather late; from the Americans' point of view, they had come just in time to save the Tommies from destruction at the hands of the Red army. Colonel Stewart's ineffective leadership, the superfluity of British junior officers, and the need to break the 339th Infantry into numerous small fighting teams combined to give the

Americans the feeling of being pushed around, sometimes to a maddening degree. Almost everywhere they went they found young and apparently condescending British officers giving them orders, frequently bypassing their own lieutenants and captains. It was the confirmed belief of many American officers that British headquarters handed out temporary promotions with abandon in order to insure that the Americans would always be outranked on every front and in every village. A common story was that in their pockets British officers carried extra "pips" so that they could instantaneously "promote" themselves to meet any occasion by affixing the necessary shoulder insignia. Some of this was certainly exaggerated-we have seen, for instance, that at Toulgas an American captain was definitely in charge of both United States and British troops, including officers-but it is indicative of how touchy the Americans felt about being subjected to British command.

One thing that rubbed many Americans very much the wrong way was the crass propaganda they were deluged with from British headquarters, especially before Ironside arrived on the North Russian scene. It did not seem that General Poole had much more respect for their intelligence than he did for that of the Russian peasants. His effusions along the know-your-enemy line often laid stress on the horrible atrocities the Bolsheviks were supposed to have committed, although the doughboys, most of whom had been in closer contact with Bolsheviks than the general, had seen nothing to bear out these stories. Sometimes the British propaganda on the enemy's characteristics seemed oddly lacking in logic ("Their natural, vicious brutality enabled them to assume leadership"); sometimes its guile was so transparent as to backfire badly ("The Bolsheviks have no capacity for organization, but this is supplied by Germany ... The Germans usually appear in Russian uniform and are impossible to distinguish.") Sometimes it got really nasty ("The power is in the hands of a few men, mostly Jews, who have succeeded in bringing the country to such a state that order is non-existent ... every man who wants something that some one else has got, just kills his opponent only to be killed himself when the next man comes along.")

On the other hand, the Americans were frequently exposed to dose after dose of Bolshevik propaganda in the form of leaflets dropped from airplanes or left along trails in the forest; and on the whole this was fairly skillful. It was written, for one thing, in language closer to what they talked themselves than what emanated from British headquarters, as can be guessed even from some of the titles: "The Shame of Being a Scab": "Say! What Are You?"; "Are You a Trade Unionist?" The line was monotonously the same, but to many of the doughboys it was not utterly devoid of sense. They were, the Communists told them, being forced to fight in a shamefulcause: "You soldiers are fighting on the side of the employers against us, the working people of Russia. All this talk about intervention to 'save' Russia amounts to this, that the capitalists of your countries are trying to take back from us what we won from their fellow capitalists in Russia... . You are kidding yourself that you are fighting for your country ..." Most of the men of the 339th scoffed at the Bolo propaganda pamphlets; but as months went by and the snows mounted higher while the temperature dropped lower, their scoffing sometimes sounded rather halfhearted.

* * *

American prisoners of war taken by the Bolsheviks were, on the whole, well treated, and except for two who died in Soviet hospitals, all were released sooner or later. (This does not take into account Americans reported missing; a few of them conceivably may have been captured-and never heard from.) Nevertheless, some of the prisoners went through rather harrowing experiences before they got out of Russia, and all of them saw much to remember. An account written by Sergeant Glenn Leitzell, of Company M, who was captured with a companion in March, 1919, and soon sent to Moscow, describes a strange, controlled freedom, granted by the Soviet authorities apparently with the idea of winning them over to the Bolshevik side. They were free to walk about the city, dressed in long Russian overcoats and fur caps furnished by their captors, visiting the Kremlin, chatting with natives who could speak a little English, and even voluntarily joining Soviet work crews for the benefit of the extra rations that followed. They were encouraged to attend meetings at a "club" where they were harangued in English on Marxist doctrine and the evils of capitalism, and rewarded with plates of hot soup and horsemeat steaks. The techniques of Communist brainwashing were in their infancy, but already they outlined the shape of things to come.

After many weeks Leitzell and some of his friends were given passports, and with a large crowd of refugees took a train for Finland. "At the border a suspicious sailor on guard searched us. He turned many back to Petrograd. The train pulled back carrying four hundred women and children and babies disappointed at the very door to freedom, weeping, penniless, and starving, starting back into Russia all to suit the whim of an ignorant under officer. Under the influence of flattery he softened toward us... . After a two kilometer walk, carrying a sick English soldier with us, my three comrades and I reached the little bridge that gave us our freedom." And so they moved on into Finland, and away from Russia forever.

For the doughboys at the front there were, of course, constant irritations which nothing could do much to ease. To Midwestern ears the British officers' upper-class accent conveyed a maddening impression of preciousness combined with arrogance. Then there was the matter of rations. In the city of Archangel and on certain fronts-notably the railroad front-the doughboys fared pretty well; but on the Dvina and Vaga, and at Kodish and Onega, they usually had to put up with British field rations. Prominent was hardtack, of a toothbreaking durability, "bully beef"-a rather tasteless tinned variety-and "M & V," a mildly loathsome mixture purporting to be meat and vegetables. There was jam; but every tin had in it somewhere a little droplet of lead which through some technical oversight dropped into the can instead of outside it when the thing was sealed. This broke teeth that chewed through hardtack with relative ease. There was also lime juice, prescribed to prevent scurvy, and roundly hated by most of the men. Almost worst of all, there was tea instead of coffee most of the time, and usually no sugar; and decent cigarettes, although they were to be had in Archangel, somehow rarely seemed to get down to the fighting fronts. Rum, which was part of the regular British issue, reached the Americans fairly often, and in the worst winter weather came to be warmly appreciated. This was against United States army regulations, and disturbed some of the Y.M.C.A. secretaries; but Ironside swore by it and was not going to see his American troops deprived of a stimulant which, he declared, was "the only means of keeping up the necessary heat in one's body" if, for emergency reasons, hot food was not available in the subzero temperatures. There were times, nevertheless, when many of the Americans would have traded their tot of rum for a good cup of hot, black coffee. There was also the annoying fact that the rum and the lime juice came in identical jugs, leading sometimes to severe disappointment when a few jugs had been fortuitously snatched from British company supplies.

With the French, in contrast to the British, the Americans got along famously. But this was only on the railroad front, for the French never fought anywhere else in North Russia. There, incidentally, the usual irritation with British officers was kept to a happy minimum, since after November no British troops were sent down the railroad. The 3rd Battalion, under Major Brooks Nichols, worked out a pleasant arrangement with Colonel Lucas, French commandant, whereby front-line duty was split between American and French companies. This was supplemented by a great deal of off-duty fraternization, including many a shared canteen of cold red wine, the poilus' substitute for rum. It helped noticeably in surmounting the language barrier.

As a matter of fact, life on the railroad front during the winter was in most respects very different from that endured by the Americans on the other North Russian fronts. The differences, in general, were desirable ones, and depended on the steady and easy communication with Allied headquarters in Archangel. Trains ran every day, bringing down rations and supplies and taking back sick and wounded. The problem of winter quarters was solved by ingenious work on scores of boxcars which were transformed into rolling barracks, complete with built-in bunks, stoves, and electric lights powered by salvaged gasoline motors. One of the best things about the cars was that when and if it came time for a rest tour in Archangel the men could stay put while their sleeping quarters were hauled up the line to the city. At Verst 455, the advance base south of Obozerskaya where the cars were put on sidings during tours of front-line duty, there were a number of more permanent structures which also contributed to the comfort and security of the soldiers. The position had been very strongly fortified by a series of blockhouses built at intervals around the perimeter of the big clearing. Heavy barbed-wire barricades, and gun emplacements for the artillery plus a high observation tower, added to the impression that 455 would be a tough bastion for the

Bolsheviks to take. Most of the winter, indeed, the Americans and French there were left unmolested except for artillery duels, and things got so tame that the chief diversion was the Y.M.C.A. hut with its films, hot cocoa, and occasional live entertainments. During the day Major Nichols kept the men busy practicing with a variety of weapons, including those supplied to the French. He even accomplished the remarkable feat of convincing them that the long Russian rifle, which had been issued in England, was a fairly respectable weapon if a man learned to use it properly.

One form of limited amusement at Verst 455 was to watch the Allied air force in operation against the Reds. The RAF faced several difficulties in the effort to keep their 1916 Sopwiths in the air, and it was seldom that more than one of them got off the ground at one time. The little aerodrome which had been cleared at Obozerskaya barely allowed space for a good take-off or landing, and before the hard frost came in November the planes often sank hub-deep in the mud. Then came the snow and the cold. One Sopwith was fitted with big skis and the pilots learned to make gingerly landings on the snow. The "hangars" consisted of canvas tents, and after each flight the engine had to be drained of oil as well as water to prevent freezing. Once the plane was airborne there was no possible landing place except at Obozerskaya, at Archangel, or behind the Soviet lines. All of this helps explain why the pilots were often a little tense when they set off on a bombing mission. Some of the RAF flyers were Russians, former members of the Czar's air corps; and one of these, on December 6, made an unfortunate error that turned the Americans on the railroad bitterly against their air support. Confused as to just where he was, he dropped two 112-pound bombs squarely on the American forward position at Verst 445, just as Company M of the 339th was being relieved by a French company. One of the bombs killed Private Floyd A. Sickles and wounded another doughboy. What little was left of Sickles was buried right there, in the crater made by the bomb.

Sickles had been a very popular member of Company M, and the rage of his comrades against the "British" pilot who they imagined had made the fatal mistake was formidable. Since their orders were to proceed to Obozerskaya, near the airfield, the situation was rather jumpy. Luckily the British officers had been alerted, and all RAF personnel were kept strictly in quarters that night. A few wild-eyed Yanks roamed the dark streets looking for revenge, but found no victims. A couple of days later trouble developed on the Pinega front, about 150 miles east of Archangel, and Company M was selected as a good one to move away from the railroad. They made a fast Christmas march between December 18 and 27, and despite the cold weather most of the men found it an exhilarating experience. The company top sergeant, Walter Dundon, insists that the mercury hit seventy-four below zero on that march. The Pinega valley was somewhat more prosperous than the rest of Archangel Province, and at night the Americans stopped in pleasant village homes where they were remarkably well received by the natives. Pinega itself, an old trading center, turned out to be a relatively nice town to spend the winter in, and most of Company M became quite fond of it before they were ordered back to the railroad in March. Captain Joel Moore, company commander, was in complete charge of the area, and he celebrated the absence of British interference by proudly flying a big American flag over company headquarters. It was an outpost where the dawn's early light and the twilight's last gleaming were practically indistinguishable in January.

Any montage of life in North Russia as the fighting men of the 339th Infantry saw it in 1918-19 would have to include the prodigious work of the 310th Engineer battalion (actually the 1st Battalion, 310th Engineers; the rest went to France). It is a good question whether any other engineer outfit in the AEF worked as hard or surmounted as many curious difficulties as this one that was shunted off to duty in the frozen north. With a total strength of about twenty officers and seven hundred men, it was split up even more thoroughly than the 339th Infantry; for it was the only battalion of engineers serving the Allied forces in the Archangel region, American, British, French, or whatever. Small units of the 310th were to be found on every front, but few of them stayed long in one place, soon moving on to points where there was new work to be done. Initially, moreover, they suffered the same awkward disadvantage as the infantry: their equipment had been sent on to France, and they were reoutfitted in England with tools and supplies which were unfamiliar to them. They quickly adjusted to this, however, and showed great adaptability in meeting the odd exigencies of an arctic theater of operations. Since the dispersal of the battalion caused an acute officer shortage, much of their work was done with sergeants and corporals in charge of groups that ordinarily would have been under lieutenants. General Ironside, who understood thoroughly the absolutely essential role played by the engineers in Archangel, cited the 310th as unsurpassed by any unit he had ever seen soldier anywhere.

A few statistics, compiled at the end of the campaign by Lieutenant Colonel P. S. Morris, commanding officer of the engineer battalion, give a rough idea of what was accomplished by these stalwarts. Often working under fire, they built in North Russia a total of 316 log block-houses. They constructed 151 billets, 30 warehouses, 167 dugouts, 273 machine-gun emplacements, a wireless station, a 60-foot observation tower, many rafts, a houseboat 120 feet long, a bridge 280 feet long, and innumerable latrines. They operated sawmills, streetcars, water works, and the Archangel power plant. They set up a topographical section of sixty men which turned out countless maps for the entire campaign, distributing them to every headquarters from Ironside's on down. Though more than eighty years have passed since the performance of these labors, it is difficult not to believe that some traces of them might still be found today by a visitor to North Russia.

With all their very material contributions to the welfare of their friends in the infantry, however, nothing the engineers did changed the face of North Russia enough to alter its exotic impact on the American soldier. It was another world, and most of them were to carry away indelible and strangely ambiguous impressions, somber yet suffused with a certain nostalgic quality. "This is Russia of the American soldier," Cudahy summed it up-"a cluster of dirty huts, dominated by the severe white church, and encircling all, fields and fields of spotless snows; Russia, terrible in the grasp of devastating Arctic cold; the squalor and fulsome filth of the villages; the moujik, his mild eyes, his patient bearded face-the gray drudgery and gaping ignorance of his starved life; the little shaggy pony, docile and uncomplaining in winds icy as the breath of the sepulcher; Russia, her dread mystery, and that intangible quality of melodrama that throngs the air, and lingers in the air, persistently haunts the spirit, and is as consciously perceptible as the dirty villages, the white church, and the grief-laden skies."

CHAPTER 8

THE SNOWS OF NIJNI GORA

IF ONE OTHER FRONT in North Russia besides the railroad was atypical, it was Shenkursk, on the Vaga River. Here, for short periods, the members of Companies A and C enjoyed a winter life that offered many of the amenities of a small city without the frenetic pressures of overcrowded Archangel. When quartered in the town the Americans lived in comfortable barracks and spent most of their duty hours working on defense construction at a pace that raised a good appetite, if it was sometimes arduous because of the weather. The company cooks managed to beg, barter, or stealsufficient eggs, butter, fruit and vegetables to make meals a pleasure compared to the ordinary fare. A good many cultivated Russians who owned summer homes in Shenkursk had now come there to wait out (as they hoped) the Communist revolution, and despite a severe flu epidemic there was a moderately active social life in the evenings. Some of the soldiers found attractive *barishnas* among the local population; for those less choosy there were a certain number of professional ladies available. In the afternoons there were teas, and ice skating on the Vaga, and many doughboys also took a sporting try at the skis with which the regiment had been so liberally furnished. There was a relatively large and well-equipped hospital, staffed by British and American medics but Russian nurses. Cossacks in colorful uniforms swaggered through the town, pony-drawn sleighs swished cheerfully through the streets on the hard-packed snow, and all in all the Americans at Shenkursk were treated to a rather pleasant glimpse of life in Old Russia, a Russia that was never to be again.

Perhaps some sense of hovering doom added to the poignancy of that last glimpse. It has been noted earlier in this account that Shenkursk stood far out ahead of the other Allied positions in North

Russia, a tender thumb thrusting deep into Soviet-held territory. Beginning late in November, American patrols had met signs of increasing Soviet activity in the area south of the city. Near the village of Ust Padenga, about fifteen miles from Shenkursk, Lieutenant Francis Cuff and a platoon of Company C were heavily ambushed on November 29 while making their way through the snow of a densely wooded patch by the river. It was the day after Thanksgiving. The odds looked very unfavorable, and Cuff ordered a fighting withdrawal. He and five of his men, covering the rear, got cut off from the rest and completely surrounded. A search party, returning later to the scene of the ambush, found the lieutenant and his squad dead in the snow, the fierceness of their last stand proved by the number of Soviet bodies lying around them. An unpleasant detail was that the officer's arms and legs had been severed, presumably by Bolsheviks. This was, however, the only such atrocity reported during the entire campaign.

The forward defenses of Shenkursk were now located in Ust Padenga and two companion villages, Nijni Gora and Visorka Gora, all three perched on the western bank of the Vaga a day's march south of the city. Of the three, Nijni Gora was the most exposed, for although it sat on a low hilltop, the hill was nearly surrounded by deep ravines and clefts filled with great snowdrifts, and the edge of the shadowy fir forest was only a few hundred feet away on the west. Sentry duty at the Nijni Gora outposts, as the year 1919 moved darkly into January, was becoming a harrowing experience. Peering rigidly out into the blackness, the nearly frozen doughboy often thought he could make out stealthily moving forms, and suspicious sounds mingled with the whistling of icy winds through the ravines and the tops of the pine trees. He sensed that Bolshevik patrols were out there reconnoitering the position; but on this front they always wore white smocks, and even as he stared, the doubtful forms would merge indistinguishably into the vague masses of snowdrifts. If a flare was sent up, it illuminated only what appeared to be snow and more snow. But the Bolos were getting bolder, and now and then a night patrol would come close enough to make an American rifle shot worthwhile. On the night of January 10, Private George Moses shot a white-clad Soviet scout within fifteen feet of the spot where he was standing guard. One thing that annoyed the Americans when they looked the dead man over was his rifle: it was a Remington.

Soon after the battle at Kodish, General Ironside had determined that he must shake off a cluster of annoying problems at his headquarters in Archangel, and go down to Shenkursk to talk the situation over with his commander there, Colonel C. A. L. Graham. Traveling by fast pony sled, he arrived on January 14 at Bereznik, the reserve base for both the Dvina and Vaga areas. General Finlayson, who had been in charge at Bereznik, had shortly before been relieved because of his health, and Colonel C. Sharman, of the Canadian artillery, was now in command. He told Ironside he did not believe the Bolsheviks were planning anything big against Shenkursk, and the general went on down the river feeling slightly reassured. That night, however, stopping at the halfway station at Shegovari for a few hours' sleep, his fears were newly aroused. Piskoff, his Russian-Canadian groom, had strolled around the village chatting with the natives, and had become so convinced that the vicinity was hostile to the Allies that he insisted on sleeping on the floor across the doorway of the general's room. Local opinion, he informed his master, was that the Bolsheviks would soon drive "all the foreigners" out of Shenkursk, and clear back to Archangel.

Hurrying on the next morning, Ironside found Graham full of confidence. He was also gratifyingly impressed with the defenses of Shenkursk, which looked strong enough to withstand a terrific siege. Spasmodic shelling was going on, but the arctic light was so poor and the range so long that the Bolsheviks were having little luck in hitting their targets. Graham took Ironside down to Nijni Gora to have a look at no-man's land, and there the general felt somewhat less optimistic. The temperature was close to thirty below zero, and as he gazed off at the surrounding expanse of snow he tried to visualize how an enemy attack might be launched there under the existing conditions. The shadowy ravines and the nearby forest looked dangerous. Captain Otto Odjard, tough CO of Company A of the 339th, showed no disposition to quail, however, and Ironside decided that at least the position was in good hands. What bothered him was that the outpost seemed to his practiced eye to be a natural for a surprise attack. This plus the ease with which Shenkursk might be enveloped, rather than directly assaulted, if the Soviet command wished to invest enough troops against it, sent him back to the town with all his misgivings again stirred up. He simply did not have the necessary men to send in a competent relief force if Shenkursk were surrounded and put under siege; yet to contemplate losing such a large part of his total command, even at the end of a siege costly to the Bolsheviks, was unthinkable. He would have to order Graham to be ready to evacuate on a few hours' notice.

Not one to indulge his fears, Ironside spent the late afternoon having tea with the abbess of the Shenkursk convent. She was a charming lady who served a marvelous cup of tea from a beautiful silver samovar, and when she expressed alarm at the possibility of Soviet capture of the town the general found himself rather embarrassed. He would have liked very much to promise her that the Allies would never abandon Shenkursk, but honor obliged him to be somewhat less positive in his assurances.

Ironside left Shenkursk on the evening of January 17. He had gone over the whole situation carefully with Graham, and made it quite clear that there was to be no thought of resisting a siege if things should shape up that way. The actual decision to evacuate Shenkursk was to be left up to Graham himself. "As I drove away in the darkness," Ironside remembered some thirty years later, "I turned and watched the flashes of the guns. They seemed to have increased in intensity and to have become more menacing. The urge to turn back and take control of the operations lay heavy on me, as I weighed in my mind the difficulties which beset Graham." But he pushed on through the snow to Archangel.

Back at Nijni Gora on the morning of January 19, 1919, Lieutenant Harry H. Mead, of Company A, awoke to the thump of heavy artillery shells bursting unpleasantly close to the log house in which he and part of his platoon had spent the night. The temperature was forty-five degrees below zero. Until early January the accumulated snowfall on the Vaga front had been unusually light, but recently nearly thirty inches had fallen. Over the surrounding white expanse a wan, subarctic dawn had begun to diffuse a glimmering light, which would reflect uncertainly for a scant few hours before total darkness fell again. From the crest of the hill on which the village sat, Mead looked out through his field glasses across the frozen Vaga River to the open plain along the opposite bank, and to the dense fir forest in the distance. From the forest, wading slowly through the three-foot depth of powder snow, long skirmish lines of Soviet soldiers could be seen advancing under cover of the intense artillery barrage. Since these troops were still out of range of rifle or machine-gun fire, Mead had a few minutes in which to consider his position.

It did not look very good. The Bolsheviks had clearly launched a major surprise attack, and Mead figured that the hill at Nijni Gora was too exposed to hold against the number of enemy fighters already in view: there were hundreds of them. The lieutenant had twenty-two men with him in the forward defenses; twenty-three others were stationed under a sergeant at the rear of the village. Half a mile to the east, down on the river bank, a company of Cossacks held Ust Padenga; but Mead doubted he would get much support from them. Nearly a mile to the north, on a high bluff, the main elements of Company A, with Captain Odjard's headquarters and one section of field artillery, occupied Visorka Gora-too distant for aid except from the field pieces. As far as Mead was concerned, the defense of Nijni Gora could be only a matter of time, and he therefore got the captain on the telephone and told him so. Odjard agreed, but ordered Mead's platoon to put up as much of a delaying fire as they could as soon as the Soviet troops came within range. Meanwhile he promised to cover them with the field guns, reminding Mead, however, that his Canadian artillerymen had recently been relieved by White Russians, whose fire might not be altogether effective. Another point, which Odjard did not need to mention, was that the three-inch field pieces were completely outranged by the Soviet guns now dropping high explosive and shrapnel on Nijni Gora, from concealed positions far back in the forest across the Vaga.

The long gray line of approaching Bolshevik infantrymen was now nearly close enough for action, and Mead knew that in a few moments bullets would begin to thud into the logs of the Nijni Gora bunkers and peasant houses where the Americans were embattled. He told his men to make ready. Suddenly the artillery barrage lifted. Instantly, to the horrified amazement of the Americans, the ravine just below their hill was teeming with white-clad Soviet troops who leaped forward to the attack with automatic weapons and rifles with fixed bayonets. They had crept into the snowdrifts before dawn, and now over a hundred of them swarmed up the hill toward the southern end of Nijni Gora as well as from both flanks.

The Americans immediately cut loose with every weapon they had, sweeping the hillside with a devastating fire. "Time after time," Lieutenant Mead recalled later, "well-directed bursts of machine-gun fire momentarily held up group on group of the attacking party, but others were steadily and surely pressing forward, their automatic rifles and muskets pouring a veritable hail of bullets into the thin line of the village defenders." Already the Americans were beginning to be wounded right and left. A platoon of Cossacks from Ust Padenga arrived at this point and deployed hastily alongside the Americans. They had barely begun to fire, however, when their officer was severely wounded, and this plus the obviously overwhelming odds threw them into a panic. They cleared out, leaving many of their weapons behind them.

One of Mead's best men, Corporal Victor Stier, rushed over to a machine gun abandoned by the Cossacks and opened up a terrific series of blasts against the oncoming Bolsheviks, who were now too close to miss. As he did so, a Soviet bullet pierced his jaw. He tried to go on operating the machine gun, but Lieutenant Mead ordered him to get back to the rear position of the village without delay. Mead then made a quick survey of the situation. Several of his men had been badly wounded. The Bolsheviks were almost on top of them, and it was a choice between certain death in hand-to-hand combat, or a fast withdrawal. "All right," Mead shouted to his little band, "let's get out of here fast."

By this time, however, despite the heavy slaughter inflicted by American fire, the Soviet troops were actually at the southern edge of the village. Mead started to lead his men down Nijni Gora's main thoroughfare, the only one where the deep snow had been packed; but he found a Communist machine gun sweeping the street. The Americans scrambled into the deep snow behind the log houses. It was waist-high, and to make a fighting withdrawal to the rear of the village was a formidable proposition. Firing desperately from behind sheds and outhouses, then plunging again with steaming gasps into the unbroken snow to struggle on to the next available cover, Mead and his men stubbornly moved toward the rear. In the subzero air the din from small arms and grenades was deafening. The Bolsheviks had the nasty advantage of controlling the open street of the village, and by now they were moving rapidly down this and bypassing some of the hampered Americans.

"I stopped behind a shed to get my breath and load my pistol," Mead recalls. "Then I started to head around the corner of the building into the snow; but for some reason I hesitated at the corner. That sudden stop saved my life. A Bolo who looked to me at least ten feet tall was waiting there, and lunged at me with his bayonet, missing by an inch. Before he got his balance I emptied my automatic into him and hurried on."

Mead is not sure just how he got back to the rear position, nor just how many of his men made it with him. One or two had fallen into the snow at every dash. It had been every man for himself, with no possibility of keeping together in squads. At any rate, Mead did make it, breathless but unwounded. He found his sergeant and the other half of the platoon doing their best to hold off the Bolsheviks, but well aware of their plight and ready for an order to retreat to Visorka Gora. Corporal Stier, he noticed, had picked up a rifle, and with the blood on his wounded jaw already frozen solid, was still firing valiantly.

The problem now facing the platoon was how to get down the hill, across the open valley, and up the road to Visorka Gora without being demolished. There was absolutely no cover between the two positions, and to reach the packed snow of the road they must go down the hill in snowdrifts shoulder-deep in places, for the Bolsheviks held the only path. Now, if ever, they needed the help of their artillery, and Mead decided to cling to the northern brow of the hill as long as possible, hoping that the Allied field guns could open up on the Bolsheviks in the village. Corporal Giuseppe De Amicis, who still had possession of his Lewis machine gun, cleared a place in the snow and turned a deadly-accurate fire into the edge of the town, where the Communist infantry were now shooting from behind every house and shed. But his stand did not last long: he was killed where he lay a few minutes later. About the same time, Corporal Stier was wounded again, this time fatally. Soviet fire was now coming from the forest as well as from the town.

To Mead's consternation, no shells came from the Allied guns up on the bluff. He was to find out why later. The Russian gunners, who had a bird's-eye view of what was going on in Nijni Gora, and could also see the hundreds of Soviet troops coming relentlessly across the river from the south, felt that even distant resistance was foolish, and deserted their guns. This would have been inconceivable for the Canadians, who were justifiably proud of their record both in France and in Russia. When Captain Odjard realized what had happened he sallied out and forced the reluctant gunners back to their places at pistol point; but by that time it was too late to be of much help to Mead's platoon.

There was nothing to do but make a try for it. Mead gave the order, and what was left of his platoon leaped off into the powdery snowdrifts on the hillside and began to struggle down. Floundering and falling against the paralyzing resistance of the snow, they were picked off by Soviet rifle and machine-gun fire with terrible ease. "One by one," Mead recalls, "man after man fell wounded or dead in the snow, either to die from his wounds or from the terrible exposure." The temperature was still forty-five below zero, and the gushing blood froze almost instantly upon contact with the air. Across the open plain the survivors stumbled, half a mile up the icy road to the edge of the bluff. Numb and exhausted with cold and exertion, full of despair at what had happened to his platoon, Mead led the remnant into the outposts at Visorka Gora, where they collapsed in the first available shelter. He pulled himself together and counted his unwounded men. There were seven, including himself, left of the original forty-seven.

The Soviet commanders seemed to be temporarily satisfied with the capture of Nijni Gora, and Lieutenant Hugh McPhail, followed by a squad of volunteers, was able to take a sled into the valley and bring in some of the wounded members of Mead's platoon who were still alive in the snow. Some of the men of Company A even thought that the Bolshevik officers, impressed by the ordeal to which they had subjected the Americans, deliberately held their fire while the rescue squad went about its work. McPhail himself doesn't remember it that way. "The Bolos did *not* stop firing," he says with the conviction of a man who has been thoroughly shot at.

At any rate, after McPhail got back to Visorka Gora, nineteen men of Mead's platoon were still unaccounted for. Six had been killed within sight of their comrades, and it was certain that others had perished in the snow; but there was hope that some might have been captured alive in Nijni Gora. Only two of the nineteen were ever heard from again, however. Corporal James Burbridge and Private Peter Wierenga appeared suddenly out of the night many hours later, their arms frozen to the elbows.

Their story was a strange one. When the Bolsheviks overwhelmed Nijni Gora, Burbridge and Wierenga fell behind the rest of the platoon, and were sure that they were done for. In desperation they dived into a log house, where a sympathetic old peasant woman agreed to hide them. There they stayed for several hours, never expecting to emerge alive. At length Soviet patrols came through the village searching every house for American stragglers. Burbridge had clung to his rifle, and now fixed the long, three-edged bayonet on the muzzle; then he and Wierenga got into the one closet in the house. When the closet door was jerked open, he drove hard and put the steel through the leader of the Bolshevik search squad. Disengaging, he fired one shot into the body of the next man, caught in mortal surprise; then both Burbridge and Wierenga broke for the nearest window, en route kicking over the lantern which was burning in the room. They went through the window in a flying leap, taking sash and all with them into a snowbank. It was now past noon, and already quite dark. The two fugitives managed to get into the edge of the nearby woods before the rest of the Bolshevik searchers had recovered from their confusion. Hardly believing their escape, they pushed deeper into the forest, expecting to hear sounds of pursuit at every step. Nothing happened. But now they were disoriented, and not sure which way to go to reach the American position at Visorka Gora. They wandered about in the frozen underbrush most of the night, eventually blundered into a brook which they knew joined the Vaga near their goal, and thus reached safety sometime in the early morning.

Other events on the night of January 19 were the arrival from Shenkursk of Lieutenant Douglas Winslow, of the Canadian Field

Artillery, with enough men to man two guns, and the arrival from Ust Padenga of the whole Cossack company which had been stationed there. So far the Bolsheviks had left the riverside village more or less alone, but the Cossacks had no wish to stay there for a repetition of what they had witnessed from afar at Nijni Gora. As it turned out, they accomplished this move so stealthily that the Soviet watchers noticed nothing at all.

Visorka Gora was now fully garrisoned, and since its defenses included five sturdy blockhouses, even the rain of artillery shells that the Communists dumped into the village during the next two days caused few casualties. The daylight hours of the twentieth and twenty-first brought repeated waves of infantry attacks against the bluff; but the Canadian gunners were in full swing, and their shrapnel was horribly effective against the Soviet soldiers attempting to cross the open valley below. At fantastic cost in dead and wounded, the Communists succeeded in occupying the deserted houses of Ust Padenga, but they made no headway against Visorka Gora.

One lucky Soviet shell, on January 22, did hurt the Americans seriously. Lieutenant Ralph Powers, Company A's lone medical officer, had set up a temporary hospital and operating room in a house near the center of the village, chosen because of its protected position and strong construction. Powers had been working for three days and nights with practically no sleep. By the light of an oil lamp, he bent over a wounded soldier who had just been brought in from an outpost. Corporal Milton Gottschalk and Private Elmer Cole stood warming themselves near the stove; Sergeant Yates Rodgers watched the doctor's operation. Outside, the booming of the big Soviet guns and the rattle of machine guns persistently counterpointed the low conversation in the room.

With no warning whatsoever a shrapnel shell tore through the roof of the building and was deflected across the room, smashing into one of the log walls and bursting as it did so. A medical corporal who was in the next room rushed to the door and looked in. Lieutenant Powers was on the floor bleeding profusely. The soldier on the table still lay there, but one of his legs had been sheared off by a jagged piece of steel. Gottschalk and Cole were dead. Sergeant Rodgers was prone on the floor, and the corporal turned him over to see if he was conscious. There was not a mark on Rodgers' big body, but he was dead, evidently from the concussion. Above the table the lamp still burned steadily.

Both Powers and the man he had been working on died a few hours later, and the incident had a depressing effect on the morale of Company A. The doctor had been greatly admired by the men, and they felt nakedly unprotected with him gone. "Curly" Rodgers, moreover, one of the few Tennesseans in the 339th, had been the most popular NCO in the company, the kind who never failed to raise a laugh with his droll wit even when things were going very badly. The Soviet bombardment had been stepped up, and many of Captain Odjard's men began to feel that fate had appointed them for doom.

Late that evening, however, orders came from Shenkursk: Visorka Gora was to be abandoned. Colonel Graham's intelligence reports had shown conclusively that the Bolshevik attack on Nijni Gora was part of a large enveloping movement, with Shenkursk the obvious prize. Although he had not yet decided absolutely on evacuation of the city, it seemed advisable to draw in his outpost: he could not afford to have them cut off. Captain Odjard's force was therefore to make a fighting retreat into the outskirts of Shenkursk, slowly enough so that the enemy would remain wary in its pursuit.

As far as the men of Company A were concerned, the decision came none too soon. The Bolsheviks had begun to use incendiary shells, and preparations for the withdrawal were barely completed when one of the main buildings of the Visorka Gora was hit. It roared into flames against the glaring reflection of the snow, and within minutes observers as far away as Shenkursk could see the red glow of the burning village in the night sky. Supplies and the wounded men were sent ahead on pony sleds, while the column came along on foot with heavily-loaded packs. The Canadians had a bad time with one of their two precious field guns. Several of their horses had been killed by shrapnel, and the rest were weakened by exposure. The gun slipped off the roadway into a deep ditch, lying nearly on its side; and all the efforts of the men and animals failed to pull it out. Any number of ponies added to the team seemed to make little difference on the slippery roadway, and the Canadian officer reluctantly ordered the eighteen-pounder to be left where it was. The gunners removed the breech block, however, and took it with them: their brigade had never lost a gun to the enemy intact, and they had no intention of smirching the record.

It was still far below zero, the men were tired and hungry, and progress along the dark North Russian forest roads was slow. The column marched for about six hours, reaching the village of Sholosha at 7 A.M. on January 23. Odjard decided to stop there for the day, resuming the retreat when full darkness came again. The men fell out and found crowded resting places in the peasant homes and huts of the village, taking only a few minutes to satisfy their ravenous hunger. It was discovered that a satisfactory cooking technique was to make a hole in the top of a firmly frozen can of "M & V," toss it into the stove, and extract it shortly afterward, "before the tin melted." The stuff had seldom, in fact, tasted so good.

In spite of their fatigue, the doughboys slept badly. Everyone was nervous, and anxious to be moving again; and the Cossacks, who had of course come along as part of the column, seemed indisposed to sleep at all. Rum had been rather generously circulated, and there was a great deal of noisy confusion in the dim streets of the village. The rum gave rise to rumors. It was said at one moment that the Bolos had followed sneakily and were about to annihilate them; a moment later the story was that they were to be reinforced from Shenkursk and head back to Ust Padenga. Nobody, in truth, knew just what was going on. Lieutenant Mead remembers that even Captain Odjard, usually master of an icy equanimity, flew off the handle and punched a Cossack officer in the face "just because he was a Cossack." Some horses got loose in the street and pranced up and down, neighing and kicking; a drunken Cossack started firing his rifle at nothing in particular; and most of the company tumbled out of their billets ready for their last battle. "I still have nightmares about that time in Sholosha," one veteran of the campaign declares. Amidst the confused alarms, Odjard decided it was time to do something. He blew his whistle for the company to fall in, and delivered a short, pithy speech. After paraphrasing Kipling's "If" in unpoetic but striking terms, he announced that the company would march on toward Spasskoe, where according to Colonel Graham's orders they were able to make a temporary stand with a view to slowing down the Bolos' enveloping tactics. The company quieted down, and again the cold march began.

Spasskoe was only about six versts-four miles-from Sholosha; but as one of the men wrote afterward, "if you chance to be all in to start with and are carrying a ton or so of Arctic outfit besides a pack and the night is dark and the enemy surrounds you, it's much longer." The road lay uphill much of the way, and passed through several small river villages whose loyalty to the Allies was doubtful. There were also signs that Bolshevik patrols had bypassed them while they rested at Sholosha: signal lights flashed from church towers, and an occasional flare indicated that elements of the enemy occupied positions on both sides of the Vega River farther north than the column had yet the Vaga River farther north than the column had yet progressed. Some of the men of Company A developed an eerie feeling, that night, that the Soviet command was deliberately letting them pull back toward Shenkursk in a kind of cat-mouse strategy that was far from comforting. Possibly so many Soviet troops were themselves on the march in the early morning of January 24 that the Americans slipped past Bolshevik sentries who mistook them for a Red army unit.

When they had climbed the last steep hill into Spasskoe they were greeted by Captain O. A. Mowat, of the Canadian Field Artillery, out from Shenkursk with a sleigh of shells and one eighteen-pounder. This was to replace Lieutenant Winslow's gun, which had been hauled into the city before the decision to make a stand at Spasskoe. The men turned in for a snatch of sleep, while the officers looked over the terrain where they were supposed to conduct a holding action. The Spasskoe bluff commanded a good view of the plain along the river bank from which enemy forces could be expected, but little was visible in the darkness except signal lights, which were still flashing assiduously. Odjard sent out a mounted Cossack patrol into the surrounding countryside to see what was what. They returned in a nervous condition at about 7 A.M.: they reported thousands of Soviet troops moving toward Shenkursk. Captain Mowat and Lieutenant Mead clambered into Spasskoe's high church tower as soon as the sparse daylight broke; to their surprise they found that for once the Cossacks had not exaggerated. Their field glasses revealed long columns of both artillery and infantry moving on the roads converging toward the town; and the plain below Spasskoe itself was swarming with the dark dots that were Soviet soldiers. Even as they watched, a Soviet shell exploded in the outskirts of the village.

The doughboys were roused to a dismal breakfast of hardtack and jam, and Odjard issued orders for a skirmish line near the edge of the bluff. On the right stood the churchyard, its tombstones barely showing above the surface of the snow and offering somewhat macabre protection against enemy fire, if a man cared to dig close behind one. This occasioned some grim jokes, but few were feeling squeamish in view of what was to be expected soon. On the left, across the road, were some big woodpiles that looked useful; there was also a good position for the Canadian field gun. Company A deployed without much enthusiasm, and the field artillerymen got ready to show their wares. Captain Mowat was still in the church belfry, which was close enough to serve as an observation post for directing the gun fire by exceedingly direct communication: shouts. Field-telephone connection had also been made with Shenkursk, now only four miles to the rear.

It was a relatively warm day-close to zero. The officer noticed, however, that the men seemed to be suffering miserably from the cold, probably as one result of short sleep and hunger. A nearby log house had a big, hot stove, and the men were allowed to go, in small groups every five minutes, to thaw out while they awaited the attack. It turned out to be largely a matter of bombardment. Evidently the Soviet commander thought this would be enough to dislodge the Americans from Spasskoe without an infantry assault; it is also likely that he had no wish to charge the Canadian field gun. The Canadians had achieved a vicious reputation among the Bolsheviks for the calm skill with which they used shrapnel as a short-range weapon against foot soldiers.

Waiting tensely behind the gravestones and woodpiles, however, the Americans were nearing the ragged edge of their endurance. The Soviet guns seemed to have the range more accurately than usual, the tall Spasskoe church serving as a beautifully clear target. Screeching shells burst in the road, in the churchyard, and among the woodpiles, spewing snow and debris on all sides. Suddenly a high-bursting missile blew up very close to the belfry where Captain

Mowat and Lieutenant McPhail were observing the action. A piece of flying steel clanged against the church bell, and in the momentary silence that followed Mowat's clear voice could be heard, intoning with the accent of a spieler at a county fair: "One cigar!" It broke the tension, and the skirmish line collapsed in a short but therapeutic fit of laughter.

Early afternoon brought disaster to the gallant Mowat. He had come down from the tower and was strolling coolly over to his single field gun when an enemy shell caught him. His men put him quickly into a sled, to be taken to Shenkursk, but it was obvious that he was badly wounded. "Tell the captain I couldn't wait," he said to one of the sergeants as the sled pulled away. It wasn't quite clear what he meant, but in some way it moved the men who heard it deeply. They were never to see him again, for he died in the hospital at Shenkursk.

Captain Odjard also brushed against death, but lived to tell about it. A Soviet shell exploded directly on the one Canadian field gun, wrecking it, killing one gunner, and cutting Odjard severely in the neck. He too went off in a sled to Shenkursk, and the company again sensed doom. Lieutenants Saari, Mead, and McPhail now held a conference, and decided that without their artillery it was useless to hold the position longer. Enemy fire was intensifying, and it would not be long before the Bolsheviks realized they had knocked out the Canadian eighteen-pounder. Mead got Shenkursk headquarters on the field phone, explained the situation, and asked for orders. There was a long wait, and shells were dropping very close to the wire, so the lieutenant took matters into his own hands. "We're on the way in," he told whoever was at the other end; and the last stage of the withdrawal into Shenkursk began.

The company pulled into Shenkursk at four in the afternoon in a state of complete exhaustion. The cooks had prepared a meal at Spasskoe just before the sudden departure from that village, and had insisted on transporting two big GI cans of hot rice and stew in a sled, carefully insulated to hold the heat. Some of the men now fell upon these like animals, spooning out the rice with their hands. Others were too tired to eat despite their hunger, and spread their blankets on the floor under the first roof they came to. A few hardy personalities decided that rum was the cure for their condition, and went after the jugs with bleary-eyed determination. One way or another the whole company was in a state of utter insensibility shortly after the full darkness of January 24 fell on Shenkursk. Compared to what they had been through for five days the place seemed secure enough to lull them off like babies.

CHAPTER 9

THE RETREAT FROM SHENKURSK

THE OFFICERS OF COMPANY A had just settled down to what they hoped would be a long winter's nap, when they were rudely aroused by messengers summoning them to a council at British headquarters. Having sleepily arrived there, they were told that all Allied personnel in Shenkursk were to be ready to march by midnight. No equipment was to be packed except what each man could individually carry.

Colonel Graham's decision to evacuate had been clinched by several recent pieces of intelligence. Scouts reported that the Bolsheviks had moved up their heaviest artillery-one 9-inch, two 6-inch, and four 4.7-inch howitzers-and this was confirmed by the size of the high-explosive craters that were beginning to appear within the town limits. Moreover, it was now a somewhat frightening experience to observe the flashes of the Soviet guns from one of Shenkursk's church towers: they came from nearly all chief points of the compass, including northeast and northwest. There was also evidence that atleast part of the route to Bereznik and Archangel was in the hands of the Bolsheviks. Communication wires had been cut and a bold raid had been made against Shegovari, thirty miles north, on the morning of January 23. It was a hit-and-run affair, apparently carried out by Bolshevik partisans rather than regular Red army troops, but it was enough to make escape from Shenkursk look like a dangerous operation. The raiders had swooped down on Shegovari before daylight, captured one American sentry, clubbed another to death, and tossed a spate of hand grenades into the houses where the garrison was billeted, seriously wounding the lieutenant in command.

The choice seemed clear: either remain in Shenkursk and be slowly but ineluctably pulverized by the Soviet artillery, or move out immediately and hope to fight through to Bereznik. By 11 P.M. on the twenty-fourth the entire town was awake and preparing for the exodus. The men of Company A, stupefied by sleep yet still exhausted, stumbled about muttering curses and trying to grasp what had happened, while their officers exhorted them to one last great effort. Company C was in better shape, but its members were not much happier about the prospect before them.

One problem was what to carry. The thermometer showed about thirty-five below zero, and it was obvious that any excess weight might jeopardize a man's chances of getting through. On the other hand, the temptation to overload was almost irresistible. In addition to great heaps of munitions, which of course were to be abandoned, more than two months' supply of clothing, personal equipment, and rations had been stored in Shenkursk, and these were now thrown open for every man to pick what he wanted. Under such circumstances human judgment can be wildly erratic. There were men who cleared everything out of their packs except food; there were others who feverishly collected the pocket watches, knives, silverware and sundry valuable souvenirs thrown away by their fellows. Still others, obsessed with the cold, packed little besides extra clothing. Painful decisions were made over packets of letters from home, diaries, and meaningful gifts that had been brought from home. A shipment of canned salmon had come in just the day before, the first the men had seen in months, and this exercised an almost magical appeal. Heavy as it was, few could resist shoving at least one can into their packs.

At staff headquarters, similar problems were being faced on a larger scale. The Canadians would hear no talk of abandoning their field guns, and it was agreed that they should go on ahead of the main column. There was some agitation among the British officers for leaving the sick and wounded behind in the hospital, since they unquestionably would be serious impedimenta; but this the American officers positively refused to consider. British propaganda, which always depicted the Bolsheviks as capable of any atrocity, had been perhaps too effective. Then there was the question of the civilian population, many of whom had good reason to fear the consequences of Communist occupation. The only solution was to let those who wished to escape come along behind the military if they would undertake to care for themselves.

The scene in the fitfully lighted streets of Shenkursk at midnight on January 24-25 was one of purposefulactivity threatening to break into chaos. Officers rushed back and forth, great clouds of steamy breath rising into the night air as they issued one order after another. Men scurried in and out of billets, packing and repacking their knapsacks. The Canadian artillery was ready to roll, but there was confusion about getting the long train of hospital sleighs cleared for the departure. About a hundred patients, two to a sleigh except for the most severe cases, had to be checked by the medical officers to see that they were warmly wrapped and fortified with medication for the ordeal they were about to encounter. It had been decided to use members of the 310th Engineer detachment at the reins, rather than the usual native drivers, and the Americans nervously stroked their little ponies. Lieutenant Hugh McPhail, thinking of the many miles of snowy march ahead, was supervising his platoon in slashing off their long, ponderous overcoats at knee length, an operation for which they were later most grateful. The civilian population seemed to be divided into two groups, equally excited and frantically intermingled: those who were making ready to follow the departing Allies, and those who, willing to remain, were busily engaged in looting the great stacks of abandoned military supplies and hiding these and other valuables in case the Bolsheviks should themselves be in a plundering mood.

At 1:30 A.M., only about an hour behind schedule, the hospital convoy, followed by the artillery, pulled away through the outer defenses of the city and headed into the dark forest. It had been determined that a force of some two hundred Soviet troops was astride the main Shenkursk-Shegovari road a few miles out of town, and an alternate route had been somewhat desperately decided upon by the British command. It was a single-track, little-used logging trail that cut straight north, across the river and back into the forest, regaining the main road about twelve miles farther on. Mounted Cossack scouts had reconnoitered it and reported that, incredibly, it appeared to have been ignored by the Soviet troops enveloping Shenkursk.

Behind the long convoy of sleighs and the artillery came the foot soldiers, British, American, and White Russian-about one thousand in all. With the horse-drawn military personnel and something like five hundred civilian refugees, the total column came to about two thousand, stretching out in the narrow trail to a length of more than a mile. The civilians, who were supposed to bring up the rear at their own risk, were mostly equipped with at least one sleigh per family; and the more lightly loaded of these soon began to overtake the plodding soldiers, sometimes forcing them off the trail. Most of the sleighs, however, were weighted down with all the household goods they could carry, as well as with children muffled in heavy robes, and were being led, rather than driven, by men and women at the ponies' heads.

The night was windless, and the tall pines of the forest stood starkly silent. An impressive quiet, in fact, lay over the long, winding column as it moved steadily forward. Snow squeaked in the cold under the marching boots, occasionally a pony huffed through icy nostrils, men grunted under their packs and rifles; but there was little talk. All felt the need to save breath, and already the going was far from easy. The artillery and the hospital sleds had cut up the trail badly, and the dimly reflected skylight from the white snow was not enough to show up all the ruts, holes, and pitfalls. "Time after time," Lieutenant Mead recalls, "you could hear soldiers near you go down with a thud under their heavy packs, and it wasn't long before they were having trouble getting back to their feet again." Company A had now been fighting and marching for six days and nights with appallingly little rest, and some of them had very nearly lost the will to go on. Just to lie inert beside the trail in the snow and sleep, and sleep-it seemed a consummation devoutly to be wished. Some, indeed, did go to sleep while they were walking, and tumbled into snowdrifts as part of delicious dreams from which they could scarcely be wakened by their comrades. The officers and noncoms outdid themselves, moving up and down the column to aid those who collapsed. Men were dragged and punched back to their feet, faces slapped and rubbed with snow, canteens of rum forced to stiffened lips; curses and commands were interspersed with pleas and promises. Somehow they all kept moving.

It had hardly been hoped that the column would get to Shegovari without clashing with enemy patrols. Graham's orders were that not a shot was to be fired except as a last resort: the bayonet was to be the weapon of defense. Miraculously, however, not one Red soldier was seen, and the fleeing Allies got back to the main road without enemy interference. This was felt to be remarkably fortunate when it was realized that two whole companies of the "Shenkursk Battalion"-part of the new North Russian army recruited from the local citizenry-had deserted to the Bolsheviks before the retreat was well under way. They had been dispatched along a parallel trail as a kind of decoy movement, since there was some doubt about their loyalty to the Allied cause, and the exact plan of the march had not been revealed to them. Ironside remarked afterward that their defection was not surprising in view of the fact that most of them had wives and families who would soon be under Bolshevik control.

Around 8 A.M. on January 25, with daylight beginning to come dully through the snow-covered branches of the forest trees, the boom of the Soviet big guns could be heard miles to the rear, opening up on Shenkursk. It was reassuring in a way, for it indicated that the Bolsheviks were still not certain whether the Allies had evacuated the town. The column had now put about ten miles behind them, and a halt was called at the first village big enough to offer temporary cover from the cold. The villagers were ready with steaming samovars of tea; everyone broke open ration tins and ate voraciously. The salmon, once defrosted, was exquisite; beans and bully beef tasted excellent, and even some greasy herring fishcakes offered by the peasant housewives were devoured eagerly.

After a little over an hour's rest the fugitives hit the trail again. Daylight had brought little rise in temperature, and even with the food inside them most of the men were now fighting a constant battle with fatigue. Every step called for an effort that really hurt. Packs began to be unbearably heavy, and the objects so carefully selected for transportation in Shenkursk began to be dropped by the wayside without remorse. Extra boots, pistols, belts, Bibles, shaving kits, packs of letters-all were tossed into the snow as if every ounce of lightening was worth its negative weight in life-blood. By afternoon men were heaving off their entire packs, and some got rid of their sheeplined overcoats, which seemed to hang on their backs like shrouds of lead. So numb they were from over-exertion that they seemed insensible to the cold. Many had long since found the Shackleton boots impossibly cumbersome, and had kicked them off to shuffle wearily on in their stocking feet. By nightfall, when they reached Shegovari, there were numerous cases of frostbite, and more pony sleighs had to be requisitioned from the natives.

At Shegovari the Canadian field battery had stopped and put their two remaining guns into "action front" position: four had been regretfully abandoned en route. The hospital convoy had gone on, and in fact continued until it reached Archangel. Rear-guard patrols had discovered that the Bolsheviks were now in close pursuit, but there was no question of the column continuing for another night's march. There were two fresh platoons of the 339th in the town, and with some trepidation it was decided that come what might a stand must now be made, at least for a few hours. Once more the Canadians proved their incalculable value to the expedition, thoroughly discouraging the vanguard of the Soviet pursuit with some splendid open-sight marksmanship.

Yet the countryside, that night, was alive with signal rockets in villages on three sides of Shegovari, and it seemed obvious that something more than the Canadian guns kept the Bolsheviks from overwhelming the retreating column. At least three thousand Soviet troops were known to be in the area, with plenty more in reserve. It began to appear that the Soviet intention was to destroy the threat of the Shenkursk salient without necessarily destroying the Allied force itself. Ironside learned later that one of Kolchak's anti-Bolshevik armies had successfully captured Perm, just west of the Urals, at the end of 1918, and thus appeared to be approaching a union with the Allied forces in North Russia in January. He therefore interpreted the drive of the Sixth Red Army against Shenkursk as a move to forestall any such union, which would have been a disaster from the Soviet point of view. At any rate, there is no doubt that at this time the Kolchak forces were a far greater threat to the Bolsheviks than all the strength Ironside could muster; and Red operations against his British and American units were therefore adequate if they evened out the front, and harassed the Allies enough to cancel any thought of a push to join Kolchak. From this standpoint, driving them out of Shenkursk was a decided Bolshevik success, even though the garrison was allowed to escape with few casualties after the initial attack at Nijni Gora.

This probably explains why the retreat from Shenkursk was not followed up more aggressively by Trotsky's Sixth Red Army. The tired Allies left Shegovari late on January 26 and withdrew to Vistafka, on the Vaga River approximately opposite Toulgas, over on the Dvina to the east. This was close enough for quick reinforcement from Bereznik, the main Allied river base, and since the Bolsheviks seemed inclined to let matters rest for the time being, the Americans were ordered to dig in and prepare more or less permanent defenses. The order was not easily carried out, the ground being rock-hard to a depth of several feet, but with such hasty expedients as barbedwire entanglements and trenches cut in the snow, something like a defensible position was contrived until more substantial dugouts could be built. Bolshevik light artillery and snipers made the work more than naturally uncomfortable, but there was no sign of a full-fledged attack. The retreat from Shenkursk was over.

CHAPTER 10

GALA ARCHANGEL

THE FALL OF SHENKURSK near the end of January, 1919, brought a lull in Soviet-American combat in North Russia. Meanwhile, in the city of Archangel, life went on in its peculiar Russian way, but under the aegis of a future peer of England.

Edmund Ironside's choice of title, "Baron of Archangel and of Ironside," when he was elevated to the peerage by King George VI in 1941, provoked this comment from a columnist in the London *News Chronicle*: "Archangel indeed! What should we say if ... Molotov were to proclaim himself First Duke of Delhi?" The leaders of the Kremlin may have felt that a more accurate parallel would be to proclaim Molotov First Duke of Glasgow, or of some other important area much closer to London than Delhi.

Since by 1941 Ironside had occupied many positions apparently far more significant than that of commander in chief of the Allied Expeditionary Force in North Russia, the title throws some light on what his year in that capacity meant to him personally. He had been Quartermaster General of India, Governor of Gibraltar, and finally, at the outbreak of World War II, Chief of the Imperial General Staff. Why "Baron of Archangel"?

The answer may be that in North Russia, everything considered, Ironside felt a greater sense of responsibility, as well as a greater sense of power, than ever again in an illustrious career. He was top man of an international army operating to help save the world from Communism; more than that, he was for all practical purposes the civil ruler of a large chunk of Russia. Chaikovsky's Provisional Government discovered at every turn that its activities must conform to the wishes of the British military of they were to continue, and that to a large extent its members were merely play-acting at statesmanship.

Chaikovsky himself, dreamer that he was, finally came to see this clearly, and left for Paris (via ice-breaker) even as Shenkursk was falling to the Reds. Nominally he continued to be President; but in fact he never returned to Russia.

Chaikovsky's departure made little difference to Ironside one way or the other. By this time he took no interest in the political maneuvering of the various elements in the North Russian government except as it affected his own problems in administering the city and the region of Archangel; all the members of the government struck him as "just timid bureaucrats." He found them woefully lacking in any realistic appreciation of the Communist threat to their country, and the necessity to win the support of the laborers and peasants in their cause. Ignoring them as much as possible, he went about the irksome duties of keeping order in a wartime seaport swollen to over twice its normal population by military occupation and by refugees of motley description.

Some of Ironside's problems were formidable, although not unexpected. His experience had taught him, as he put it, that every army base turns into "a sink" in war, and must be frequently cleaned out. He had a good administrative officer in General Henry Needham, but there were many things in the cleaning process that Ironside felt called for his personal attention. Shortly after taking over from Poole, for example, he had become aware that the city jail was bursting with prisoners, and that nobody knew just who they were or why they were there. The head jailer was a big man with a bushy beard whose conception of his job was encompassed by two ideas: keep them alive, and keep them. Among the hundreds of prisoners were many who had been there long before the capture of Archangel by the Allies; to these had been added many more, most of them vaguely accused of being either pro-Bolshevik or anti-British, or both. None had yet been brought to trial under the Provisional Government.

When Ironside entered the jail for a good look, he was nearly overpowered by the smell. The windows had been sealed with tape, and although there were steam baths in the building, they had not been used. The tattered prisoners were crowded into dank compartments, sometimes as many as sixty to one room. None had been given any work to do, and there was no system of regular exercise.

Speaking to a few men at random, Ironside was shocked to find that some of them were Austrian prisoners of war who had been in jail at one place or another for nearly four years without having their cases reviewed. He was already feeling rather grim about the whole thing when the jailer showed him twenty small boys, orphans of the revolution, who had been picked up for stealing food.

Ironside was by no means an insensitive man, and he took immediate steps to remedy these medieval conditions. The problem was intensified by the fact that it really was necessary to screen out genuine criminals, Bolshevik agitators, and troublemakers from the rest; and in the absence of reliable records on the prisoners this was almost hopelessly difficult. The general put some of his intelligence staff to work on the weeding-out process. Gradually the captives were separated into three categories, somewhat unscientifically designated, by Ironside, "the bads, the less bads, and the probably harmless." Hundreds were put into work companies, to be kept busy loading and unloading vessels under guard; others were allowed to enlist in "Dyer's Battalion" (named after its Canadian commander) of the Slavo-British Legion, for military training under close supervision. The forlorn little boys were put temporarily in the care of noncommissioned officers, and some were soon the happy mascots of British and American army units.

There was no question but that Archangel was honeycombed with Bolshevik sympathizers and agents. In the laboring districts of the city, which were very fertile ground, propaganda leaflets and posters appeared regularly, and the British had much trouble trying to trace these to their sources. As in every civil war, moreover, it was egregiously easy for spies and provocateurs to mingle with the population; no tell tale signs in appearance or accent existed. Getting across the Allied lines was no great difficulty either, since the frozen forest and tundra of the province stretched over an area that Ironside's limited forces could not possibly check thoroughly. To add to the headaches of the intelligence officers and the military police, there were numbers of odd characters in the city whose activities were mysterious and therefore suspicious, even if nothing definite seemed to connect them with the Bolsheviks. A typical specimen was an attractive woman known as "Dolina," who claimed to be an actress from Petrograd. She cultivated the Allied officers so assiduously that Lieutenant S. M. Riis, naval attache at the U.S. embassy, reported her as a possible spy, although the frequency with which she entertained guests in her room also suggested a less sophisticated motive.

Prostitution, in general, was a problem hard to separate from that of security. Certain night spots popular with the soldiers, such as the notorious Cafe de Paris, were staffed largely by waitresses who doubled as whores; so, according to one American report, did a good many of the regular female customers. Sometimes these establishments were placed off limits, but often this merely resulted in making the task of surveillance more difficult. Although there undoubtedly was a certain amount of nonprofessional activity going on, the prevalence of prostitution in Archangel in 1918-19 is probably fairly well indicated by the American statistics on venereal disease and prophylactics. The venereal rate reported by the chief surgeon was about the same as that for the American Expeditionary Force in France, and well over three thousand prophylactic treatments were given in the nine months the Americans were there. It must be remembered, in this connection, that some elements of the 339th Infantry did not get back to Archangel more than once during all the time they were in Russia.

One quixotic personality Ironside was glad to turn over to the Russian authorities to deal with was Madame Botchkareva, former leader of an organization popularly known as the Battalion of Death. This was a unit of the Imperial Russian Army composed of female volunteers who allegedly went to the front line and fought Germans and Austrians. After being wounded several times, the Madame made her way to the United States and achieved a certain wartime fame by appearing at patriotic rallies to tell of her exploits. Later, in England, she talked the War Office into sending her to Archangel with Poole's invasion force-for what purpose was not exactly clear. For some time she hovered about Allied headquarters at Shenkursk, attempting ineffectually to interest various officers in her story. Lieutenant Mead, of Company A, had an embarrassing interview with her during which, as he recalls, she kept trying to exhibit her scars; he was in some doubt about just how she had come to merit the appellation of "Madame." Eventually she got an audience with Ironside, who likewise found her anything but a romantic figure with her "broad ugly face, mottled complexion and squat figure." Taking pity, however, he sent her to General Marushevsky for assignment. But the little martinet of the North Russian army gave her no satisfaction, instead issuing what Ironside referred to as "one of those curiously conversational Orders of the Day in which Russian generals so often indulged." The gist of it was that Madame Botchkareva was to be stripped of her uniform, since "the summoning of women for military duties, which are not appropriate for their sex, would be a heavy reproach and a disgraceful stain on the whole population of the northern region."

This, incidentally, was a typical effusion for Marushevsky, who had soon disappointed Ironside by showing more interest in a figmentary honor than in the development of an effective fighting force. The pint-sized monarchist insisted on wearing a uniform ostentatiously reminiscent of his service under the Czar, and was constantly up to his medals in elaborate paperwork. Many of his lengthy orders of the day, instead of showing some awareness that the forces under his nominal command were up against a ruthless and determined enemy, concerned themselves with profanity overheard among the enlisted men, incorrect uniform, or intoxication, and were likely to end with expressions like: "How pitiful is all this and how deeply disgusting!" Nothing in Ironside's twenty years of military service had prepared him for dealing with a general officer like Marushevsky.

Fortunately, a second expatriate general who arrived in Archangel about the middle of January showed more promise. This was Eugene K. Miller, whose apparently Anglo-Saxon name was belied by a distinguished record of thirty years in the Russian army. Although he was even more of a monarchist than Marushevsky-and this disturbed Ironside, who understood very well that Russia was quite done with czars-he had one thing the British general had found remarkably rare in Archangel: a burning desire to overthrow the Bolsheviks by military power. Miller took the position of governor general in the Provisional Government as well as commander in chief of the North Russian armed forces, and was soon enthusiastically engaged in building up his new army as fast as he could. This was a great relief to Ironside, who from the moment of the Shenkursk disaster had begun to think very seriously about evacuation of the Allied forces from North Russia. He as yet had no orders pointing to such a conclusion, but he was beginning to feel that it was inevitable; and he knew that when it came the fate of the province would have to depend entirely on native defense efforts against the Bolsheviks.

Quite aside from such military problems as security and recruiting, Ironside was obliged to consume much time with troublesome economic matters. During the entire Allied occupation, for instance, the currency situation was more or less chaotic. At first the invaders had paid for whatever they bought, in goods or labor, with czarist rubles; but as a limited supply had been brought in, and the Russians tended to hoard them, these were soon driven out of circulation by paper rubles issued by the Bolshevik regime. This Soviet currency was abundant but subject to explosive inflation, so that its possession before long became meaningless. Many Bolshevik prisoners of war taken in the fall of 1918 were found to have twenty or thirty thousand paper rubles in their pockets; but these would buy practically nothing. In November the British imported great packs of new currency, printed in London and guaranteed by the Bank of England at the rate of forty rubles to the pound sterling "at the cessation of hostilities." It was discovered, however, that these by an incredible oversight had been printed from a design adorned with Russian imperial crowns-hated emblems of the old regime which could never be accepted by the people of North Russia. Rubber stamps were made, and each emblem laboriously obliterated before this currency could be put into circulation, an immensely time-consuming project. Meanwhile a very active barter market had developed; and indeed this continued to be the favored method of exchange whenever possible, since the phrase "at the cessation of hostilities" was regarded as somewhat ambiguous. For a few pounds of sugar or flour, or a few packs of cigarettes, a man could obtain anything from jewels to magnificent fur coats. An American intelligence officer estimated the buying power of one cigarette, around Christmastime, as equal to twenty-five cents.

It need hardly be said that the American and British soldiers in Archangel were very quick to react to this situation, and "skolkoing"-skolko means "how much"-became a favorite off-duty recreation. Huge supplies of food had been shipped into Archangel to feed not only the troops, but the civilian population, and the temptation to steal from the warehouses and stacks on the quays was irresistible to many. Ironside notes with something like horror that even officers were caught on the streets bartering goods which had been "requisitioned" from Allied supplies. Not only food but equipment of all kinds disappeared nightly, and doubling the guard details seemed to do little good. To the Americans on the combat fronts, the supply company of the 339th Infantry looked highly suspect, and it was a most unpopular outfit. Cudahy made the point bluntly enough: "… over across the harbor at Bakaritza, a well-fed Supply Company watched over mountains of rations and supplies that had been brought all the way from far off America … These supplies never reached the front, but the Supply Company, with American business shrewdness and American aptitude for trading, acquired great bundles of rubles, and at the market place converted these into stable sterling, and came out of Russia in the springtime with pleasant memories of a tourist winter; likewise a small fortune securely hid in their olive drab breeches."

If there was one commodity that was not easy to dispose of on the black market, it was alcohol. Any metropolis in wartime is likely to be far from dry, but Archangel, it seems, very nearly set itself afloat. Vodka was one of the few things it was easy to buy, and buy cheap. According to an American naval intelligence report, the Provisional Government had appropriated five million gallons of grain alcohol once belonging to the czarist regime; this was used for the manufacture of vodka in what Ironside called "almost unlimited quantities," selling for the equivalent of a shilling a bottle. On top of this, the British themselves had brought in an enormous quantity of Scotch-several sources say forty thousand cases-for the use of their officers, and although many of these gentlemen applied themselves with the best will in the world, this was so much an oversupply that hundreds of cases somehow got into civilian hands. An American Red Cross official, naturally outraged by this state of affairs, demanded at British headquarters why so much whiskey had been shipped in. He was assured that it must have been an error.

In picturing the liquor situation in Archangel in the winter of 1919, it must be remembered that a large part of the population, both civilian and military, was without employment. Most of the city's productive enterprises had come nearly to a halt, and even had they been operating full tilt there would have been thousands of refugees for whom no work could have been found. The military unemployment was largely the result of General Poole's defeated expectation that many thousands of Russians would answer the call to the colors and require a tremendous training and administrative staff to get them ready for action. Hundreds of excess junior officers, including many expatriate Russians who had filtered into Archangel by way of England, hung about the cafe and street corners with nothing to do, or made a show of performing military jobs which, in truth, amounted to nothing. The intense cold, added to hunger, idleness, and anxiety, made drinking an almost compulsive activity for many civilians; for the surplus officers it was a pastime. Twenty hours a day of darkness and the dim twilight even at noon didn't help either: it was very difficult to know when to stop drinking.

All of this helps to explain why many an American combat soldier, when fortune gave him a few days' furlough in Archangel, found the city rather depressing. There were the usual contrasts, always shocking, between life at the front and life in the rear, but in North Russia they were ironically intensified. After the stark realities of vigil on the Dvina or Vaga, the alcoholic gaiety of Archangel-despite its drab streets and open sewers-seemed incredible. To make matters worse, Colonel Stewart and his headquarters staff gave the impression of being both cowed by the British and strangely uninterested in the problems of the fighting fronts. Stewart, of course, had a good Freudian reason for trying to ignore the fact that the Americans under his command constituted a majority of the forces in combat with the Bolsheviks. He knew that he stood in constant violation of President Wilson's orders, although to be sure he got no encouragement, either from the American embassy or from the American Military Mission under Colonel James A. Ruggles, to out them into effect. The truth of the matter, it must be acknowledged, was that by this time any attempt to do so would have caused an international incident of considerable impact, and might have jeopardized the safety of the entire Allied expedition.

The Americans in from the front, however, knew nothing of all this, and to them Stewart's behavior was unforgivable. Without question his personal failings magnified the bad impression he made on his men. Three lieutenants of the 339th swore to their fellow officers that they reported at American headquarters in Archangel one day, and were pleasantly surprised to be greeted by Stewart with a handshake and the inquiry, "How are you, lieutenant? When did you get in?" Later in the day, however, they met the colonel at two separate social functions. They were astonished, both times, to have him again extend his hand to each of them with a rather glassy stare, and inquire, "How are you, lieutenant? When did you get in?" Running a close second to Stewart in unpopularity was Major Young, the officer who had begun his career in North Russia as commander of the 3rd Battalion, on the railroad front. Having been relieved-the doughboys said it was for incompetence-he was put in charge of summary courtsmartial for the regiment, a job which he seemed to relish. His sentences were stiff, and Colonel Stewart showed little inclination to modify them when they came before him for review.

Even the noble efforts of the Y.M.C.A. and the Red Cross often fell flat with the men in from the combat fronts. To the extent that these organizations managed to get their cocoa, candy, cigarettes, and entertainment out close enough to the fronts to benefit the men on the line, they were tremendously appreciated. Transport, however, was a tough problem, almost all the sled convoys being loaded with goods deemed more essential by British headquarters. In contrast to the meager trickle of comforts that reached the men at the front, Archangel seemed almost too well taken care of. There were movies twice a week, band concerts, dances, teas, a library, boxing matches, toboggan parties, several hostess huts, minstrel shows, canteens, etc., etc. The Red Cross put out a weekly paper, piously named *The American Sentinel*, which was well edited, but poorly supplied with battle news by military headquarters. Here the tired combat soldier, in for a few days around Christmastime, for example, could read the cheery news that prohibition was a sure thing back home in Michigan; that troops were already being returned from the western front to the

U.S.A.; and that what he was doing in North Russia was "giving the world the best present it could possibly receive, the promise of peace." One feature he conceivably might have enjoyed was a satirical column called "Who's Who in Russia," a typical entry of which read: "—, Ivan Petrovich Podparuchik (Lieutenant), Russian Forces. Born 1892, Moscow. Member of bourgeois, or Samovar-type of Russian family. Cadet School, Orianbaum, 1914-1917. Captured by Bolsheviks November, 1917. Escaped, July 1918. Fled to Archangel. Belongs (theoretically) to infantry. Wears spurs, always. Favorite amusement, dancing all night. Specialty: Bowing to acquaintances in—cafe."

On the whole, however, the American infantrymen were likely to feel too bitter for light satire on this topic. What Cudahy wrote afterward was probably more expressive of the way they felt:

> So it was that Archangel became a city of many colors, as gallant, uniformed gentlemen strode down the Trotsky Prospect, whipping the air with their walking sticks, and looking very stern and commanding, as they answered many salutes, in a bored, absent-minded way.
>
> There were officers of the Imperial Army, weighed down with glittering, ponderous honor medals, and dark Cossacks with high gray hats, and gaudy tunics, and murderous noisy sabers. Handsome gentlemen of war from England, from Serbia, Italy, Finland, France, and Bohemia, and many other countries, all arrayed in brilliant plumage, and shining boots, and bright spurs ... And, of course, there were large numbers of batmen to shine the boots and burnish the spurs, and keep all in fine order, and other batmen to look after the appointments of the officers' club, and serve the whiskey and soda.
>
> In the afternoons there were teas, and receptions and matinees, and dances in the evening, when the band played and every one was flushed with pleasure and excitement. Such flirtations with the pretty *barishnas*, such whispered gossip and intrigue and scandal in light-hearted Archangel!
>
> At Kodish, at Onega, on the Vaga, and at Touglas, far off across the haunting snows, sick men and broken men, men faint from lack of nutrition, and men sickened in soul, were doing sentry through the numbing, cold nights, because there were none to take their places in the blockhouses, and no supports to come to their relief ... far, so far off from gala Archangel.

One thing that jarred gala Archangel considerably was the Allied retreat from Shenkursk. As long as that important bastion, two hundred miles away, was held against the Bolsheviks, Archangel seemed safe from attack; but now there was nothing to the south to impede the Communists except a lot of insignificant villages and the wavering Allied troops themselves. Aside from any actual military advantage, the possession of Shenkursk had been psychologically important; its loss was a serious blow to the prestige of both the Allies and the Provisional Government. Like the winter of 1776 in America, it was a time "to try men's souls," and a good many North Russian souls decided that to throw in their lot irrevocably with the Allies might in the end turn out to be a very serious mistake. The Red Army was clearly getting stronger.

Ironside's chief task, after the bad news from Shenkursk followed so closely his return to Archangel, was to try to calm the ministers of the Provisional Government and their local adherents. It seemed to him that only when they felt themselves suddenly in danger were they ready to face the fact that they relied almost entirely on Allied military protection for their free existence in Russia. Now they bothered him with anxious inquiries as to the intentions of the Allies: would North Russia be abandoned to the fury of the Bolsheviks? The general had waited in vain for a statement of policy from England, or from the Allies at the peace conference in Paris; but he told them that in his own opinion Great Britain "would never desert those Russians who had sided with us in the days before the Armistice." At the same time he was obliged to remind them of what the theory had been all along: North Russia would build up her own independent army, capable of defending the region if and when the Allies should leave. He was luckily able to point to General Miller's strenuous conscription and training activities, which were already beginning to show results. About five thousand natives had now been put into uniform and their numbers were rapidly swelling.

However, American authorities in Archangel, as well as Russian, were upset by the defeat at Shenkursk and what it seemed to imply. Even while it was happening, DeWitt Clinton Poole, the American charge d'affaires, wired the State Department an apprehensive report, citing the ugly circumstances under which the 339th Infantry was fighting: "The enemy greatly outnumbers us both in men and artillery; his morale, numbers and efficiency have increased. We are more and more put upon the defensive, subjected to more and more frequent attacks and bombardment suffering many casualties. We have no reserves." Nevertheless, Poole, who was as implacably set against Bolshevism as his mentor Ambassador Francis, was in no mood to recommend American withdrawal from North Russia. "I am convinced after careful inquiry," he said two days after Shenkursk was abandoned, "that the large majority of the people of this region favor the present intervention."

Poole based this statement on what may be regarded as a dubious assumption: that the Provisional Government truly represented the feelings of a "large majority" of the people of Archangel Province. He did not have the acquaintance with the peasants that Ironside had as a result of his frequent travels; nor, it may be presumed, did he have the gift for sensing the pulse of the laboring class in Archangel that belonged to his perceptive underling, Felix Cole. He was thus still inclined to estimate very optimistically the degree of popular support the Allies could count on, and to suggest to the Department of State that what was needed was a bigger and better intervention. He even reported as "representative," with the implication that it made sense, the belief of one member of the Provisional Government that "the occupation of Murmansk and Archangel without further advance into the country has been unfortunate; it has lent color to the Bolshevik charge that intervention is selfishly inspired, seaports along being taken and with a view to permanent occupation." According to this theory, the farther the Allies penetrated into Russian territory, the *less* successful the Bolsheviks would be in rallying the native population to the defense of the Fatherland against the invaders. Ironside had another theory, which he expressed in a graphic metaphor: "To me it was like a great sticky pudding. A hand could be thrust easily into it. Everywhere it gave way so long as the thrust continued. Immediately the thrust ceased the mass began to close steadily in on the hand, wrist, and arm. There then came the horrible fear that the hand could never be withdrawn."

As the winter advanced, Ironside found life in the icebound city of Archangel more and more irritating. Although he was a competent administrator, he had never enjoyed desk soldiering, and his heart was with the troops at the front. At headquarters he was harried by an endless queue of agitated persons who wished to consult him on matters most of which he considered trivial or beyond solution; in the field he could attend directly to what he viewed as his real business in North Russia: holding off the Bolsheviks. He was a sociable man, but social life in Archangel had little appeal for him. There were too many drunken and useless officers hanging about, and the gay activities of Archangel's upper-class residents seemed to resemble far too closely the behavior of the two little pigs in the nursery tale who so badly misjudged the power of the big, bad wolf.

Visiting the fronts, however, had involved certain difficulties with the coming of the snow in November. Before that, the general had been able to keep in touch with his combat units by river or by air; now the only easily accessible front was the railroad, and that was the most secure of all and consequently the least interesting to him. He gave careful consideration to various means of transport, but found only one that seemed feasible. Flying was altogether too undependable in the face of the cold, snow, and lack of good landing fields. Apparently there was not a riding horse in Archangel Province able to carry Ironside's tremendous weight. A few Ford trucks that the expedition boasted were tried and found very much wanting: even on packed trails they had to proceed in low gear, and after a snowstorm they simply stalled. Reindeer sleighs were available, and this means of travel had an appealing dash; but experienced natives discouraged their regular use. Although faster than the little Russian ponies, the reindeer were not so long on stamina, and also required special fodder.

In the end the ordinary pony sleigh proved the best solution to the problem. It was a marvel of functional design. There was not an excess piece in its open frame of light pine or birch saplings laced with thongs, and its big runners curved up at the front with just the right arc to ride easily over bumps and through snow-drifts. With a good bed of hay in the body of the sleigh, a sleeping bag, a couple of blankets or robes, and a flask of rum for emergencies, a man could swish along snowy trails under the North Russian stars in almost womblike comfort, even when the temperature was far below zero.

The North Russian pony was a perfect match for the sleigh he pulled. Very small but very stalwart, the breed had developed an almost incredible resistance to the arctic climate and the relatively careless treatment given by their masters. Ironside, who was used to the meticulous attention paid to the big horses of the British artillery and cavalry, was astonished to find that the ponies remained in excellent condition even though they were never groomed. At the end of a long, cold journey, they were simply let into a crude stable and furnished with plenty of hay; "never any such thing as bran-mash or a bag of oats." If no stables were available, the ponies were left to stand in the open, sometimes resembling figures of ice sculpture by morning. A slap on the rump, however, and a little massaging of their nostrils after breaking off the icicles, got them ready to go again.

Ironside found to his delight that he could make excellent time in his sleigh, once a pony-express system of relays had been set up to furnish fresh horsepower as often as possible. Much to the dismay of some of his staff officers, he decided to risk traveling the far-flung trails of the North Russian forest without military escort. Although a good pony could draw a heavy load, and the typical sleigh would hold two men besides the driver, it naturally made much faster progress with only one rider; and to have taken even a squad with him would have meant a cumbersome number of sleighs. He therefore used only two, one for himself and one for his faithful Russian groom, Piskoff. At first they frequently changed drivers as well as ponies; but early in the winter one driver, a Russian peasant boy of sixteen named Kostia, attached himself so doggedly to them, and drove so well, that they made him a permanent member of the party. Kostia, in fact, turned out to be more permanent than Ironside ever anticipated, for he accompanied the general out of North Russia and remained in his service for twenty years. He was to prove of great value, also, to the British intelligence service during World War II.

It would be interesting to know whether the Bolsheviks ever realized that the commanding general of the Allied forces spent many a night cruising serenely through the lonely stretches of the forest, with nothing to guard him from capture but two men and a boy. At any rate, Ironside never ran into trouble except once. It was about 2 A.M., on a leg of his January trip to the Dvina front. The night was still, and the general dozed comfortably in his sleeping bag, occasionally coming to when a startled partridge or grouse would take off from an overhead branch, dusting the sleigh with powder snow. The runners squeaked slightly on the packed trail-it was about thirty below-and the sleigh swayed with a gentle, soporific rhythm as the pony trotted briskly along.

Suddenly Ironside sat bolt upright. From somewhere off in the woods had come a shout, followed immediately by the crack of a rifle. Both the general and his driver dove out beside the sleigh into the snow as more shots banged out and bullets cut the underbrush along the trail. Ironside quickly pulled out a rifle that was stuffed into the hay of the sleigh, and ran up the trail to where Piskoff and Kostia were furiously shooting their automatics at the flashes made by the Bolshevik rifles. He had fired two shots when a pony's high-pitched scream was heard; then another shout, and silence. Cautiously they made their way down an intersecting trail to the right, and after going about twenty yards came upon a dead pony and an overturned sleigh. The snow was red with the blood of a wounded man who lay near the pony. He was in bad shape, but with a stiff shot of rum Piskoff revived him long enough to discover that he had been part of a propaganda team trying to make their way to Archangel. Another sleigh had managed to escape. The Bolshevik died before any more could be done for him, and Ironside and Piskoff carried his body back to one of their own sleighs. They then continued toward the next Allied outpost, Kostia nearly beside himself with joy at having been in action against the enemy. Ironside himself, who was more addicted to danger than ninety-nine generals out of a hundred, was by no means displeased.

There is no doubt that Ironside's jaunts to the fighting lines contributed much to the tremendous popularity which he won from the men under his command, not excluding the Americans. The sudden appearance of the general's gigantic figure, clad from head to foot in heavy furs, invariably seemed to make the troops feel better, especially since he had a facility for remembering names, and took a genuine interest in the details of their life at the front. In this, of course, he was the precise opposite of Colonel Stewart, and the American officers and men transferred to him with double intensity the admiration and loyalty they would have liked to feel for their own commanding officer.

Nevertheless, American morale in North Russia by the end of January, 1919, was severely on the wane. Ironside was one of the few exceptions among British officers who were able to elicit respect from the doughboys; most of the "limeys" they despised. As the weeks and months went by they came to believe that they had really been forgotten by the United States War Department, and they still had no clear idea of why they were fighting the Red army. The Communist propaganda pamphlets which they picked up on their icy patrol trails raised this question again and again, and the unpleasant answers supplied by the Bolsheviks made more sense to some than the evasive replies they got from their own officers. Although details were lacking, it was now widely known among the men of the 339th that Americans had suffered desperately in the defense of Shenkursk, and that the town had afterward been abandoned. In the bitter cold and what seemed like perpetual darkness, they sat in their blockhouses and pondered still the tiresome question that had irked them from the beginning: what was it all about? And now, to many, another question arose like a specter: would they ever get out of it alive?

CHAPTER 11

A CRUEL DILEMMA

IF THE MEN OF company A, 339th Infantry, could have seen a copy of the *New York Times* for Sunday, January 19, 1919-the day they were so disastrously assaulted by more than a thousand Soviet troops at Nijni Gora-their distress would hardly have been alleviated. The paper was bulging with signs that everything in the U.S.A. was getting pleasantly back to normal. All the big department stores were featuring January clearance sales. Broadway was alive with new shows, and Walter Hampden was a great success in his performance of *Hamlet*. Motorcar ads filled the back pages, most of them, like that for the Jordan, plucking hard on the Johnny-comes-marching-home theme: "Somewhere in this great land there is a wonderful girl waiting for a wonderful boy ... ." But it is possible that the most annoying item of all would have been the banner headline on the front page: ALLIED UNITY MARKS OPENING OF THE PEACE CONFERENCE.

It will be recalled that the Department of State, upon being asked what change the armistice would make in the fate of the American troops in North Russia, had replied that any decision must await President Wilson's discussions with Allied leaders at the peace conference in Paris. The President had arrived in Europe, amidst huge acclaim, in December; but it was only after a month of triumphal tours, lectures, and dinners that he was ready to start his fateful conversations with Lloyd George and Clemenceau in Paris, and the peace conference did not formally begin until January 18. The vexatious Russian question, however, had come up several times during Wilson's travels, notably in London, where David R. Francis was waiting for his doctors to make up their minds to operate. The old ambassador was ailing painfully, but he was also in a state of acute anxiety to see Wilson and explain to him what ought to be done about the Bolshevik menace.

Although Francis had been considered important enough for the cruiser *Olympia* to make a special trip to Archangel to pick him up, he now found that his counsel was not in great demand by his chief of state. Notes to the effect that he was at Wilson's disposal for an audience finally produced a reply saying that the President's mind had been "running in the same lines" as the ambassador's with regard to Russia; but this encouraging word was dampened by Wilson's failure to set any time when he could be seen. At Christmas, Francis thought he would have his opportunity, for, as he proudly wired the embassy staff at Archangel: "Invited banquet Buckingham Palace which King giving President and which can attend by consent of young eminent Johns Hopkins specialist whom Department ordered from France to London for me."

The royal banquet was, as Lloyd George put it, "a dream of magnificence." All the great war leaders of the Allies were there, "arrayed in resplendent uniforms of every cut and colour." Francis, however, was again frustrated in his effort to talk to Wilson, for the social eddies of the dinner never seemed to move him within earshot of the President. "While he was talking to the King and the Premier," he wryly recorded later, "... I was talking to the ladies." He did manage to air his feelings to the King of England. The monarch happened to encounter Francis as he escorting Mrs. Wilson from the banquet hall when the affair was coming to its conclusion. "Mr. Ambassador," said the King, "what do you think we ought to do about Russia?" Francis promptly replied that the Allies ought to overthrow the Bolshevik government; and the King, to his great satisfaction, said that he thought so too.

Francis left the hospital, after his operation, on February 1, and immediately headed for Paris, where Wilson was now in daily consultation at the peace conference. Hovering near the bustling corridors and antechambers, he was able to arrange talks with some of Wilson's advisors, but not with the President himself. To Secretary of State Lansing, General Pershing, *et al.*, Francis outlined his plan for solving the Russian problem. It was beautifully simple in theory, and featured the ambassador himself as the leading actor. He would "occupy the Embassy at Petrograd" with the aid of 150,000 troops, one-third each from America, England, and France. He would then announce to the Russian people that the Allies had come to enable them "to hold a free election." Under these benign circumstances, Francis was convinced, the regime of Lenin and Trotsky would crumple very shortly.

According to Francis, the various important people to whom he presented his plan all said, "You tell that to the President." This he was more than eager to do, but still the chance evaded him. What he apparently did not know was that while he was in the hospital in London, the peace conference had considered the possibility of further armed intervention in Russia, and had taken a dim view of it. This was, in fact, one of the first big points on which Lloyd George, Clemenceau, and Wilson were in agreement, however reluctant. "Is anyone of the Western Allies," asked Lloyd George, "prepared to send a million men into Russia?" He doubted "whether a thousand would be willing to go. All reports tend to show that the allied troops in Siberia and in Northern Russia are most unwilling to continue the campaign and determined to return to their homes." There was then some talk among the conference delegates about a volunteer army of perhaps 150,000 men. Lloyd George quickly demanded what contributions America, Italy, and France would make toward the raising of such an army: Wilson and Orlando (the Italian premier) each said "None"; and even Clemenceau, the old "Tiger" of French politics, who would have liked nothing better than to see the Bolsheviks demolished by force, replied that France had no men to spare.

This, of course, was on a purely practical level. In the more ethereal realm of principle, the Big Four at the peace conference enjoyed less unanimity. As far as Clemenceau was concerned, the Communists were no better than thugs and murderers; they had betrayed France in her hour of trial (by the Treaty of Brest-Litovsk), and no honorable nation could recognize their claim to rule Russia, much less deal with them as equals in international relations. Lloyd George, although it was under his leadership that England had sent armed forces against the Bolsheviks in 1918, had now come to feel that this was perhaps inconsistent with the British axiom of non-interference in the internal affairs of any country. The response of the

Russian people-North Russia was a perfect illustration-had not been what England had hoped: instead of regarding the Allies as saviors, they seemed on the whole inclined to regard them as invaders. "To say that we ourselves should pick the representatives of a great people," he declared to the conference, "is contrary to every principle for which we have fought." The evidence from British agents in Russia convinced him that although the majority of the people were not Bolsheviks, they would support the Bolshevik government in preference to anything that smacked of the czarist regime; and the governments of Admiral Kolchak, General Denikin, and M. Chaikovsky all left much to be desired in that respect. Everything considered, Lloyd George felt that the time had come to pull out of Russia, and he was even in favor of dealing with the Communists as the *de facto* government.

President Wilson was much of the same mind. This was not surprising, since the views expressed by Lloyd George resembled closely those held by the President as far back as the previous summer, when Wilson had unsuccessfully resisted British and French pressure for intervention. Knowing, as by now he did, the belligerent use to which American soldiers had been put by the British in North Russia, Wilson must have experienced feelings, of bitter irony as he listened to Lloyd George explaining the futility of military intervention. He did not, however, indulge in embarrassing recriminations, instead supporting the British prime minister before the conference with further observations along the same line. The tolerance of the Russian people for Bolshevism, he observed, was founded on a basis of real grievance against the wrongs of the old order: "The seeds of Bolshevism could not flourish without a soil ready to receive them." Moreover, he went on, "we should be fighting against the current of the times if we tried to pre vent Russia from finding her own path in freedom. Part of the strength of the Bolshevik leaders is doubtless the threat of foreign intervention. With the help of this threat they gather the people around them." This analysis, it must be noted, was exactly the reverse of that made by Ambassador Francis and DeWitt Clinton Poole, who reasoned that the more resolutely the Allies plunged into Russia the more enthusiastically the people would turn against the Communists.

With this concord between Lloyd George and Wilson, and with grudging agreement from the French and Italian delegations, the Paris conference decided, on January 21, to take a step toward bringing about peace in strife-torn Russia. The step, however, was not what, to some, might have appeared the obvious one, namely ordering all Allied troops to get out of Russia as soon as possible. There were difficulties in the path of any such simple solution as that. What they agreed to do, on a motion from Lloyd George and President Wilson, was to invite all the warring factions in Russia, including the Bolsheviks, to sit down with the Allies at a conference table and see what could be done toward settling their differences. At first it was suggested that they come to Paris; but this Clemenceau unalterably opposed. He was not going to have the French capital contaminated with scum like that from which Bolshevik commissars were made. It was therefore decided that some place easily accessible from Russia would be more practical for the meeting, and an aid figured out that the island of Prinkipo, near Constantinople, was a likely spot. Accordingly, on January 23, there went out to the world by wireless and cable a lengthy message, phrased by Woodrow Wilson, inviting "every organized group that is now exercising, or attempting to exercise" authority in Russia, to send representatives to Prinkipo to meet with the Allies in peaceful discussion.

In after years David Lloyd George was often mordantly critical of Wilson for being a dreamy idealist who "shunned the sight or study of unpleasant truths that diverted him from his foregone conclusions." The joint action of the two statesmen in proposing the Prinkipo conference, however, was proved by events which followed immediately to have been a partnership in fantasy. The response of the three principal White Russian "governments"-Kolchak's in Siberia, Denikin's in South Russia, and Chaikovsky's in North Russia-resembled what might have been expected if, in the early days of the American Civil War, Yankees and Confederates had been invited to settle their dispute over a table in Havana. The Whites were horrified and indignant. At Archangel, where the reaction was typical, the Provisional Government decided unanimously that the Prinkipo proposal was totally unacceptable, and in the absence of Chaikovsky directed General Miller to frame a reply to the Allies. This he did, in eloquent terms, and by January 27 the Allied officials in Archangel had been told that under no conditions would representatives of the North Russian government sit at the same table with "brigands, robbers, and murderers" who "had stooped to nationalizing women." (The notion that the Communists were determined to make a kind of government monopoly out of sex was an alluring one which, although without factual roots, died hard.) Chaikovsky, en route to Paris, was interviewed in London on February 1, and summed up the White attitude rather neatly: "Either we prevail over them or they prevail over us"; and similar sentiments were received a few days later from Siberia and South Russia.

Meanwhile, to the consternation of the Allies, a message came in from the Soviet government accepting the Prinkipo invitation, and asking for the exact time and place of the meeting. The acceptance, however, was couched in terms which some of the delegates to the peace conference found embarrassing if not insulting. Not only did the Bolshevik leaders state outright that from their point of view the only powers really worth dealing with were the Allies themselves, since the White Russian forces opposed to the Soviet forces "depend exclusively on the aid which they receive" from the Allies. They went on from that to sketch a number of material concessions in mining, timber, and territory that they were prepared to consider, "in view of the great inclination which foreign capital has always displayed to exploit Russia's natural resources for its own advantage," if the Allies would agree to end hostile action against the Soviet government.

It may be reasonably doubted whether the Communist leaders' offer to go to Prinkipo was made altogether in good faith, although there is no doubt that they earnestly desired an end to the warfare which was bleeding Russia almost to the point of collapse. They must have known that there was no genuine likelihood of the Prinkipo conference becoming a reality. Under no illusions about the undying hatred of their White foes, they also had their own bitter reasons for disbelieving that the Allies sincerely wanted to bring the civil war in Russia to a conclusion. In order to grasp some sense of how the Prinkipo proposal must have struck Lenin and Trotsky, it must be remembered that the White Russian armies were in fact fighting largely under Allied auspices. They were heavily dependent on arms, uniforms, and food supplied by the Allies; and in North Russia most of the soldiers actually in combat against the Red army were American, British, or French.

The truth is that in allowing himself to put any faith in the Prinkipo will-o'-the-wisp, Woodrow Wilson had blinded himself to reality and deluded himself by his own passionate desire for peace on earth. On the very day when the proposal was sent out, American doughboys were stubbornly retreating from Nijni Gora to Shenkursk, killing Soviet soldiers as they went. In the light of this cold fact, and the statistical truth that in January, 1919, there were more American soldiers fighting the Bolsheviks in North Russia than those of any other nation, some of Wilson's noble phrases in the Prinkipo document must have evoked hollow laughter in the Kremlin. The Allies, said Wilson, "recognize the revolution without reservation, and will in no way, and in no circumstances, aid or give countenance to any attempt at a counter-revolution." (He meant the democratic revolution of March, 1917, which overthrew the Czar; but this was a curious way to address the Bolsheviks, to whom "the revolution" meant only the one they pulled off on November 7, 1917. It was also a curious way to address monarchists like General Miller and Admiral Kolchak, who certainly thought of themselves as counter-revolutionists.) The allies had no intention, Wilson went on piously, "to favor or assist any of those organized groups now contending for the leadership and guidance of Russia as against the others." Finally, he stipulated that all parties interested in accepting the invitation to Prinkipo must first observe "a truce of arms" during which no aggressive military action should take place.

From the Bolshevik point of view, this was preposterously two-faced. It was most glaringly so with respect to North Russia, for there was absolutely no sign that the Allied troops on that front had been ordered to cease fire, or to negotiate for a truce. Indeed, General Ironside got no instructions to that effect either from Paris or London, and only through him could a truce in North Russia have been arranged. It was as if the parents of a boy who has been assiduously heaving rocks through a neighbor's windows should gravely petition the neighbor to stop heaving them back, and talk things over-while at the same time the boy heaves a few more.

By the middle of February it was becoming clear to the peace conference that Prinkipo was a fiasco: only the Bolsheviks had accepted the proposal, and their acceptance looked more like a propaganda triumph than anything that would help solve the Russian problem. Lloyd George had gone temporarily back to London to mend political fences; President Wilson was on the point of going to the United States for similar reasons. A new figure, however, had appeared at the conference table-one destined to loom large on the horizons of history for more than a generation. Winston Churchill had been made Secretary of State for War in Lloyd George's new cabinet on January 14; he was now, therefore, the government official directly responsible for the Allied campaign in North Russia. He arrived from London on February 14 expressly to try to accomplish something on the question of policy toward Russia before Wilson sailed for the United States.

At a meeting of the Supreme Council that evening, Churchill faced up to the problem with characteristic bluntness. Wilson had already risen to leave, but he paused when Churchill began to speak, and listened closely, leaning one arm on Clemenceau's chair as he stood there. Great Britain, Churchill said, had soldiers in Russia who were being killed in action. "Their families wish to know what purpose these men are serving. Are they just marking time until the Allies have decided on policy, or are they fighting in a campaign representing some common aim? The longer the delay continues, the worse will be the situation of the troops on all the Russian fronts."

This gave Wilson an opening to express a feeling that no doubt had been rankling for some time. One thing he was very sure of, he said, was that Allied troops "are doing no sort of good in Russia. They do not know for whom or for what they are fighting. They are not assisting any promising common effort to establish order throughout Russia." His conclusion was that the Allies ought to withdraw their troops from all parts of Russian territory.

Now Churchill began to show his hand. Complete withdrawal of all Allied troops was logical and clear policy, he conceded, but its result would be the destruction of all non-Bolshevik armies in Russia. It would be "equivalent to pulling out the linch-pin from the whole machine. There would be no further armed resistance to the

Bolsheviks in Russia, and an interminable vista of violence and misery was all that remained for the whole of Russia."

This fine Churchillian period must have distressed Wilson, but he stuck to his point. The existing Allied forces in Russia could not stop the Bolsheviks, he said, and not one of the Allies was prepared to reinforce its troops. Churchill thereupon admitted that conscripting troops for service in Russia was out of the question, but he was not ready to agree that volunteers were unobtainable. Also there was the possibility of greater material assistance: technical experts, arms, munitions, tanks, airplanes, and so forth.

Wilson's reply to this was a curious one, and demonstrates how painfully ambivalent he still felt on the whole question of Soviet Russia. On one side, he pointed out that sending war materiel to anti-Bolshevik armies would certainly, in some areas, "be assisting reactionaries. Consequently, if the Allies were asked what they were supporting in Russia they would be compelled to reply that they did not know." Then came the other side of the coin. He himself, he said, felt "guilty" because the United States had sent "insufficient forces" to Russia, but it was not possible to increase them. It was certainly "a cruel dilemma." American soldiers were being killed in Russia, yet if they were taken out many Russians might be killed in consequence. Still, they could not be kept there "forever," and the consequences of taking them out would in any case only be deferred. It is worth noting in connection with this that Wilson had recently been briefed on the heavy American casualties at Shenkursk, and had asked the War Department what consideration it was giving to the plight of the 339th Infantry. The Secretary of War had quickly bounced this ball back by reminding Wilson that the Supreme Council itself was responsible for the reinforcement and safety of all Allied forces in North Russia. The President had thus finally come to have a real sense of the fate to which he had exposed American troops by submitting them to a British command which ignored the limitations he had announced for intervention.

But it was now growing late at the Quai d'Orsay, and Wilson was due to depart if the steamer *George Washington* was not to be kept waiting. Churchill saw that the best he could hope for that day was to keep the door from closing entirely on Allied anti-Bolshevik action;

he said he would like to know whether the delegates "would approve of arming the anti-Bolshevik forces in Russia should the Prinkipo Conference prove a failure." Wilson answered that although he would not express any "definite opinion," he would agree to "cast in his lot with the rest." He then hurriedly left to catch the boat train.

The next day, with Wilson temporarily out of the way, Churchill exercised all his great skill in attempting to make the delegates to the peace conference perceive his view of what Soviet victory might mean to the future of Europe. He had already told his fellow cabinet members, in England, that the civil war in Russia was an inseparable part of the Great War; "if we ignore it we shall come away from the Peach Conference rejoicing in a victory which is no victory, and a peace which is no peace." Now, in Paris, he took the same line: Russia, he insisted, "is the key to the whole situation, and unless she forms a living part of Europe, unless she becomes a living partner in the League of Nations and a friend of the Allied Powers, there will be neither peace nor victory." In Churchill's searching mind there already rose a frightening vision of an alliance between a revived Germany and a Russia controlled by the Bolsheviks. It was time to do something positive; it was almost too late. He proposed the immediate establishment of an "Allied Council for Russian Affairs." It would have political, economic, and military sections; but the task which must be done without delay was "to draw up a plan for concerted action against the Bolsheviks." Then if the Prinkipo plan finally came to nothing, "the Supreme War Council would be in possession of a definite war scheme," and the decision would be taken "either to act, or to withdraw their troops and leave everyone in Russia to stew in their own juice."

Whatever one's opinion of Churchill, it is difficult not to admire the boldness with which he presented this suggestion to the Paris peace conference. He knew that his own prime minister, Lloyd George, was opposed to the continuance or expansion of Allied military intervention in Russia; he knew that Woodrow Wilson was equally if not more opposed. He knew that behind both of these great leaders stood millions of ordinary people who were sick and tired of war, and whose chief sentiment toward Russia was that the Russians should be left alone to settle their internal problems by themselves.

But he felt with tremendous urgency that if ever the Soviet government was to be overthrown it must be within the next few months, and he was determined to push his conviction before the conference against all odds and the expectation of failure.

From Clemenceau, not surprisingly, Churchill got gruff support, although the old Frenchman was dubious about how easy it would be to overcome the Red army. He was ready, he said, to make new sacrifices; but he did not "court defeat in Russia, after having been victorious on the Rhine." From the American contingent at the conference table, however, came immediate resistance. "Colonel" Edward M. House, Wilson's crafty personal advisor, had been left behind by the President to watch over American interests, and he and Secretary of State Lansing refused to take any action on the military question until a weekend had intervened, and an "opportunity for consultation" had been given. The conference therefore turned to the question of whether anything further ought to be done about the Prinkipo proposal. Churchill suggested that another telegram should be sent to the Bolsheviks, pointing out that in accepting the invitation to go to Prinkipo they had not met one of the conditions, namely the cessation of hostile military activity against the anti-Bolshevik forces. They should be told, he said, that unless they would cease firing on all fronts and withdraw their troops at least five miles within the next ten days, the Prinkipo proposal "will be deemed to have lapsed."

It is impossible to believe Churchill thought for a moment that the Communist leaders would agree to any such truce. He knew perfectly well that a truce must be mutually arranged between the contesting forces, and that the anti-Bolshevik groups in Russia had already proudly refused any cessation of hostilities-to say nothing of the Allied forces fighting in North Russia. His desire was to salvage Allied prestige from what had turned into a propaganda victory for the Bolsheviks. He did not want anyone to be able to say, as he put it, "You made a false movement, and you abandoned it. The Bolsheviks were about to accept, and you withdrew." Although he did not quite come out and say so, a conceivable solution was to offer them something they could not possibly accept.

At this point in the discussion, however, A. J. Balfour, the British foreign minister, spoke up with distressing candor. He wished to ask, he said, a question of fact. It was being said that the Bolsheviks had only pretended to accept the Prinkipo invitation, since they had not ceased hostilities against the anti-Bolshevik forces. "But have the Allied troops abstained from hostilities? Or, to put the question another way: have all the Allied military operations been defensive in their character?"

It may well be imagined that an embarrassed silence fell upon the conference table at this moment. Everyone looked at Churchill, and he fielded the question as best he could. In the last three weeks, he pointed out, the Bolshevik forces had made heavy attacks on all fronts. It was not a very satisfactory answer, and it seems to have discouraged the assembled statesmen. The shadows were lengthening on a late Saturday afternoon, and some of the delegates were doubtless feeling the need of a drink. Mr. Balfour remarked that "a good many points of great difficulty had been raised," and proposed adjournment until Monday afternoon. The meeting broke up without anything having been done on the Russian problem.

Meanwhile, through the gray waters of the Atlantic, the *George Washington* was steaming steadily away from the tangled affairs of postwar Europe. Mentally, however, the tangle was still very much present in the brain of Woodrow Wilson; and there was, besides, the ship's wireless to maintain an invisible but persistent connection with the peace conference. On February 17 Secretary Lansing sent a radiogram outlining Churchill's proposal for planning Allied military action against the Soviet government, adding that the American representatives at the conference had opposed the idea, and were delaying action on it as long as possible. Wilson got off the following reply: "Greatly surprised by Churchill's Russian suggestion. I distinctly understood Lloyd George to say that there could be no thought of military action there... ." He would not be in favor of any course, he said, contrary to "the earliest practicable withdrawal of military forces. It would be fatal to be led further into the Russian chaos." A few days later he was reassured by another message from Paris: "Churchill's project is dead and there is little danger that it will be revived again by the Conference." Thus, partly through Wilson's opposition, Winston Churchill saw his dream of crushing Communism in its infancy pass from the realm of hope into the limbo of lost causes. He had not entirely given up, as we shall see; but any idea of a massive Allied campaign against the Bolsheviks must now be forgone.

A kind of pathetic footnote to these high-level negotiations took place aboard the *George Washington* when Wilson finally got around to hearing Ambassador Francis' views on Russia. The ambassador had been invited to return to America with the President's party; and not having been advised otherwise by the State Department, he had accepted. He was not privileged to dine at the presidential table and so again found himself deprived of the President's ear; but he let it be known that he was ready to consult with the chief executive at any time. One day Wilson appeared at Francis' cabin and listened patiently while the ambassador described his scheme for a crusade to Petrograd. He did not protest against the plan on principle, but merely observed that he and Lloyd George both had serious doubts about the possibility of raising the necessary volunteers. He then left, saying that he would "give further consideration" to the ambassador's recommendation. As it turned out, however, this was the effectual end of Francis' doughty public service: he never again was consulted by Wilson. Of course the ambassador was not aware at the time that the curtain had descended, and continued to send messages to the American delegation at the peace conference urging that there be no withdrawal from North Russia, and insisting, as he always had, that "Bolshevik doctrines destroy family relations and if they predominate they will mean return to barbarism."

Apparently it was Churchill's exhorting the Supreme Council to plan large-scale intervention that precipitated Wilson's decision, once and for all, to withdraw American troops from North Russia. The President clinched matters by making the decision public, and by February 20 the Archangel wireless had picked up the electrifying news: Wilson had authorized "the withdrawal of American troops in North Russia at the earliest possible moment." It was not official notification-no orders were received by Colonel Stewart-but it seemed to be authentic, and the glad word traveled to the outstretched columns of the expedition with great speed. To thousands of American soldiers it sounded like a reprieve. At the same time they appreciated keenly a cartoon from the February 5 issue of the Detroit *News* which was widely handed about when it reached them: it showed a doughboy

clinging desperately to the tail of an enormous, raging beast labeled
"Russia." "The Hard Job Is to Let Go," read the caption.

After forty years, during most of which relations between the
Soviet Union and the West have been featured largely by mutual
distrust, the dealings of the Paris peace conference with Russia can be
viewed with little exaggeration as a prologue to the Cold War. On
both sides were the two-edged weapons of arrogance and propaganda,
and the treacherous armor of self-deception and ignorance.
Paradoxically, with respect especially to future Soviet-American
relations, this familiar armament of the cold war was wielded against
a background of a small but intense shooting war between Soviet and
American soldiers in North Russia. The full irony of the Prinkipo
episode cannot be appreciated without taking that into account.

The negotiations in Paris in 1919 are of interest not only in
having set a lamentable pattern for Soviet-American relations, but in
revealing two divergent attitudes toward the Communist power on
the part of Western statesmen and diplomats which continue today.
On the one hand there was the I'd-rather-die-than-say-yes school,
represented by men like Clemenceau and Ambassador Francis, to
whom Communism was sheer anathema on moral grounds. On the
other hand was the live-and-let-live school, represented by men like
Lloyd George, who had no love for Marxism but were moved by
practical considerations, antipathy for the old regime, and belief in
"self-determination of peoples," to let Russia alone. The practical
considerations were often paramount here; for example Lloyd George's
notion of the extent to which the Bolshevik regime represented the
will of the Russian people seems to have fluctuated inversely with how
close Kolchak's armies got to Moscow.

In the end Woodrow Wilson went along with the live-and-let-
live school, although his motives were to some degree peculiar. Few
men of his time were more thoroughly imbued with moral idealism,
and under ordinary circumstances the moral appeal against Bolshevism
might have been expected to affect him very strongly. Over against
this, he was more intensely devoted than Lloyd George to the idea, as
a matter of principle, that force was no solution to the problem of
Communism, and that the Russians should be left to "find their own
path." Yet perhaps Wilson's chief reason for shoving aside the Russian

problem without a satisfactory settlement was his consuming zeal for world peace. He came to Paris with this as his great goal, and the League of Nations as the program which above all might bring it into reality. The Russian tangle was an intolerable hindrance, an impossible delay. He knew it was serious, but he hoped that in the long run it would work itself out; meanwhile he was not to be deflected from the great task to which he felt destiny had appointed him.

Wilson's final tragedy-the rejection by the American people of the League of Nations-takes on a glint of extra irony in the light of his attitude toward Russia in 1919. For in a sense his refusal to face the terrible difficulties of that problem with full responsibility was an omen of the ignorant isolationism that kept the United States out of the League.

As for Winston Churchill, whether or not he is now judged to have been right in his desire to crush Communism in the cradle, he at least sensed fully the magnitude of the Soviet problem for the future, and was ready to make the most energetic effort to do something practical about it, hang the cost. He was consistent and unwavering-"the most formidable and irrepressible protagonist of an anti-Bolshevik war," Lloyd George called him. The alteration in the course of world history that might have been brought about by the implementation of his plan is tremendous if incalculable. His own feelings about the behavior of the Allied governments toward Russia in 1919 he expressed later, in *The Aftermath*, in a passage of superb sarcasm:

"The fitful and fluid operations of the Russian armies found a counterpart in the policy, or want of policy, of the Allies. Were they at war with Soviet Russia? Certainly not; but they shot Soviet Russians at sight. They stood as invaders on Russian soil. They armed the enemies of the Soviet Government. They blockaded its ports, and sunk its battleships. They earnestly desired and schemed its downfall. But war-shocking! Interference-shame! It was, they repeated, a matter of indifference to them how Russians settled their own internal affairs. They were impartial-Bang!"

CHAPTER 12

SPRING-A LITTLE LATE THAT YEAR

ALTHOUGH THE FIRST RESPONSE of the American soldiers in North Russia to news of their prospective withdrawal was enthusiastic, it was not long before a dismal reaction set in. It was all too clear, after the defeat at Shenkursk, that they had accomplished little toward what was alleged to be the goal of the expedition: the overthrow of the Communist regime. Regardless of whether that goal seemed to make much sense, it was discouraging to know that their hardships and the death of some of their comrades had been of no avail. On top of that, the promise of withdrawal at "the earliest possible moment" clearly meant after the spring thaw; and even at the end of March, in Archangel Province, there were few signs of spring except a perceptible lengthening of the days.

February, meanwhile, had been relatively quiet on the fighting fronts, allowing much time for mournful thought. Some of the talk in the dim log billets of the native villages began to echo ideas and even phrases from the Bolshevik propaganda pamphlets so often found along the trails when the doughboys stomped through the snow on their daily patrols. Headquarters in Archangel were seriously disturbed by the appearance of a typed sheet headed FACTS AND QUESTIONS CONCERNING THE NREF which was reported to be circulating widely on the river fronts; it was alleged to have been written by an American officer, although nobody could say whom. It pulled no punches, and was assuredly grounds for court-martial if the author could be identified.

England has undoubtedly many capable officers [the sheet observed], but they are not in Russia. However, we ourselves are woefully lacking in that respect. The manner in which this expedition has been mishandled is a disgrace to the civilized world... . The majority of the people here seem to prefer Bolshevism to British intervention... . WHERE IS OUR MONROE DOCTRINE? ... We are fighting against enormous odds in men, artillery and material... . We wonder what propaganda is at work in the States, which enables the War Department to keep our troops here... . We have no heart for the fight... . We are fighting neither for Russia or Russian wealth, but for our lives. We have earnestly endeavored to find some justification for our being here, but have been unable to reconcile this expedition with American ideals and principles instilled within us. We are removed 200 miles from our base, with an open country intervening, with no force except in a few villages to guard our lines... . There is no military reason why we should be more than 20 miles from our base.

At the same time, material conditions of some of the American troops were deplorable. An overworked sanitary officer, after a tour of the fronts, reported on February 28 that a large percentage of the men were in bad health. In general they were still subsisting on the winter ration devised by Sir Ernest Shackleton; and as the officer pointed out, this had been calculated for men in a garrison situation, whereas most of the Americans at the front were engaged in strenuous patrol and work activity. A patrol through deep snow with the temperature thirty below zero, or carrying one end of a pine log a couple of hundred feet under the same circumstances, was not what Sir Ernest had in mind when he figured the calorie requirements. There was usually a shortage of bread and coffee; the meat was often moldy; there was seldom sugar for the lime juice to make it potable. "Our men at the front," stated the report, "are complaining of hunger and lack of food to a greater extent than in any Army organization I have ever investigated. The men are suffering from malnutrition, without any possible doubt... . I found men at the farthest outposts getting a piece of bread no larger than an egg and a piece of inedible fatty meat as their entire noon meal. Beans and tea had both run out before the ration detail reached the outpost and the men were melting snow to have a drink with the bread."

The remedy of the British command for the rapidly skidding morale brought on by the shape of things in February was to insist on regular and aggressive patrols even when the Bolsheviks showed little disposition to attack. This was orthodox military theory; but in North

Russia's snowbound terrain it sometimes produced miserable results. The cold white fluff had piled up until any departure from the beaten path meant impossibly slow going, and most patrols stuck close to the trail. Some of the American officers-John Cudahy, for instance-realized that snowshoes or skis were the answer, and took men out to practice with this ungainly equipment whenever possible. Few of them, however, reached what could be called operational efficiency even on snowshoes; on the skis they seemed hopeless. Meanwhile, under Trotsky's whiplash authority, the Red army had trained the "2nd Ski Battalion of the Northern Dvina," which was estimated by Allied intelligence to have four hundred riflemen capable of traveling and fighting in deep snow.

A typical consequence of this state of affairs was an episode near Toulgas on March 1. A patrol of seven from Company B, led by Corporal Arthur Prince, was moving southward along a forest trail when, from the depths of the woods, there came a furious crackle of rifle fire. Bullets whipped through the deep snow as they took cover in drifts. Prince ordered the patrol to crawl back toward Toulgas. This they attempted to do; but only one of them made it. The Soviet ski troopers easily stayed opposite them in the woods, and continued to shoot whenever one of the Americans showed himself above the snow. Before they reached the outskirts of the American position two were dead, three badly wounded, and Corporal Prince had disappeared. The seventh man got back to Toulgas in a distraught condition, and Lieutenant Cudahy led a rescue squad out into the snow to get the wounded. But by this time the Bolsheviks were in the woods surrounding Upper Toulgas, and they pinned down the whole American party with relentless fire for nearly three hours. Back in Toulgas, the Canadian gunners finally figured out where the Bolshevik attackers were concealed, and drove them off with a few shrapnel shells. Several other Americans were wounded, and as a result of severe exposure three died, including perhaps the most popular noncom in Company B, Sergeant William Bowman. A search party, later, found no trace of Corporal Prince except confused tracks in the snow and some blood; he was presumed to have been wounded and captured. (Prince, long given up for dead, was to turn up in Germany in August, 1920, having spent seventeen months recuperating from his injury in Soviet hospitals.)

No doubt it was occurrences like this, and the fear of more, that explained a rash of self-inflicted wounds among the Americans at the front in North Russia late that winter. The board-of-inquiry report on a typical case makes pathetic reading: the stubborn insistence of a soldier that his rifle "just happened to go off," putting a bullet through the center of his hand; gradually turning, under repeated questions, into a shamefaced or sullen confession of an overpowering urge "to do something to get out of all this."

There was, however, only one suicide during the entire American campaign in North Russia. Sergeant Edward Young, of Company G, had been wounded in the fall, and the wound had not healed properly. He remained on duty, but as the winter waned he became morose and strange. When it was decided, early in March, to move Company G from Pinega back to Archangel, Young and Sergeant Michael Macalla went ahead in charge of an advance party. While they were stopped for the night in a little village called Gabach, poor Young ended his troubles by shooting himself through the head with a revolver. This gave rise to a nightmarish experience for his friend Sergeant Macalla.

It was decided that he might as well proceed the many miles to Archangel, taking Young's body with him in a pony sleigh, while the rest of the group came along on foot. The weather was subzero, and the corpse was frozen solid; no effort was made to put it in any sort of coffin. It was simply wrapped in a couple of army blankets and bundled into the sled beside Macalla. While he naturally was in a somber mood for the journey, it never occurred to Macalla that there was anything particularly weird about it until the second day. He had spent the night with a peasant family, sheltering the sleigh and pony in the stable, and had been warmly received. When he awoke in the morning, however, the hospitality had vanished. Some curious villager had unwrapped the bundle on the sleigh enough to see what it was, and Macalla now found himself regarded with staring horror. The natives watched him hitch up and leave as if a curse were departing from their village; and inevitably he himself now began to feel odd about his mission. At that night's stopover the villagers seemed to guess immediately what Macalla's burden was, and it was with difficulty that he persuaded anyone to take him in. Nobody would let the sleigh inside a stable, so it was left outdoors for all to see. "I don't believe a soul in the village slept that night," Macalla says.

The third night of this ghoulish trip was spent in a community where a wake had been in progress all day for one of the inhabitants. The death house was the only place offered Macalla to sleep in, and the logic of the situation seemed to his now somewhat fuddled brain to call for the presence of Young also. He carried in the remains of his friend, and slept on the floor alone with the two dead bodies.

The culmination of the melancholy journey came when Macalla got lost in a snowstorm and spent the next night in the almost negligible shelter of a clump of trees. The cold was intense, and he was sure he would freeze to death until he remembered the two blankets wrapped around Young's body. "I guess I was a little out of my head by that time," Macalla remembers. "I talked to Young as if he were alive, and told him I had to take his blankets; that they couldn't do him any good anyhow. So through that long night I sat huddled on the sleigh next to him and dozed off now and then. In the morning I thought my feet were frozen, but I finally got the blood circulating and once more we pushed on." At last, not in very good shape, he reached the outskirts of Archangel and was relieved of his lugubrious charge.

If the *esprit* of the Americans was suffering at the end of the winter, that of the British and French was no better. Indeed, it soon grew worse. News of the retreat from Shenkursk produced much disquiet in the War Office in London, and it was decided that some reinforcement of the Archangel troops was immediately necessary, as much for the sake of boosting morale as anything else. A battalion of English infantry from the Yorkshire Regiment was ordered to proceed from Murmansk to Archangel, and feverish preparations ensued for this difficult five-hundred-mile journey. The last two hundred miles had to be made either on foot or by sleigh.

Under personal supervision of the famous Shackleton (who was now actually in the British army as a major at Murmansk), the battalion was outfitted with arctic clothing of the latest design, since subzero weather could be predicted all the way. Transportation of equipment was a problem. In the Murmansk region sleighs were usually pulled by reindeer; they could feed on the abundant arctic moss merely by nuzzling through the snow at mealtime. This moss, however, was exceedingly scarce in the Archangel sector; and reindeer disdain hay. Pony sleighs were the only solution, but so few were available at Murmansk that the Yorkshires had to move their equipment by stages, the sleighs going back and forth several times.

Despite this hindrance, first contingents of the long column got off to a good start early in February, and under Shackleton's fond surveillance (for it was the kind of assignment that delighted him) came through to Archangel by the middle of the month in excellent condition. Ironside met them at Onega, congratulated them on their march, and promised that they would soon be in the front line relieving Americans who had been fighting Bolsheviks all winter. For the moment everyone seemed encouraged, and Shackleton bounced cheerily into Archangel and gave an impromptu lecture on antarctic exploration before a large crowd at the Y.M.C.A.

The pleasant complexion of things resulting from the arrival of the Yorkshires, however, soon darkened. Apparently they had entertained mistaken notions of just what they were to do on the Archangel front. A few days of conversation with British and American soldiers who had fought at Kodish convinced them that this was no winter carnival. Having been sent to the Allied base at Seletskoe, they were ordered on February 26 to march to the Kodish front to take over the line. To the astonishment of their commander, who had been with them only a few days, the men refused to fall in. Colonel Lavie, a veteran of several years' service in France, walked over to the billets and personally ordered the battalion to fall in without their weapons. They no sooner had done this than two sergeants stepped forward and volunteered the information that the men had made up their minds not to fight.

While Colonel Lavie's inward reaction to this news is not on record, his behavioral reflex made a sharp impression on all present. Without an instant's pause he ordered a corporal to take a squad of men immediately to get their rifles. He went and stood in front of the sergeants, but said not a word until the corporal returned with the riflemen. Then he ordered the two spokesmen to the guardhouse under close arrest, and set the troops off on a long tiring march through the forest to no place in particular, thence back to their billets. It occurred to most of them that they had seen the last of the two sergeants, and their mood was rapidly softening. They marched for the front the next morning, without complaint. Ironside, appalled by the whole incident, came down to Seletskoe and arranged to have the sergeants court-martialed; they were sentenced to be shot, but since King George had forbidden execution of British soldiers after the armistice, they were given life imprisonment instead.

Exaggerated reports of the British mutiny soon reached the French troops assigned to the railroad front. Not to be outdone, they staged their own rebellion on March 1, the date when they were supposed to relieve American troops for front-line duty. Most of one company positively refused to leave their barracks at Archangel, lying stubbornly on their bunks even when visited by Ironside himself. As the general recalled it afterward, about all he could get out of them was the expression. "I don't give a damn" (*je me fiche bien*), together with prepositional phrases involving the war with the Bolsheviks, whatever their country might think of them, and whatever punishments the authorities chose to impose. They were put under guard of a detachment of marines from a French cruiser lying in the harbor, to await evacuation to France. About the same time a few of the French soldiers down the railroad went on a night rampage, got drunk, broke into the Y.M.C.A. hut at Verst 455, smashed a piano, and replaced a sign reading "These seats are reserved for officers" with one reading "The officers will be under the ground." As Ironside summed things up, in what seems rather an understatement, "we were drawing terribly near to the end of our tether as an efficient fighting force."

To the regimental credit of the 339th Infantry, nothing comparable to the British and French incidents occurred in their ranks. Most of them were at the fighting fronts, and whatever their feelings were, the threat of enemy attack demanded fundamental military discipline. Late in March there was one flurry of recalcitrance in Company I, which had been resting at Archangel and was about to return to the front. Ordered to load sleds of equipment, some of the men grumbled and said they couldn't see why they should go back to fight again when there were thousands of Russians in Archangel who did nothing but drill and eat. The top sergeant reported this to Captain Horatio Winslow, who decided to telephone Colonel Stewart before things got out of hand. In the meantime, however, a first lieutenant forcefully ordered the men again to load up the sleds, and with a single exception they then obeyed. It turned out afterward that the one man who appeared to refuse was of Polish background, and had not understood the order. By this time Colonel Stewart had arrived, and the men quietly listened to a lecture which included a reading of the pertinent articles of war featuring the phrase "punishable by death or such punishment as the court martial may direct." He finished by asking if there were any questions. Someone promptly threw him the favorite query of the year: Why were they in Russia? Stewart had the sense to reply that he didn't know why they were there, but that one thing was certain: they must fight now to protect themselves, or they might be wiped out. That ended the discussion, and the entire company marched across the ice of the Dvina and boarded troop trains for the front. By the next day they were actively skirmishing with the Bolsheviks, and there was no further sign of disobedience.

Unfortunately the United States War Department, which for a good part of the winter had acted almost as if it had never heard of the troops in North Russia, chose to make public an account of this episode that made it sound quite serious. Newspapers across the country eagerly pounced on the item, writing it up with as much sensation as possible. The result was to be that when the men of the 339th, most of whom had fought valiantly under exasperating conditions, finally reached home, they would frequently be accosted by snide inquiries as to why they had "mutinied" in Russia.

Actually, the question that had been bothering the American troops ever since the armistice, and had finally precipitated the reluctance of Company I, was severely agitating a good many civilians back home by the time the winter was over. Gradually it dawned on the parents and wives of the soldiers in North Russia that their young men were fighting in an undeclared war for undeclared reasons months after the armistice. Protest meetings were held in various places in Michigan, and Congress was made acutely aware that something appeared to be rotten in North Russia. Senator Townsend asserted that he was receiving "literally hundreds" of letters every day from his Michigan constituents complaining that "their boys and their husbands are in that Godforsaken country practically lost, so far as the United States is concerned." A young Congressman from New York named Fiorello La Guardia denounced Ambassador Francis for incompetence, and demanded the return of all American troops immediately. Senator Hitchcock, chairman of the Foreign Relations Committee, explained repeatedly under pressure that the United States was not at war with the Soviet government, and gave the same old reasons for the retention of American troops in Russia-guarding supplies, helping the Czechoslovaks, etc.

In England the home-front reaction to what was going on in North Russia was interestingly different, thanks largely to the efforts of Winston Churchill. The explanation he gave for Allied troops still being there was simple, but eloquently put: he admitted that the original reason for sending them had passed away, but "the troops sent in obedience to it are still on those wild northern coasts, locked in the depth of winter, and we must neglect nothing required for their safety and well-being." In short, he told the House of Commons on March 3, 1919, it might well be necessary to send reinforcements to North Russia in order to make sure the exhausted troops already there would get safely away when spring came. Nothing was said about overthrowing the Communists, although this certainly was still very much on Churchill's mind. There was already enough agitation from British labor against the Allied intervention, without suggesting that the reinforcements might be used for any aggressive purpose. The thing to do, as Churchill perceived it, was to bill the whole thing as a rescue operation, and an exceedingly noble one at that.

Leading British newspapers were accordingly encouraged to picture the situation at Archangel as one of grave peril, and by early April most London editors were agreed that reinforcements were urgently required. "The cold facts," said the *Times*, "... will, we hope, put an end to this cry about withdrawing from Russia. We could not withdraw if we would, for our Army at Archangel is frozen in.... We shall, therefore, want more men for Northern Russia, and, regrettable though this need of reinforcement is, we hope that it will be accepted without opposition." With the public thus primed, the government issued a call for volunteers to go on a relief expedition. The response was lively. There seemed to be plenty of young men around who had not had enough action to suit them during the Great War, and in whom the appeal of the army actually aroused nostalgic yearnings. The mission, moreover, was a real winner: to save their countrymen and their Allies from being overwhelmed by hordes of Bolsheviks. There was no difficulty in organizing two infantry brigades-eight thousand men-and they had their pick of the latest army equipment to take with them. It was expected they could be ready to sail for Archangel by the middle of May.

Undoubtedly it is true that in British military and political circles there were many who believed the dispatch of a relief force to North Russia was a real necessity. The War Office had been highly disturbed by reports of Allied mutiny, and by indications that the White Russian units were unreliable. Its degree of agitation is suggested by a message sent to Ironside in April for transmission to his troops-meant to be a morale tonic in the highest tradition of British stiff-upper-lipmanship, but in fact redolent of anxiety. It was full of hortatory expressions like "undaunted," "resolute and faithful," and "fighting for dear life and dearer honour"; but Ironside, after considering it carefully, felt that it had better be stuck in a file drawer instead of communicated to the troops.

Ironside himself, incidentally, by now had less fear about his ability to get all Allied troops safely out of North Russia, even if no reinforcements arrived and the White Russians went into a general collapse. He had a strong naval flotilla ready to operate on the Dvina as soon as the thaw would permit; it would not be long now. From his point of view the eight thousand fresh troops expected from England were to be used primarily in a new offensive against the Bolsheviks, the aim being either union with Kolchak's Siberian army, or, at least, setting up General Miller's Russian regiments in a good position from which they could make the union after Allied departure.

In the light of all the evidence it is impossible to conclude that Churchill's true view differed substantially from this; indeed it was all he had been able to salvage from his great plan for direct Allied overthrow of the Soviet regime. The British had definitely decided now to evacuate North Russia by the autumn of 1919; but to do this hardly called for a "rescue" force eight thousand strong, unless each of the newcomers was to carry out a tired comrade on his back. The Allied troops who had wintered in North Russia had suffered considerably, but nearly all of them were still ambulatory and capable of shooting their rifles.

As it turned out, they were obliged to shoot several thousand rounds more before their ordeal was over. In the first week of March the Bolsheviks launched new attacks on the Vaga River at Vistafka, where Americans, Canadians, and White Russians had been holding on since the retreat from Shenkursk. Massive artillery fire was followed on March 5 by several waves of infantry attack. These were driven back with the aid of expert gunnery on the part of the supporting Canadians, but the force at Vistafka was cut off from their access to the north by a Soviet flanking movement, and for a couple of days was in danger of annihilation. They were saved by Russian infantrymen and Cossacks who were dispatched from Kitsa, a few versts down the river, after having been given an extra-large rumration. In this case intoxication proved the better part of valor, for the tipsy contingent blundered into the wrong trail and wound up right in the rear of a totally unsuspecting force of Bolsheviks camped in a ravine on one side of Vistafka. Surprised and pleased, the Whites unlimbered their machine guns and went into action, while the Bolsheviks attempted to escape across the still frozen Vaga, thus coming directly under the guns of the Canadians and the rifles of the Americans. It was a haphazard victory, but satisfactory enough to the victors.

This was only temporary, however. A much heavier Soviet assault began on March 9, with an artillery bombardment so concentrated that some of the Canadians were heard making comparisons to Vimy Ridge, where they had been just two years earlier. The Soviet infantry attack, which came after a few hours of this, pushed very close to the Vistafka dugouts and blockhouses, and obviously involved many hundreds of men. To the one-hundred-odd Americans holding the forward dugouts there, under Lieutenants Mead and McPhail, withdrawal seemed to make sense, for they were hopelessly outnumbered; but no orders came.

It began to look like Nijni Gora all over again, and the spirit of Company A was far from optimistic. Their ragged hopes had been revived by the promise of going home "in the spring"; but under the pressure of an enemy with apparently no end of reserves, many of them now doubted that they ever again would see green grass. As if in mockery of their plight, the Soviet guns threw over a few teargas shells, the first used on the North Russian front. A chance shell also destroyed a building containing some sacks of newly-arrived mail that nobody had found time to distribute.

Crouching behind their log defenses, the Americans waited grimly while Soviet high explosive pounded the village of Vistafka to ruins. Their dugouts were what the field manuals called "shell-proof," but during the day of March 9 several of them were knocked out, with a dozen men wounded and three killed. One of the wounded was Lieutenant Mead, who was caught in the chest by a flying piece of steel that brought the war in North Russia to an end for him: by nightfall he was in a hospital sled on his way toward Archangel. Meanwhile Lieutenant McPhail, with twenty men, was hanging on to a forward dugout at the southernmost edge of Vistafka, completely out of communication with the rest of the Allied force. The men asked the lieutenant if they could make a run for the rear positions; but McPhail, a man of dogged temperament, told them they could not unless orders came through to that effect.

In mid-afternoon a runner got to the forward dugout with word of Mead's wound, and an order to fall back. The Bolsheviks now had machine guns sweeping the village streets; it was strictly a case of every man for himself. One by one they scampered across the open area to a safer position, the snow kicking up in lethal spurts all around them as they ran. Miraculously, all twenty made it without being hit. As McPhail brought up the rear, dodging from one scant cover to another, he came upon a smashed American dugout with two doughboys pinned down by heavy broken beams, but still alive and conscious. McPhail put his powerful shoulders to the beams, but could not lift enough to get the men out. He promised a rescue squad as soon as possible, and hurried on to the rear position. The two soldiers were extracted from the debris of the dugout when darkness fell; but both were badly hurt and died later.

It had now become clear to the Allied commander at Bereznik that there was no further point in trying to hold Vistafka, which was nearly surrounded, and reduced almost to nothing by the Soviet artillery. Americans, Canadians, and White Russians therefore pulled back into Kitsa, where they awaited the next Bolshevik move with considerable apprehension. Reliable reports indicated that the Red Sixth Army had something like four thousand men ready to advance. But nothing happened, except that a steady stream of Russian peasants came up the road on their way north, trying to get away from the big battle that presumably was about to commence. Days went by, and still the Bolshevik commanders did not press the advantage they had won at Vistafka. American morale lifted again, and there were even those who thought the Soviet troops had been hit so hard by American and Canadian marksmanship that they were ready to call quits for the time being.

While this may well have been the feeling among the Soviet infantry, who as usual had been forced to attack recklessly and who had suffered correspondingly heavy casualties, it is unlikely that the Bolshevik commanders held off for any such reason. The probable explanation lies in a very different direction. For although, during this period, General Ironside had been unable to get any reliable news of how Admiral Kolchak's anti-Bolshevik forces were progressing in their drive westward from the Urals, Leon Trotsky labored under no such lack of information. He knew that on March 1 Kolchak had kicked off a new drive for Viatka, the point on the Trans-Siberian Railroad at which, if he reached it, he would branch off north to try to join Ironside's troops.

When the total pattern of Soviet warfare in 1919 is examined, it thus appears that Trotsky's strategy was to strike at the Allies in North Russia precisely whenever Kolchak was pressing him hard enough to make the plan of junction between the two anti-Soviet forces look feasible. Despite tremendous losses, the Red army opposing Ironside had such a commanding numerical superiority by the end of 1918 that from then on it was able to push the Allies back almost at will and keep the gap between them and Kolchak approximately constant. Any large-scale slaughter of American and British troops, however, would have been undesirable at this time, from the Soviet standpoint. Public opinion in the United States and Great Britain was clearly in favor of getting the troops out of North Russia as soon as possible, and it would have been a mistake to reverse this by creating a motive for vengeance.

Kolchak's success west of the Urals continued until mid-April, and this together with news that more British troops were marching from Murmansk to Archangel may have been the explanation for the last major Bolshevik attack against American troops, before they were pulled out of front-line positions near the end of that month. The trouble started at Bolshie Ozerki, on the road between the railway town of Obozerskaya and Onega, General Ironside's westernmost outpost. The idea of the Soviet strategists evidently was to plant themselves firmly astride this vital road, preventing any further reinforcements or supplies coming in by land from Murmansk, and threatening to move east and hit the Allied troops on the railroad from the rear. If successful, this maneuver would certainly stimulate early Allied evacuation of North Russia.

The Bolsheviks struck suddenly from the south on March 17, with a large force of ski troops and cavalry which completely destroyed a small French garrison at the village of Bolshie Ozerki. A lucky bonus they received by this surprise was trapping the French commander of the Allied railway force twenty miles from his headquarters at Obozerskaya. Colonel Lucas had exhibited a remarkable fondness for staying at his desk all winter, despite frequent attempts by Ironside to get him out on visits to his outposts. Possibly the bright March sun finally had encouraged him to make such a trip, although it was still very cold; and on the sixteenth he had gone by sleigh along the broad trail leading westward. Passing through Bolshie Ozerki, he spent the night at the village of Chinova, a few miles farther. The next morning an American patrol from Company H, which was stationed along the Onega River, came in with a report of the Soviet strike at Bolshie Ozerki, but without information as to how large the enemy force there was.

Lucas's impulse was to get back to Obozerskaya as quickly as possible, even if he had to fight his way back. His guess was that Bolshie Ozerki was occupied only by a small Bolshevik raiding party, and he therefore set out on March 18 with an escort of thirty

Americans under Lieutenant Edmund Collins. Their ten sleighs moved briskly along the snowpacked trail without encountering any sign of enemy activity, and Lucas began to think there would be no trouble after all. They were only about a mile from Bolshie Ozerki when this pleasant illusion was dispelled by a sharp burst of machine-gun fire from a concealed position. One of the ponies panicked, and in a minute all the others were bolting in confusion. Most of them charged off into the deep snow and threw their occupants out into the drifts. The doughboys got their rifles into action, but it was clear that the road into the village was commanded by a very thoroughly entrenched nest of machine guns. After desultory resistance during which one American was killed and Colonel Lucas got separated from the others, Collins ordered his men to head back toward Chinova. This they did, most of them on all fours through the snow until they were well out of range of the Soviet machine guns. Lucas wandered about in the woods all night, and was picked up by an H Company patrol the next day with both hands frozen.

By this time the Allied troops on the railroad were aware that the Communist move at Bolshie Ozerki was no mere raiding party. The parish priest had come in to Obozerskaya with a tale of thousands of Soviet troops moving into the district, supported by much artillery, and this news was hastily wired to General Ironside. Disgusted by Lucas's adventure, the general relieved him of command by wireless and went himself down to Obozerskaya to see what was happening. He found a great flurry of activity. The American engineers were working twenty-four hours a day to build log barricades, and even new blockhouses, on the Bolshie Ozerki road about twelve miles west of the railway, in anticipation of a heavy Soviet attack. By field wireless it was learned that the Onega force, on the other side of Bolshie Ozerki, had just been reinforced by three companies of the 6th Yorkshire Regiment, marching through from Murmansk. While the dispatch of these troops to the Archangel front had probably been one cause of the New Bolshevik strike in the first place, they were now most welcome arrivals, and Ironside ordered them to combine with the Americans in an attack from the west.

Before daylight on March 23, Lieutenant Collins led a platoon of Company H along the trail until within shooting distance of the

Bolshevik outposts, and then deployed them in the woods near the trail. Meanwhile one company of Yorkshires circled through the forest to the north, and a second did likewise to the south, while the third company was held in reserve. The attack was well coordinated, but the deep snow proved to be a severe obstacle. Freezing by night to a hard and very slippery crust that would bear the weight of a man, it thawed in the morning sun to become a heavy, wet, clinging mass, far different from the fluffy powder of the winter. Slowly the troops worked their way forward against what seemed to be a limitless number of chattering Soviet machine guns. Anything resembling a running charge was out of the question in that snow, and while Allied casualties were so far light, it was obvious that an attempt to actually take Bolshie Ozerki would mean wholesale slaughter. Lieutenant Collins, exhorting his men, got caught in an exposed position, and went down with a wound from which he was to die the next day. Hours had gone by with very little progress, and ammunition was running low. The British colonel in command of the Onega column decided to call off the attack for that day and try again later.

Over on the other side of the Bolshevik position, Ironside made up his mind that artillery was the answer. All available guns and howitzers-most of them manned by Russians-were pulled out of Obozerskaya and hauled twelve miles to the front, where the engineers had now roughly completed several new blockhouses, and where Companies E and M of the 339th were awaiting the enemy onslaught. Under Ironside's supervision, the Allied guns systematically pulverized the fortifications of Bolshie Ozerki, killing practically all of the Soviet garrison.

Scout reports now showed, however, that the Bolsheviks who had been in the village itself were only a very small part of the force that had moved up from the south to cut the Allied communications line. Moreover, troops and horse-drawn equipment were still pouring into the area at a feverish pace. An American doughboy who was captured on March 22 and taken down to the Red stronghold on the railroad at Plesetskaya said later that he saw dozens of ponies, dead from exhaustion, along the winter trail from there to Bolshie Ozerki. The Soviet general in charge of the operation evidently was intimidated by the Allied artillery bombardment on the village, and instead of attacking quickly, when he might have been successful, he gave Ironside time to construct a new defensive position while Soviet reinforcements came up. All told, three Bolshevik regiments were now ranged against the Allies: the 2nd Moscow, the 96th Saratov, and the 2nd Kasan.

The all-out Soviet assault began on April 1, aimed at the Allied force to the east, in the direction of Obozerskaya. The Red general had a ridiculous superiority of numbers, but this very fact worked against him. Few of his troops had been able to find shelter in the immediately surrounding countryside, and had been forced to bivouac for several nights in deep snow with the temperature around zero at midnight. Most of them were thus in miserable condition for the attack. Also, because of their number, their officers drove them forward with prodigal abandon against the American and British barricades and blockhouses. From behind these solid fortifications, with enormous piles of ammunition standing ready, the Allies mowed them down with devastating automatic gunfire as they stumbled through the snow. Trench mortars, rifle grenades, and field artillery were also in action, and the Bolshevik losses were staggering. When darkness fell on that cruel All Fools' Day, many of the Bolshevik infantrymen crawled forward to the American barricades and gave themselves up; many more remained where they were and froze hands, feet, and other appendages that night.

April 2 was a repetition of April 1, except that the Allied force to the west of the Bolsheviks attacked them fiercely, even as they attacked the Allied force to the east. The Reds had tied watchdogs to trees several versts in their rear, and these barked a warning as the Allies came through the woods. The Americans of Company H, and the men of the Yorkshire regiment, found the circumstances no better for offensive operations than the Bolsheviks did; but their attack at least gave the enemy two fronts to think about. It was a chaotic battle. A whole company of Yorks got lost in the forest; a platoon of Poles, who had been in Archangel all winter but had seen little action, discovered that they had no taste for it and refused to move forward. Captain Ballensinger, CO of Company H, persuaded them to advance at the point of a pistol, thus mimicking what was taking place on a larger scale in the Soviet lines, where commissars with automatic rifles urged their unwilling troops to the attack.

Lieutenant Clifford Phillips, an amiable young officer of Company H, caught the real spirit of battle, and led his men into the Bolshevik machine-gun fire like a crusader about to recover the Holy Land from infidels. "I have never seen a look like it before or since," his company commander said later of the expression on Phillips's face that day. "It was a look that made me watch him all the way out. It made me hunt him up with my glasses, while I was watching the enemy." Whatever else the look meant, it meant Phillips's death, for a Soviet bullet hit him in the chest soon afterward. He had been extremely well liked, a young man who in the fall had taken intense interest in the Russian peasants and their homes and customs; indeed, he had been roundly reprimanded by British censors for writing of these things in letters sent home. Now quite beyond censorship, he was carried back to the Allied field hospital at Onega, where he died.

Two more days of attack brought the Bolsheviks little but a casualty list of shocking proportions. Apparently in a fit of despondence, the colonel of the 96th Saratov Regiment rode his white horse through the trampled snow right up to an American barricade, where he was shot as thoroughly as if he had been in front of a firing squad. Some doughboys of Company M ran out, got his long, curved sword, and presented it exultantly to their popular commander, Captain Joel Moore. Also, after one wave of assault had been driven back, an American patrol poking among a pile of enemy dead found the commissar of the 2nd Moscow Regiment, alive and untouched, but more than willing to surrender. And now the weather began to play a decisive part in the battle. By April 5, with the sun coming up at 4 A.M. and not setting until 8 P.M., it had turned warm enough to make slush of the packed snow on the forest trails at midday. The Soviet general, afraid of losing his artillery and hundreds of sleighs in the deep mud which could be looked for soon, ordered a retreat; and the Allied troops on either side of Bolshie Ozerki pushed through and regained contact with each other. According to accounts which appeared later in Communist newspapers, Soviet losses in the two weeks of battle, including wounded, frostbitten, captured, and killed, had been nearly two thousand men-more than the Allies lost all winter.

This was the last big fight for Americans in North Russia. Sporadic artillery duels and patrol actions continued throughout April, but spring had come at last, and any large movements through the soggy forest and tundra were now impossible until summer. Colonel Stewart was still without any official orders for American evacuation from Archangel, but it was assumed by all that President Wilson's promise would be carried out. Accordingly, the men of the 339th spent much of the month showing the ropes to replacement outfits of General Miller's new North Russian army, about ten thousand of whom were now judged to be ready for action. One by one the American companies were drawn in to Archangel, abandoning some towns completely, after extensive booby-trapping, and handing over others to the White Russians. On the Dvina and Vaga there was a delay because of the huge masses of ice just beginning to break up in the rivers; but the Americans were at any rate taken from the front-line positions and allowed a much-needed period of rest.

The slow and tantalizing breakup of the river ice nevertheless produced a good deal of nervous tension among the troops. One threat was the expected appearance of big Soviet gunboats on the upper Dvina, where they would be able to operate among the ice floes for several days before the lower part of the river became sufficiently unclogged to let the Allied flotilla move upstream. Luckily, the Canadians had managed to transport two heavy guns-sixty-pounders-by sleigh from Archangel, using a total of 118 ponies to pull the enormous weight; these had come through just before the thaw. They were a match in range and caliber for anything the Bolsheviks had on the river, as they demonstrated convincingly during the first week of May, before the Allied gunboats arrived. From their positions near Toulgas, the sixty-pounders successfully blasted the Soviet flotilla back up the river, although there were some exciting moments when the Bolsheviks got a few six-inch guns, on barges, into action against them.

There was also a last scene, so to speak, in the drama of American-British friction, in mid-April, at Kitsa on the Vaga River. There Company F of the 339th was stationed in such a position that, once the river became impassable, they would be caught in swampy forest and unable to reach the Archangel road. The CO, Captain Ramsay, informed the British colonel in command, on the other side of the river, that he would order his men to cross on the ice at the first sign of breakup, since after that it would be too late. The colonel, an irascible man, said the Americans would do nothing of the kind. They would stay where they were until told to do otherwise, and if they moved they would be fired on by the Canadian artillery. The Canadian officers, however, observed that they would not fire on the Americans under any conditions; Captain Ramsay proceeded to move his men across on the ice at the first sign of breakup; and the British colonel, no doubt fuming, did nothing. A small party of engineers, bringing up the rear of the American company, soaked Kitsa with oil and burned it to the ground, as they departed, to prevent enemy occupation.

On the seventeenth of April, to the surprise of nearly everyone, there arrived at Archangel Brigadier General Wilds P. Richardson, United States Army, together with his staff. They came in by ice-breaker, and pursuant to his orders General Richardson immediately took over command of the American Expeditionary Force in North Russia from Colonel Stewart. It was not perfectly clear just why he had been sent. Apparently it was the result of a delayed chain reaction, begun in the fall of 1918 by Ambassador Francis' conviction that an American general ought to be in North Russia, and pushed on in the spring by the story of unrest and "mutiny" in the 339th Infantry. Richardson was supposed to supervise the final withdrawal of American troops, and take steps to bolster their sagging morale.

In this latter enterprise he was no great success. He was the type of regular army officer, perhaps more frequently found among those who have seen little combat, who regard war (as he put it) as "a great game." Addressing units of the 339th, he told them that he never ceased regretting that he had not been with them during the winter combat. This raised what Ironside described as "a shout of laughter," which was hardly the effect Richardson must have hoped for. He exhorted them to keep up "the right spirit," and not commit any act "by company or individual that you will be ashamed of." They were in North Russia, he assured them, "to do a certain duty, determined by the highest authority in our country ... and by the best minds in the world in connection with this great war which we have been waging." The men listened quietly, and thought about home.

One of General Richardson's theories, by no means original, was that military courtesy and close-order drill were excellent ways to raise morale. A lieutenant colonel he sent to the railroad front submitted a shocked report to the effect that many of the enlisted men habitually forgot to salute; that their personal equipment was "very dirty"; and that there were wild irregularities of uniform ("All kinds of head-gear are freely worn"). Frequent drill and rigid inspections were ordered, and the men returned to Archangel from the fronts to discover that Camp Custer had come to Russia. An unpolished pair of shoes or a missing button meant plenty of trouble. But they took all this fairly cheerfully: it was a kind of purgatory through which they must pass before the great day of going up the gangplank for the home trip.

By the end of May practically all American troops were in Archangel itself, or close vicinity. The first four thousand British of the "relief force" docked on May 27, having sailed from England in troop ships with hulls reinforced against the floating ice of the White Sea. The weather was fine; the city was bedecked with flags; the anti-Bolshevik part of the population was, as a newspaper account phrased it, "in ecstasies." The American reaction to the newcomers was somewhat less than ecstatic, but since it had been rumored that the 339th would ship for France in the vessels the British had come on, it was not an unpleasant sight to see the volunteer brigade march away from the quays. After a ceremonial exchange of pleasantries between Generals Miller and Marushevsky, on one side, and General Grogan, the newly-arrived British commander, on the other, the brigade prepared to go up the Dvina just as the Americans had, some nine months earlier.

On Memorial Day there was a big parade. It included, besides detachments of the 339th Infantry, some sailors from the U.S.S. *Des Moines*, and Russian, British, and French troops. At the Archangel cemetery a memorial service was presided over by Ironside, Richardson, Miller, and charge d'affaires DeWitt Clinton Poole.

General Richardson gave a speech of strictly traditional timbre ("…
responded to their country's call … deep reverence … supreme
sacrifice …"), and a bugler sounded "Taps" over the numerous
American graves in the cemetery. It was the last official appearance
of American troops in North Russia, and within a fortnight the 339th
Infantry sailed out of Archangel harbor, never to return. With them
went eight Russian brides, and an assortment of young Russian
orphans who had been adopted as mascots. The medical units and the
310th Engineers followed shortly, and by June 28 all were gone. The
great moment had come.

Yet when the transports actually emerged from the Dvina's
mouth and steamed away into the waters of the White Sea under the
midnight sun, many of the Americans standing at the rails looked back
on North Russia's shores with an emotion that was far from elation.
What bothered them still was the feeling of bafflement-the distressing
sense of having spent nine months in a painful struggle to accomplish
something very difficult, and now giving up without ever having
understood it. "When the last battalion set sail from Archangel,"
Cudahy declared, "not a soldier knew, no, not even vaguely, why he
had fought or why he was going now, and why his comrades were left
behind-so many of them beneath the wooden crosses."

And even beyond that, there was the sway, escaping analysis,
that any country comes to hold over men when they have lived there
close to the earth, witnessing the change of the seasons, and the
natives' time-worn patterns of birth and life and death. North Russia
had become part of them. "That night scene with the lowering sun
near midnight," one of them wrote later, "gleaming gold upon the
forest-shaded stretches of the Dvina River and casting its mellow,
melancholy light upon the wrecked church of a village, is an
ineffaceable picture…. For this is our Russia-a church; a little cluster
of log houses, encompassed by unending forests of moaning spruce and
pine; low brooding, sorrowful skies; and over all oppressive stillness,
sad, profound, mysterious, yet strangely lovable to our memory."

CHAPTER 13

THE END OF SOMETHING

THE DEPARTURE OF THE American troops from North Russia, while it was numerically more than balanced by the influx of the British relief force, caused considerable misgiving among the non-Bolshevik Russians of Archangel. The Americans had been well liked, especially by many peasants of the region, and whatever small enthusiasm these had been able to muster for the war against Bolshevism had been fed largely by American participation. If the Yankees were giving up the struggle, it seemed reasonable to a good many peasants that the time had come for them to give it up too.

Apparently this conclusion was also reached by a significant number of soldiers in General Miller's new North Russian army. There was a steady trickle of desertions. What was worse, even before the Americans sailed for home there occurred the first successful mutiny; and it occurred at a spot just recently taken over from U.S. troops by an all-Russian company. At Toulgas, in the early-morning hours of April 25, about three hundred members of the 3rd North Russian Rifle Regiment murdered seven of their officers and went over en masse to the enemy. They then turned around and attacked the remnant of loyal Whites, consisting of little more than a section of field artillery, in an attempt to take Toulgas for the Bolsheviks. The gunners managed to limber up their field pieces and get away, but only because the Canadian artillery across the ice-clogged river, at Kurgomen, had by this time realized what was going on, and dumped a heavy curtain barrage on the attacking mutineers. Even so, the Bolos were soon firmly established at Toulgas, in the very solid blockhouses and dugouts which the Americans had spent a good part of the winter reinforcing.

The Toulgas mutiny was of course a severe blow to General Ironside, and even more to General Miller, whose ultimate hopes for saving North Russia from Bolshevism were entirely pinned to the idea of a reliable White Russian army. Miller, who in Chaikovsky's absence had tended more and more to make himself a one-man government, was also having his troubles with unruly civilians as the days lengthened into spring. His well-known sympathy for the late Czar, and his insistence on wearing his pre-revolutionary uniform, would have been sufficiently irritating to the socialists and laborers of Archangel even if he had not shown a dictatorial disposition. Nearly everything he did convinced them that if worst came to worst a victory for the Communists would be preferable to a White government run along the lines Miller seemed addicted to. It was therefore not surprising when certain socialist leaders began to make public denunciations of Miller and his Provisional Government, and by the middle of March the workers were being urged to turn against both the government and the Allies, and throw in their lot with the Bolsheviks. Miller struck back by arresting the ringleaders and redoubling his search for Bolshevik agents and agitators, in his army as well as among the civilians. They were tried as rapidly as they were found, and many of them were shot during March and April. An American Y.M.C.A. secretary commented: "The execution of suspects made Bolsheviki right and left. The inquisitorial processes of the Russian puppets of the Military Intervention were necessarily so much like those of the old regime that they went far to dispel all illusions … when night after night the firing squad took out its batches of victims."

Oddly enough, Miller and Marushevsky accompanied this tough policy with a lenient one whereby any Bolshevik sympathizer who wished to cross the lines into Soviet-held territory before mid-April would be allowed to do so, and would even be given rations for the journey. Hundreds took advantage of this, since the implication was that when the offer had expired any remaining Bolsheviks would be hunted down relentlessly. The difficulty was that the category of "Bolshevik sympathizers" never remained static, but shifted in proportion to the strength of rumors to the effect that all the Allied troops would soon be evacuated from North Russia. As Churchill pointed out, once a Russian made up his mind that this was going to happen, "his safest course was to make terms with his future masters at the expense of his departing Allies."

Actually, it was a matter of months before complete Allied evacuation was anything more than a rumor for the populace of Archangel, even though Ironside had been told by the War Office in April that full withdrawal must be finished by the end of September, 1919. The general knew that an announcement of evacuation would have a paralyzing effect on White Russian morale, and he carefully concealed his orders as long as he could. Even Miller was led to believe that the fresh British troops who came in the spring were genuine replacements, and might well remain through the winter of 1919-20. Ironside fostered this rosy impression at a press conference on June 6, just as the second contingent of four thousand, commanded by General L. W. deV. Sadleir-Jackson, was beginning to disembark at the Archangel quays. He told newspapermen that he now had "all that is needed to carry out the plan for this summer, which is to transfer the base of the Russian National Army from Siberia to Archangel." Barracks, warehouses, and necessary supplies would be ready and waiting for Kolchak's army. As for the actual junction of the two forces, Ironside made it sound almost as easy as General Poole had, back in the early days of the campaign. "I shall move up the river and take Kotlas," he announced coolly, adding that Vologda and Petrograd would also undoubtedly be occupied during the summer.

Much of this was exaggeration for the sake of encouragement. It is true, however, that Ironside now had more reason than Poole for thinking he could advance to Kotlas without great difficulty: the new troops were in top condition and full of volunteer enthusiasm. They were splendidly equipped, and officered by men whose reputation as soldiers had been won on the battlefields of the western front. General Grogan's troops were already on the Dvina and Vaga fronts, eager to fight, and Ironside lost little time in trying them out. He planned a co-ordinated attack for June 20, with White Russian units moving farther up the Dvina as the newly-arrived artillery and naval flotilla pushed back the Bolsheviks with a heavy barrage, and a battalion of the Hampshire Regiment struck in from the flank after a nine-mile circuit through the forest.

The ground had now dried out sufficiently for fairly easy marching on the trails, and the only serious natural impediment was the North Russian mosquito, a voracious type that seemed to breed, in the muskeg and swamps, by the million. The Hampshires survived the mosquito attacks with a great deal of swearing and slapping, and arrived at their jump-off point on schedule. Everything appeared to be in order; but the British generals had miscalculated one important factor. That was the extraordinary character of the Hampshires' battalion commander, Lieutenant Colonel Sherwood-Kelly. He was not of the regular army, but his war record was very brilliant; he had shown himself to be a bold and intelligent leader. Ironside and Grogan were therefore dumbfounded when Sherwood-Kelly withdrew his battalion, just at the crucial moment, without having fired a shot.

Ironside had experienced some misgivings about the state of Sherwood-Kelly's mind when they first met, but nothing that led him to anticipate behavior of this sort. The occasion was the general's inspection of the new troops, which had ended with his delivering a talk on their mission in North Russia. They were here, he told them, for a most important purpose: The destruction of Bolshevism; and he went on to explain why it was necessary for Bolshevism to be destroyed. During this speech, he was surprised to hear from Sherwood-Kelly, who of course was standing nearby, a series of muttered remarks which he interpreted as a kind of hallelujah chorus. "I thought that I was unconventional enough to stand anything," Ironside said afterward, "but this was more than I could tolerate." He did nothing, however, except to wave the lieutenant colonel into silence and mention the incident to General Grogan; for he was anxious above all to send a real fighting army into the field, and Sherwood-Kelly's reputation was tremendous.

When Ironside put the young officer on the carpet the day after the attack fizzled, he got little satisfaction. Sherwood-Kelly claimed, rather vaguely, that he had thought he was about to be outflanked by the enemy, and had retreated for the safety of his men. As far as Ironside was concerned it was a clear case of insubordination, and certainly deserving of a court-martial if the culprit had been a regular amy officer. Under the circumstances, he concluded that

Sherwood-Kelly was "worn out" by his responsibilities, and sent him up to Archangel for shipment back to England.

But that was not the end of the affair. A few weeks later there appeared over Sherwood-Kelly's signature, in the letters column of the London *Daily Express*, the following:

> I have just returned from North Russia under circumstances which compel me to seek the earliest possible opportunity of making known in England certain facts in connection with North Russia which otherwise might never come to light… . I know that my action will render me liable to professional penalties … but I am prepared to take all risks in carrying out what I know to be my duty to my country and to my men.
>
> I volunteered for service with the North Russian Relief Force in the sincere belief that relief was urgently needed in order to make possible the withdrawal of low category troops, in the last stages of exhaustion, due to the fierce fighting amid the rigours of an Arctic winter.
>
> The wide advertisement of this relief expedition led myself and many others to believe that affairs in North Russia were about to be wound up in an efficient and decisive manner. And we were proud to be accorded the privilege of sharing in such an undertaking… .
>
> Immediately on arrival at Archangel, however, towards the end of May, I received the impression that the policy of the authorities was not what it was stated to be… . I was reluctantly but inevitably driven to the following conclusion:
>
> That the troops of the Relief Forces which we were told had been sent out purely for defensive purposes, were being used for offensive purposes, on a large scale and far in the interior, in furtherance of some ambitious plan of campaign the nature of which we were not allowed to know… .
>
> I discovered … that the much vaunted "loyal Russian Army," composed largely of Bolshevik prisoners dressed in khaki, was utterly unreliable, always disposed to mutiny, and it always constituted a greater danger to our troops than the Bolshevik armies opposed to them.
>
> This was tragically demonstrated early in July, when the Russians mutinied and murdered their British officers.
>
> I formed the opinion that the puppet-Government set up by us in Archangel rested on no basis of public confidence and support, and would fall to pieces the moment the protection of British bayonets was withdrawn.

One can imagine the ferocity with which Winston Churchill must have chewed on his cigar if he read this expose of his plans for

North Russia. Evidently Ironside never did read it, for he remained puzzled about Sherwood-Kelly's conduct for many years afterward.

The July mutiny referred to in Sherwood-Kelly's letter was indeed a tragedy, not only for the five young British officers who were killed but for Ironside's dream of a self-sufficient North Russian army. It took place in two companies of "Dyer's Battalion," which had received more special attention and training than any other in the Slavo-British Legion. In concept this was a salvage battalion: under the general's careful shepherding even some Bolshevik prisoners were enlisted, in addition to various riffraff from the prisons and streets of Archangel. It was Ironside's faith that British discipline and good officers would make soldiers of these men; and in *esprit de corps* they did seem to be the best unit of Russians in the Allied force. But despite their excellent marching and apparent pride in their organization, about one hundred of them deserted in the early morning of July 7, after a cold-blooded slaughter of a group of officers who were caught asleep in their billet on the bank of the Dvina. Four Russian and three British officers died instantly; two more of the British died soon afterward. One, a captain, was wounded in seven places as he fought his way out of the billet; he then swam two hundred yards to a British boat anchored in the river and gave the alarm.

Ironside could scarcely believe the faithlessness of the Russian troops toward the officers who had worked so hard with them. "No one," he said, "could have trained and looked after their men better than they had." What this meant, as he saw it, was that any really successful stand by General Miller's forces after the British departure was most unlikely. He was reluctantly coming around to the conclusion that there did not exist in North Russia any sufficiently widespread determination to halt Communism. As if to prove the point, another and larger mutiny occurred at Onega on July 20, leaving the whole right flank of the Allied position wide open to Soviet attack. The only consolation was an intelligence report showing that the mutineers did not join the Bolsheviks, but instead dispersed and made for their homes, where they hurriedly got rid of anything that could have been used to prove their service under Allied command. The inference was clear that a large percentage of the conscripts in General Miller's army had little if any political sentiment. What they wanted was to get out of uniform and go back to farming.

Meanwhile the prospects of Kolchak's anti-Bolshevik army, which early in June had still been thought bright, took on a decidedly grayish hue. His spring offensive had rolled to a standstill, and now Trotsky's Second and Third Red Armies were beginning to push him back. On July 1 the Reds recaptured Perm, and it became obvious to British military advisors serving with Kolchak that there was no further expectation of his joining hands with Ironside's troops: Perm was more than four hundred miles from Kotlas. Ironside was therefore informed by the War Office that British junction with Kolchak had now positively flown off into the realm of lost schemes.

Incidentally, the fighting between the Reds and Kolchak's Whites near the Urals, during this period of the civil war, was thrown into an ironic light as a result of fumbling Allied attempts to aid Kolchak from the east. Despite the usual disclaimers by the statesmen at Paris of any intention to interfere in Russian civil affairs, they had decided by the end of May to offer as much help to Admiral Kolchak as possible, short of sending an Allied army into Siberia. Woodrow Wilson's doubts about Kolchak's reactionary leanings were stilled, after much discussion, by making the admiral promise to be good in return for aid from the Allies; he was informed on May 26 that he would be helped with "munitions, supplies, and food" if he would guarantee a democratic Russia and no return to the pre-revolutionary regime. (The London *Morning Post* commented that if this "be not interfering in the domestic concerns of Russia, we do not know what is.") Kolchak, to no one's surprise, soon declared that he had never had any thought of usurping power in Russia; and the way was thus open for increased Allied support. (England, it will be remembered, was already helping Kolchak with large quantities of supplies and weapons.) Unfortunately for him, this accord with the Allies was reached just at the moment when the Soviet armies were turning the tide, and the Kolchak forces were beginning a long, demoralized retreat that was to end in total defeat. Both sides, on the Ural front, were so badly clothed by this time, according to a British correspondent, that a war theoretically involving high moral principles "is reduced to individual combat for the possession of poor rags. Paradoxical as it may seem, the fine British uniforms served out to a few White units have stimulated the Reds to fight in order to capture the wearers."

What between mutinies and the bad news from Kolchak, July was a gloomy month for General Ironside and General Miller. Marushevsky, who was still puttering ineffectually about at Allied headquarters in Archangel, recalled later that there was a notable change in Ironside's demeanor about this time: he lost the look of cheerful confidence which he had managed to maintain all though the winter and spring, and which so often had bucked up the courage of his officers and men. Moreover, by the end of the month he felt morally obliged to tell Miller that all British soldiers must be gone from Archangel before autumn. He tried to soften the blow by adding that England would undertake to evacuate as many as thirteen thousand Russians from Archangel when the time came to go, including all members of the government, Russian officers, and anyone who was likely to suffer serious reprisals at the hands of the Bolsheviks. This offer Miller rejected flatly, saying that he would continue the struggle against Communism even if the Allies abandoned him completely. It was then his awkward duty to preside, on August 2, at the first anniversary celebration of the Allied landing in North Russia, and lead a cheer for the English, French, and Americans. Ironside was not able to bring himself to attend this social event.

About the only solace Ironside could find during the long, bright, but depressing summer days was in working hard over his evacuation plans, and carrying out a few last military operations with his fresh British troops. There had been no further incidents like the one involving Sherwood-Kelly, and most of the soldiers seemed to be spoiling for a fight. An attempted mutiny among the Russian troops on the railroad at Obozerskaya was nipped in the bud, and a company of Australians came down from Archangel to toughen up that front. They got in a sneak attack on the Bolshevik lines one evening, bayoneted several dozen Soviet soldiers, set fire to four blockhouses, and quickly withdrew with very few casualties among themselves. It was more or less pointless, but it gave Ironside something encouraging to report to Miller.

August 10 had been chosen as the date for officially letting the population of Archangel in on the secret that the Allies were about to pull out altogether. It was felt that the effect on civilian morale might be lightened by the fact that this was also the date picked by Ironside for striking a last, hard blow at the Soviet forces; with any luck a victory could therefore be simultaneously announced. The official British reason for this last offensive was to facilitate "disengagement," and permit full evacuation while the Bolsheviks were still staggering. The enemy, as Winston Churchill expressed it, "was to be given a blow so severe that before he could recover not a British soldier, nor a loyal Russian who claimed asylum, would remain on shore." This, of course, was not counting any British soldiers who might be killed in the attack.

The British force that hit the Bolsheviks at dawn on August 10 was actually the one Ironside had planned to use for driving down to Kotlas. Although the objective now was much less ambitious, he decided to go all out and not pull the punch in any way. The operation, both in plan and execution, had a very modern look, perhaps as much because it called for rapid penetration and extended movement as because of the abundance of new equipment that was used. Sadleir-Jackson was put in command, and his orders were to attack after a heavy bombardment, under a smoke screen, and continue attacking until Soviet resistance broke completely. Expected depth of penetration into the Soviet front on the Dvina was ten miles. Communication arrangements were elaborate, and Sadleir-Jackson was in close touch with the commander of the naval flotilla by field wireless, as well as with each of his subordinate unit officers. There was an observation balloon, and a squadron of airplanes that easily swept the skies of what little air resistance the Bolsheviks were able to offer.

The attack was an overwhelming success. The Soviet front turned out to be in a very pulpy condition: the British troops smashed through like a fist through wet paper. Apparently the Bolsheviks were taken by surprise, and by the end of the day more than two thousand of them were prisoners. Their casualties in killed and wounded were heavy, and eighteen field guns and two thousand rifles were lost to the attackers. The British lost only 145 in killed and wounded.

Although Soviet resistance on August 10 appeared to have been amazingly weak, it was easily subject to misinterpretation. It has already been pointed out that Trotsky undoubtedly was co-ordinating Red army efforts in North Russia with what was going on elsewhere; and during the first two weeks of August, Kolchak's disintegrating army was fading away rapidly. Its broken northern wing was in fact two hundred miles east of the Urals, and there was absolutely no danger now of any junction between Kolchak and Ironside. Indeed, Trotsky must have been astonished at the intensity of the British attack on the Dvina. The last thing he wanted to do was to impede in any way the withdrawal of British troops from North Russia, and he was well informed that they were scheduled to get out by summer's end. From the Soviet point of view, the British "disengagement blow" must have looked altogether superfluous. It is even possible that, when the blow struck, Soviet commanders did little to prevent large numbers of their men from being taken prisoner. Two thousand Bolshevik prisoners in Archangel would mean simply that many more mouths for the Whites to feed, and that much more of a potential fifth column for the Reds.

None of this occurred to General Miller, whose sour summer mood gave way to elation at news of the great victory over the Bolsheviks. Even though his Russian field commanders told him they expected a general collapse of the North Russian front after British evacuation, he insisted that they must fight on to throw off the Bolshevik yoke in Russia. In this heroic stance he got support chiefly from an organization of Archangel businessmen, who had become acutely aware of what would happen to their extensive property holdings if the Communists took over. At their urging, Miller put out an order forbidding the departure from North Russia of any able-bodied male between the ages of seventeen and fifty. This, of course, ran counter to the actions of the British, who were determined to transport out of the country, to the best of their ability, all Russians desiring to leave, and who were already issuing permits for that purpose.

Another event immediately after the big British attack on the Dvina was the arrival at Archangel of General Lord Rawlinson, a famous figure of the Great War, to superintend the forthcoming evacuation from both Archangel and Murmansk. This was to some extent a blow to Ironside's prestige, but it had been dictated by public clamor in England following news of the July mutinies. Ironside took it in good grace, although his plans for evacuation were now nearly complete and required little more than Rawlinson's approval. As a matter of fact he soon fell under the spell of Rawlinson's strangely magnetic personality. They had barely met in France, but Rawlinson quickly put Ironside on familiar terms by using the sobriquet popular with the huge young general's troops on the western front: Tiny. It was the beginning of what Ironside described as "a very precious friendship," for the two were to see much of each other in years to come.

Like many others, Ironside was struck with Rawlinson's marvelous air of informed equanimity. Nothing seemed to escape him; nothing disturbed him. Urbanely ignoring Bolshevik shell fire while touring the fronts, he would intersperse shrewd military comments about the terrain with allusions to history and esthetic observations on the landscape; he spent many of his evenings in his quarters painting pictures. Ironside recalled hearing a well-known news correspondent in France express something like horror at the calm cheerfulness with which Rawlinson ordered men to what he knew would be certain death. "I wondered at the time," Ironside commented, "whether [the correspondent] expected him to look dismal when he talked to his men." His impression was that Rawlinson never worried about whether he had made correct decisions, and never "spent a sleepless night over past events." It was a perfect disposition for a general.

But the Allied intervention in North Russia was now entering its last phase, and Lord Rawlinson was to have little chance to demonstrate his *sang-froid* in that theater of operations. The rest of August and most of September were taken up with multifarious preparations for withdrawal. A thousand difficult decisions had to be made. Archangel was in a turmoil of activity, for not only were all Allied diplomatic offices to be removed together with the British army, but thousands of citizens were now agitating to go along. Thousands of others were agitating for continuation of the Allied intervention, not realizing that the decision had long since been made irrevocable. Ironside was deluged with "petitions and deputations" from various organizations begging him not to give up the anti-Bolshevik cause.

President Wilson received a plaintive message from a group of regional officials predicting disaster if the Allies departed: "... we look into the future with anguish ..." One delegation even sailed for England and made a personal appeal to Churchill at the War Office, but of course to no avail. Communications flew back and forth between London and Archangel, making provision for the large amount of shipping necessary for the evacuation of the troops and their supplies. Some six thousand Russians registered for shipment out of Archangel, many of them, according to Ironside, with false names and credentials; a great flurry of hasty marriages took place, since married couples stood a better chance of filling the requirements. One big problem for Ironside and Rawlinson was deciding what military supplies could or could not be safely left in Russian hands. Felix Cole, observing all this from the American embassy, put his finger neatly on the difficulty of leaving much equipment: "It may result in adding the majority of the present Russian forces here, fully equipped, clothed, and armed, to the Red Army." In the end, huge quantities of materiel were destroyed, much to General Miller's dismay.

The actual withdrawal of British troops, elaborately planned, began on September 10. It was done in five definite stages, one stage per day, so that transfer of the frontline positions to full Russian control could be made gradually. What Ironside feared more than Bolshevik attack was a mass mutiny on the part of Miller's troops; but nothing of the sort happened. Miller even carried out a successful attack of his own, on a small scale, to divert enemy attention from the British evacuation. By September 26, the troop transports were at the quays ready to be filled, and that night the whole force embarked.

Ironside spent his last night in Russia aboard the yacht of a British admiral. They were tied up at a dock near the big cathedral. It was a pleasant fall evening with just a nip in the air, a foretaste of another early Russian winter. The general sat on the quarterdeck chatting with the admiral and glancing occasionally at the empty streets of Archangel. Miller had declared a twenty-four-hour curfew, with all lights out at 8 P.M.; the city was like a deserted place. After a good dinner, Ironside went to bed early in order to be up to see the transports get under way in the morning. Kostia, his Russian servant lad, who as usual spent the night sleeping across his doorsill, woke him at four o'clock, and he went on deck. It was chilly, and there was a light fog.

For two hours the transports moved silently and steadily by; then nothing but the mist. Around nine o'clock a tugboat captain, who had been checking embarkation piers for stragglers, came by to say that he had found only one: a soldier who claimed to be "Captain Snodgrass's servant." He had waited patiently on the pier with the captain's baggage, somehow had missed his master, and perhaps would be there still, a monument to the British Empire's thoughtful provision for the personal needs of its officers, if the tug had not picked him up.

A few minutes later the figures of General Miller and his aide, looking as Ironside said, "strangely forlorn," appeared on the pier and walked toward the yacht. Miller had come to pay his parting respects to Ironside. He was piped on board, and a quarter-hour of stiff conversation and formal compliments passed between the two generals. Ironside wished him luck in his campaign against the Bolsheviks; but as the British had already made quite clear their belief that it could not be successful, Miller was able to reply only with a bow. He then went down the gangplank with the aide, and slowly walked away. "I was half hoping," Ironside wrote of that moment, "that he might turn and wave his hand to us in farewell, but he never once looked back.... He was a very proud and gallant gentleman."

The admiral's yacht now moved into the channel of the Dvina and slowly made its way out toward the White Sea. The sun had broken through the mist, and cast its golden light on the same brilliant display of fall color along the banks that Ironside had enjoyed just one year earlier, as he arrived in Russia to commence the strangest assignment of his career. Slowly the cupolas of the Archangel cathedral sank lower behind the curtain of forest treetops; and suddenly they were gone. By the morning of September 28 the curfew in Archangel was lifted, and a Russian colonel was hailed on the street by another of General Miller's officers with the question: "How do you like the Russian city of Archangel?"

The aftermath of Allied intervention in North Russia is a brief and bitter story. For a little while General Miller's battalions had better success against the Bolsheviks than anyone had expected, but it was only a question of time. Short of food, ammunition, and money, and plagued by a succession of ever more serious mutinies, the Whites moved steadily toward defeat. The Sixth Red Army took it easy,

E.M. Halliday

waiting for winter to come to their assistance. By February, 1920, the
end was obviously near. In Siberia, Admiral Kolchak's armies were in
a state of dissolution, and he himself was shot by a firing squad on
February 7. In the south, Denikin was in retreat. As if in a last frenzied
attempt to deny the reality of it all, the prominent citizens of
Archangel held a fancy theatrical and ball on the night of February
15. Even as they danced, however, one of Miller's officers was
negotiating with the Bolsheviks at Vologda to learn what surrender
terms could be had. The answer, as might have been expected, was:
"Unconditional."

On February 17 Miller explained the drastic situation to what
was left of the White government in Archangel, and it was decided
to move the center of resistance to Murmansk by means of pony-sleigh
convoy. This difficult and doubtful maneuver was to begin on the
afternoon of February 19; but by that time Miller had seen things in
another light. A powerful icebreaker was in the Archangel harbor, and
by noon on the nineteenth he and his staff were aboard, as also were
a select group of army and navy officers, members of the government,
and a certain number of wealthy merchants together with their
families. The records do not indicate just how this change of plans
was negotiated, but one hint is afforded by the identity of the captain
of the icebreaker. It was none other than Commander Chaplin, who
had turned up at the last moment like the unshakable mystery man in
a spy movie. Just as he had played a key role in the very opening of
counter-revolutionary efforts at Archangel in 1918, now he played a
key role in the final scene. On February 26 the icebreaker reached a
port in Norway, and the anti-Bolshevik leaders of North Russia were
free to fight another day.

Meanwhile, on February 21, the 154th Red Infantry Regiment
had marched into Archangel with no sign of resistance from the
populace, who on the contrary received the conquerors with as much
enthusiasm as they had shown the Allies eighteen months before.
Murmansk fell into Soviet hands two days later, and the struggle
against Communism in North Russia was over.

AN AFTERWORD

EDMUND IRONSIDE, HAVING HELD the most important job in North Russia for nearly a year, returned to England in October, 1919, to find himself unemployed. Everyone paid him compliments on his leadership of the Archangel expedition, but the War Office revealed that he was home too late for an active-duty appointment. He was to go on the waiting list at half pay; and since his permanent rank of colonel grouped him with many much older men-he was still under forty-he could expect a wait of months, or even years. Yet, at his age, the War Office was absolutely unprepared to grant him retirement. Disconsolately, Ironside took a small cottage in a London suburb and tried to amuse himself by digging in the garden, and by watching with some amazement the behavior of his small daughter, who was virtually a new acquaintance after his absence of a year.

All this changed abruptly on November 11, when he discovered that, with Lord Rawlinson's recommendation, he had been promoted to the permanent rank of major general in recognition of his service in North Russia. In the rarefied atmosphere of this upper echelon the competition for peacetime appointments was less severe, and within months General Ironside found himself in the Middle East, again supervising the extrication of British troops from uncomfortable situations. "I seem to have become a specialist in retreats," he observed somewhat ruefully. Meanwhile, he had been knighted by George V, and was rapidly becoming one of the best known of the younger generals in His Majesty's forces.

While the next twenty years took Ironside steadily up the stairs of military prestige, none of his assignments compared in unique quality with the year in North Russia. There were several relatively placid years in India; there was the almost honorary appointment, in 1931, as Lieutenant of the Tower of London; there was a year as Governor of Gibraltar. Everywhere he was impressive, with his enormous, handsome bulk, his unconventional approach to conventional problems, his extraordinary facility with languages, and his positive yet easygoing manner, quite free of any pomposity. He never lost his fondness for bulldogs; there were nearly always a couple at his heels. In civilian dress he habitually favored the sporting tweed, and his collection of smoking pipes became as familiar as the bull terriers and the sport jackets. Yet he took none of his assignments routinely, and his air of nonchalance was deceptive. At Gibraltar, for example, he insisted on a series of improvements that turned the venerable landmark into a modern fortress just in time for the outbreak of World War II.

It was then that Ironside reached the pinnacle as Chief of the Imperial General Staff. Britain's military operations in the first months of the war were under his direction, with close co-operation, of course, between him and his old friend Winston Churchill. The name of Ironside became a public metaphor expressing England's determination to survive against Hitler's armies. After Dunkirk, however, it was felt in government circles that the old warrior should give place to a younger man. He himself shared this view, and his suggestion that he be made commander of the British Home Forces was accepted-"a spirited and selfless offer," Churchill called it. Sir John Dill therefore became CIGS on May 27, 1940, while Ironside began to work out a plan for a last-ditch stand against the German invasion that was expected all the following summer. Although he retired from active service altogether late in July, it was basically his defense plan on which the nation counted during the terrible days of the Battle of Britain, when the *Luftwaffe* was pounding London to pieces as a prelude to the invasion that never came. The title of Lord Ironside, conferred in 1941, expressed England's gratitude for more than fifty years of devoted service.

Ironside had broken both thighs in an airplane accident in 1921. In September, 1959, he fell and broke one of them again. Taken to a London military hospital, he seemed to be recovering when he died of heart failure on September 22.

* * *

Other leading figures in the allied intervention at Archangel passed into history with varying degrees of public attention. Chaiokovswky, Miller, Marushevsky, and Chaplin became members of the European *emigre* set and continued to agitate forlornly against the Bolshevik regime. Ambassador Francis resigned his now meaningless post in 1921, and lived out his last six years stoutly insisting that Russia might have been saved from Communism had he been allowed to return to Petrograd with fifty thousand troops. Felix Cole remained for many years in the U.S. foreign service, but never achieved the prominence that might have been expected from his perspicacity in Russian affairs. Instead, he was minister to Ethiopia in 1945; ambassador to Ceylon in 1948. DeWitt Clinton Poole, on the other hand, took from his experience in Russia a lifetime orientation. He spent eighteen years with the Princeton School of Public and International Affairs as an expert on Communism, and at his death in 1952 was president of the National Committee for a Free Europe-sponsors of Radio Free Europe.

Of the 5,500 members of the American Expedition to North Russia, few ever reached prominence. Colonel Stewart slipped rapidly into oblivion except in the unflattering recollections of his surviving troops, and little was heard from the other officers of the regiment. Of them all, only John Cudahy drew national attention, becoming Franklin D. Roosevelt's ambassador to Poland in 1933, minister to Eire in 1937, and ambassador to Belgium in 1939.

It may be truthfully said that Cudahy never got over his experience in North Russia. In 1924 he published a strange, anonymous book about the campaign: *Archangel: The American War with Russia*, by "A Chronicler." He took an epigraph from Shakespeare: "Nothing extenuate, nor set down aught in malice." Certainly nothing is extenuated, for the book is a harsh indictment of the expedition from beginning to end. The passages describing battle actions-especially those Cudahy saw himself-are emotionally overwritten nearly to the point of incoherence: clearly words were unable to communicate adequately the intensity of his feeling. This makes all the more curious the name he chose for his only daughter: Toulgas.

Yet it was not really war in North Russia that disturbed Cudahy: it was war itself, the sheer madness of human destruction as a means of settling disputes. He was to see war on a far greater scale twenty years later. As U.S. ambassador, he lived through the shattering German attack on Belgium in May, 1940, and saw the Nazi troopers take over the country. (A few days later he visited the beach at Dunkirk just after its evacuation by three hundred thousand English soldiers: "a scene of havoc and desolation beyond the power of language.") His sympathy for the plight of Belgium was intense-he wrote a superb defense of King Leopold against British and French charges of having betrayed the Allied cause-yet he refused to let his hatred of Nazism dislodge his sense of honesty and fairness to all. This got him into trouble when he stopped over in London on his way back to the States in the summer of 1940. He told reporters that after making a thorough investigation at first hand, he was convinced that the average German soldier had conducted himself fairly decently when Belgium was occupied.

"I was a soldier in the last war, and I think these Germans behaved better than United States soldiers would have done," he said with a maximum of indiscretion. He then went on to suggest that unless several million people in occupied Belgium and France were going to be allowed to starve in the winter of 1940-41, the British might have to relax their blockade enough to let American food come in. Loud roars instantly went up from the British press, the American press, and the American Legion, and a hurried message came from Washington: Cudahy was to return immediately for conference with President Roosevelt.

He was not publicly rebuked, but the upshot was his quiet exit from the foreign service. Within months, however, he was back in Europe, this time as a correspondent in Germany for *Life*. In this capacity he wrote several extremely interesting articles, including a report of the last interview ever granted by Adolf Hitler to an American. Although he tried to be scrupulously objective, putting down little except what he asked Hitler and what Hitler replied, his article annoyed Roosevelt, who cited it as an example of how the Nazis were duping Americans into thinking there were no evil German designs on the United States and the free world.

Back in the States in the summer of 1941, Cudahy went on a national radio hookup and argued vehemently for peace. It was far from the usual isolationist harangue: he urged Roosevelt to propose "an international government with power to enforce the solution of this and all the endless wars of Europe." But the time was hardly propitious, and for his pains Cudahy lost some of his old friends from the Archangel days, many of whom were ready and willing to go to war again by 1941.

After Pearl Harbor, John Cudahy stayed home in Wisconsin, becoming chief of civilian defense for the state. His tense life came abruptly to an end on September 6, 1943, when he fell from his horse while riding on the family estate.

* * *

Two other officers of the 339th Infantry were moved to put a full-scale account of the North Russia expedition down on paper: Joel R. Moore, former captain of Company M, and Harry H. Mead, lieutenant of Company A. *The History of the American Expedition Fighting the Bolsheviki*, as their book was called, came out in 1920 after several months of hard and hasty compilation. Rather chaotic in its organization, it nevertheless possessed the great virtue of having been written when most of the events recounted were fresh in memory. Moore and Mead were assisted in the actual publication of the book by another ex-officer, Lewis E. Jahns, who handled business matters and set up the "Polar Bear Publishing Company" to do the job. It was a one-shot proposition; no further works appeared under the imprint of this Detroit establishment. Jahns dropped out of sight shortly afterward, but Moore and Mead remained close friends until Moore died in 1953, after many years as warden of the Michigan State Prison at Jackson. Mead, who had roomed with Frank Murphy at the University of Michigan law school before World War I, got into local politics as Murphy's manager in a successful campaign for mayor of Detroit in 1930; later he handled Murphy's two campaigns for governor of Michigan. Semi-retired, as of 1960, in the hamlet of Milford, near Detroit, Mead pursued happiness with a gusto possibly born of his hair-raising escape at Nijni Gora forty years before, driving a bright red Mercedes sports car back and forth to the office, swimming daily in his pool in the summer, and frequently skiing with alarming abandon when Michigan provided a winter with enough snow.

Cudahy, Moore, and Mead were all early presidents of the Polar Bear Association, founded in Detroit in 1922 to tie veterans of the North Russia campaign to one another by something a little more substantial than the mystic cords of memory. At its regular biennial reunions a fairly large percentage of the Americans who went to Archangel gathered to celebrate the exotic days of 1918-19. Aside from its necessarily exclusive membership, the association was a typical veterans' organization, busying itself with resolutions calling for such things as a bonus, a special campaign medal (never granted), and repeal of the Eighteenth Amendment. Nostalgia and alcohol flowed freely as the glittering snows of Kodish, Shenkursk, and Bolshie Ozerki were fought through again: it sometimes appeared that the answer to Villon's famous question, *Ou sont les neiges d'antan?* was obviously "Detroit." One notable fact was that the winter temperature in North Russia seemed to get lower every couple of years, threatening to reach absolute zero before the turn of the century.

A more sober feature of the reunions is the Memorial Day service conducted at the White Chapel Cemetery, near Detroit, where a magnificent stone figure of a polar bear commemorates those who died in North Russia. Many of them are buried in a special plot at White Chapel; and the tale of how they came out of Russia makes a curious epilogue to the Archangel campaign.

One day in August, 1919, General Ironside was puzzled to encounter a long convoy of Russian carts on an Archangel street, headed for the wharves. On each cart was a wooden box about six feet long. He was told that the boxes contained the bodies of American soldiers: they had been dug up from the cemetery in Archangel and now, the last of their regiment to leave, were about to begin their long, quiet voyage back to the United States. Apparently this struck Ironside as grotesque, for he laughed when he understood what was going on.

Grotesque or not, the disinterment was part of the U.S. War Department's official policy, which was to return all American bodies from enemy soil. The difficulty in North Russia was that more than a hundred Americans had been buried in areas retaken by the

Bolsheviks before the Allied evacuation, and there was no way to retrieve them. For ten years after the end of the expedition this bothered the relatives of the abandoned dead, and formed a topic of agitated discussion at meetings of the Polar Bears. Many felt particularly distressed at the thought of American soldiers lying in unmarked graves beneath the ground of an atheistic nation. Michigan congressmen were actively concerned, and in the spring of 1929 Senator Arthur Vandenberg successfully pushed through a bill appropriating $200,000 for the recovery of the bodies in North Russia.

There was still the problem, however, of just how they were to be secured. The Soviet Union had not been recognized by the United States government, so no direct dealings through diplomatic channels were possible. It occurred to Colonel Edwin S. Bettleheim, Jr., an official of the Veterans of Foreign Wars, that perhaps the VFW could get permission from Moscow to enter Russia as a private agency interested in recovering the bodies; and after a certain amount of negotiating this was arranged. Bettelheim proceeded to Paris, where the War Department had deposited funds to the credit of the VFW, and was joined there by a captain from the graves-registration service of the U.S. Army, together with three sergeants who were experts in the unpleasant work of digging up remains. All four of the army men were also VFW members, to make everything legitimate.

Arriving in Moscow early in August, Bettelheim's group found that five members of the Polar Bear Association, headed by its 1929 president, Walter Dundon, were there by courtesy of the Michigan legislature, which had put up travel money. Their function was supposed to be assistance in locating battlegrounds and burial places. All of the Americans were immediately taken under the wing of Soviet officialdom, and were advised to outfit themselves with Russian peasant costumes so that their activities in North Russia would be no more conspicuous than necessary.

The actual recovery operations, not surprisingly, were nearly as confused as the 1918-19 campaign itself had been. After a rail journey to Archangel the party broke up into several groups, some going to one front and some to another, although most of the bodies they were looking for were known to be on the Dvina and Vaga rivers. Bettelheim and the graves-registration men bought a good-sized boat, with facilities for sleeping and cooking, and used that as their headquarters as they went from village to village. They were glad to be out of Archangel, where living conditions were, if anything, worse than they had been ten years earlier. The weather was bad: alternately hot, cold, and rainy. As Bettelheim remembers it, the members of the little expedition began to get on each others' nerves rather soon. One of them was a religious cultist, and evidently took a peculiar view of recovering dead bodies; he was also given to staying up all night singing hymns. One disappeared for a couple of weeks without explanation, and then showed up again; it was thought that a female was involved. Then there was a certain amount of trouble with the natives, who were not very sympathetic to the idea of digging into old graves looking for what might be left of perished American soldiers.

It is hardly necessary to say that not much was left. The bodies had been buried either in the crudest sort of board coffins, or none at all; and ten years of the North Russian climate had reduced them to a few bones, and shreds of rotten cloth. Identification was difficult: in many cases even the metal "dog tags" had crumbled away to rusty dust. Russian peasants, asked where the "Amerikanskis" were buried, were as likely as not to lead the searchers to graves that turned out to be British when probed. Nevertheless, after two months' work, eighty-six remains which were believed to be those of American soldiers had been dug up: the bones were washed in lysol, wrapped in linen, and put into boxes for shipment.

Although the living veterans of the AEFNR had returned to the United States in 1919 without any great fuss being made over them, at least before they reached Detroit, the scant relics of the dead late-comers were accorded meticulous homage all the way from France to the White Chapel Cemetery. Reaching Le Havre in November, they were transferred to full-size coffins, the large amount of excess space being filled with blankets. An honor guard of French sailors and soldiers was in constant attendance until the flag-draped coffins were ready for embarkation; a memorial service was conducted on November 18, attended by various French and American officials, delegations from patriotic societies, etc. When the *President Roosevelt* docked at Hoboken about ten days later, it was greeted by a seventeen-gun salute form Fort Jay, a guard of honor, and the U.S. army band;

then a second memorial service was held. Finally, a funeral train took most of the coffins to Detroit, where of course even more elaborate ceremonies had been arranged; three were sent to Arlington National Cemetery, which also provided special rites.

The skeletons of thirty-nine American soldiers were still left in North Russia after the recovery expedition of 1929; in 1934 another group went in and located nineteen more. The rest were never found, and presumably will remain beneath the Russian tundra forever-permanent envoys, and poignant reminders of the tragic first chapter in the relationship of the twentieth century's two greatest powers.

The ranks of the Polar Bear Association naturally thinned rapidly in the 1970's and 1980's, and today not a single survivor is left. It has, however, been revived as the Polar Bear Memorial Association, which meets every Memorial Day in Detroit's White Chapel Memorial Park to recall and honor the men who fought-and especially those who died-in the snows of North Russia. A military detail, including a bugler, from the recently reactivated 339th Infantry Regiment, is always there in uniform to formalize the occasion.

On a more frequent-in fact everyday-basis, there is at Frankenmuth, Michigan, a few miles from Detroit, a remarkable military museum called Michigan's Own, which has an impressive display of memorabilia from the North Russia expedition among its exhibits. This was gathered, organized, and documented over many years by the museum's founder, Stanley J. Bozich, who quite possibly knows more about this aspect of the story than anyone else anywhere.

In Russia, too, there doubtless is no-one left who fought against the Americans in 1918-19. Across the still gloomy reaches of North Russia few signs remain of the obscure struggle: here and there an abandoned village where timber wolves nose the ruins of old log houses; in the depths of the forest an occasional heap of rotten pine where once a blockhouse shielded American soldiers.

But in the annals of the Cold War the Soviet-American combat of 1918-19 has not lost its significance. It was a painful beginning, and clearly it must be weighed in any realistic analysis of today's difficulties between America and Russia. "We remember," said Nikita Khrushchev in Los Angeles in September, 1959, "the grim days when American soldiers went to our soil headed by their generals to help our White Guard combat the new revolution ... all the capitalist countries of Europe and of America marched upon our country to strangle the new revolution.... . Never have any of our soldiers been on American soil, but your soldiers were on Russian soil. These are the facts."

The obvious Western reply, grown hoary after forty years of repetition, was that the expedition to North Russia did not have as its aim the overthrow of Bolshevik power; or at any rate, as no less an authority than George F. Kennan once put it, that American soldiers in North Russia took "no part in any actions other than ones of a defensive nature." The record, however, speaks otherwise; and it must be conceded that Sir Winston Churchill more accurately echoed the motif of the campaign when he stubbornly observed, in 1953: "The day will come when it will be recognized without doubt throughout the civilized world that the strangling of Bolshevism at birth would have been an untold blessing to the human race."

NOTES

(Many sources are indicated below by names of authors only: for titles, see the bibliography which follows.)

NOTES: *Chapter 1*

My chief authorities for this chapter are Cudahy (who was at Toulgas), and Moore, Mead and Jahns (hereafter referred to as Moore & Mead). Captain Robert Boyd, who was in command of Allied troops on this front, has provided very helpful comments by letter. The statement that Trotsky directed the Soviet attack is found in both Moore & Mead and Cudahy; I have not been able to find verification in Trotsky's own writings, however. Ironside's account of Toulgas is evidently confused: he claims that General Finlayson took personal command of the operation. This is disputed by all American sources, including Captain Boyd.

NOTES: *Chapter 2*

The background of American intervention in North Russia is covered in great detail by Kennan (*The Decision*); also by Strakhovsky in his *Origins*. The statement about "some professional historians" is illustrated by Browder, who claims that American soldiers landed at Archangel "in June" to help "in protecting Allied supplies stored there"; he gives no sign of knowing what they in fact did. The incident of the American officer ordered to report to Archangel *via* Vladivostok is told by Cudahy. The *Yank* reporter who tried to find out about Soviet-American combat was myself. The activities of the U.S. Cruiser *Olympia* and her crew in North Russia may be followed in the daily log of the vessel, which is deposited in the National Archives. Lenin's vituperative telegrams to the Murmansk Soviet are to be found in naval intelligence records at the Archives; also in Kennan (*The Decision*) and Strakhovsky (*Origins*). Ambassador Francis' character can be inferred from a reading of his memoirs; Kennan (both volumes) and Noulens (vol. 2) also have interesting remarks to make about him. Both Felix Cole's letter to the Secretary of State and Wilson's famous *aide memoire* are printed in full in the State Department's *Foreign Relations*, 1918; likewise the British reasons for intervention in North Russia. Stakhovsky (in *Intervention*), and Kennan (in *The Decision*) both gave detailed accounts of the Allied landing at Archangel; Cole's experience is told in a dispatch in *Foreign Relations*, 1918. The U.S. Navy's account is given in an intelligence report in the Archives; it is printed in Strakhovsky. Maynard was the fellow general who commented on Poole's optimism. The episode of the *Olympia* bluejackets who pursued the Bolsheviks is told in Moore & Mead, but the details are obscure. Some accounts even call the sailors "marines," much to the disgust of surviving members of the *Olympia*'s crew. They definitely were sailors, chosen for their rifle marksmanship. The log of the *Olympia* does not mention the wounded officer, thus throwing some doubt on the matter since it goes into detail on wounds sustained by enlisted members of the landing party. The quotation that ends the chapter is from Wilson's *aide-memoire* of July 17.

NOTES: Chapter 3

Moore & Mead, Cudahy, and Dupuy are the chief sources for the early history of the 339th Infantry. The Lowell Thomas incident was told to me by Mr. Mead. General Poole's cable of August 12 is found in the Archives. The description of Archangel in 1918 is based on Moore & Mead, Ironside, and Cudahy. Strakhovsky's *Intervention* is the best source for information on political maneuverings in that city during 1918-19; the volumes of *Foreign Relations* also give considerable detail; and Ironside makes many comments. Francis, as well as well as all of those just mentioned, tells the story of the kidnaping of the government ministers. For the tangle involving Francis, the State Department, and Colonel Stewart, *Foreign Relations*, 1918 is the essential source. The typed transcription of Lansing's message to Francis, September 26, is found in the headquarters records of the 339th Infantry, now at the Archives.

NOTES: *Chapter 4*
For all of the combat descriptions, Moore & Mead have been heavily relied on. In this connection it should be noted that they were in close contact with other members of the 339th when they compiled their volume, and drew upon eyewitness accounts and diaries furnished by many. The military intelligence report describing Stewart's behavior on the railroad front is printed in Strakhovsky's *Intervention*. Dorothea York gives the most detailed account of the activities of Company A throughout the campaign. Naval intelligence reports in the Archives give the clues for straightening out the comedy of errors involving Company K and the *Olympia* landing party early in September. Operational records of the 339th, also in the Archives, supplement with many details the drive for the Trans-Siberian at the end of September.

NOTES: *Chapter 5*
Ironside's biographical background is derived from various articles on him which appeared in 1939-40, when he was Chief of the Imperial General Staff: see the *Reader's Guide to Periodical Literature*. The account of his appointment as commander in chief for the North Russia expedition is based largely on his own memoirs. So also the account of his first weeks in North Russia, with supplemental information from the Archives. Chaikovksky's difficulties with General Poole are described in detail by Strakhovsky (*Intervention*); the Torcom episode comes from Noulens and Ironside. The recalcitrance of the 1st Archangel Regiment at the end of October is reported in *Foreign Relations, 1918*, as well as by Ironside and by Strakhovsky. Noulens gives a somewhat contradictory account.

NOTES: *Chapter 6*
Stewart's cablegram to the War Department is in the Archives. DeWitt Clinton Poole's Thanksgiving address is taken from *Foreign Relations, 1918*; also the messages of the American and British governments about the effect of the armistice on the troops in North Russia. The general situation of the civil war in Russia in December, 1918, is of course described by many writers; Stewart's *The White*

Armies of Russia is one useful source. Ironside's telegram on Soviet morale is on record in the Archives. The description of the Russian mutiny on December 11 is based principally on 339th Infantry records in the Archives. Ironside, Strakhovsky (*Intervention*), and Moore & Mead also describe it. Strakhovsky insists that no American troops took part in the incident, and scoffs at Moore & Mead for saying that they did; but the official records bear out Moore & Mead. Ironside says that the mutinous leaders were not shot, but were allowed to cross the Bolshevik lines and go to their homes. This is contradicted by the other accounts, as well as by a cablegram from DeWitt Clinton Poole to the State Department, printed in *Foreign Relations, 1918*. Ironside's Christmas trip is described in his own book; Colonel Stewart's in Moore & Mead, and in intelligence reports now in the Archives. Boyd's remarks are quoted by Moore & Mead. The account of the battle of Kodish, and its accompanying events on the railroad, is based on Ironside, Moore & Mead, and Archives documents. Incidentally, the one-sided casualty rates at Kodish (as well as in nearly all the fighting in which Americans took part) are surprising even after allowance has been made for superior American equipment, training, morale, and luck, and for the exaggeration that so often inflates battle statistics. In the whole campaign, American losses were 144 killed in action or dead from wounds, with 305 others wounded. Approximately 100 others died by accident or from disease; and the rate of non-combat casualties (i.e., men taken out of action by frostbite or sickness) was high. But Soviet losses, conservatively estimated, must have been in the thousands.

NOTES: *Chapter 7*

Since this chapter consists of a melange of impressions, rather than straight narrative, its sources are manifold and overlapping. Every book devoted specifically to the campaign which appears in the bibliography was drawn upon; also much miscellaneous material in the Archives, a file of the American soldiers' paper, *The Sentinel*, and conversations with veterans of the campaign. Albertson's book is useful with regard to doughboy-peasant and doughboy-Tommy relations. Sergeant Lietzell's account of his capture is given in Moore, *Company 'M'*; parts of it are also in Moore & Mead.

NOTES: *Chapter* 8 *and* 9

Life in Shenkursk is sketched in some detail by Dorothea York; also by Steele in *Snow Trenches* (a novel). The fate of Lieutenant Cuff is told by Moore & Mead, and by Costello. Ironside recounts his January journey to Shenkursk. Details of the attack at Nijni Gora, and the subsequent retreat, are compiled from York, Moore & Mead, the Archives, and conversations with Mr. Mead and Mr. Hugh McPhail. Sharman specifies the actions of the Canadian field artillery during these episodes.

NOTES: *Chapter* 10

Ironside relates his visit to the Archangel prison, and implies that it occurred in the fall; a naval intelligence report in the Archives suggests that it was several months later. Naval intelligence also describes the activities of "Dolina." The impressions of Marushevsky and Miller are gained from Ironside and Strakhovsky (*Intervention*). Currency problems are outlined by Ironside, Moore & Mead, and in naval as well as military intelligence reports in the Archives. The statement that in mid-winter the Americans constituted a majority of the Allied forces on the combat fronts is borne out by strength reports, in the Archives, issued from both British and American headquarters. In January, 1919, for example, 4,200 Americans were reported at the front, as compared to 3,000 British (including Canadians). In contrast to this, there were nearly 3,000 British in and about Archangel, as compared to 900 Americans. Little can be found in British accounts of the campaign to indicate that this was the situation: one picks up the impression, instead, that the Americans were merely an adjunct to the British forces. At the same time, Ironside makes a point of praising the good service rendered by his American troops, unlike some British sources. The official British naval history of the campaign, for instance, observes that since the American force "was composed almost entirely of untrained troops," it was "of little value." It should be added that Canadian accounts are fair to the Americans.

Costello relates the incident of the three lieutenants who reported to Colonel Stewart. DeWitt Clinton Poole's comments on the military situation are printed in Foreign Relations, 1919. Ironside tells the details of his sleigh journeys in his memoirs.

NOTES: Chapter 11

Francis' curious telegram reporting his invitation to the King's banquet is in the Archives; Lloyd George's description of the affair is in Memoirs of the Peace Conference, while Francis gives his impressions in Russia from the American Embassy. Transcripts of the peace-conference conversations dealing with Russia are printed in Foreign Relations, 1919. Strakhovsky (Intervention) reports Miller's reply to the Prinkipo proposal, as well as Chiakovsky's reaction. The Soviet reply is in the Foreign Relations. Churchill gives a dramatic version of his encounter with Wilson in The Aftermath; this is paralleled by a transcript of their statements printed in Foreign Relations. The latter volume also prints a telegram conveying to Wilson the reply of the Secretary of War to an inquiry evidently made by the President about the fate of the 339th Infantry. Wilson's telegram expressing dismay at Churchill's "Russian suggestion" is in Foreign Relations; Francis tells of Wilson's visit to him on the George Washington. The reception at Archangel of the President's decision to withdraw the 339th is reported in The American Sentinel. Lloyd George's comment on Churchill is found in Memoirs of the Peace Conference.

NOTES: Chapter 12

"Facts and Questions Concerning the NREF" is on file with 339th Headquarters records in the Archives; also the sanitary officer's report. Cudahy narrates the episode at Toulgas on March 1; the fate of Corporal Prince is told by Moore & Mead. The story of Sergeant Macalla's journey with the body of his comrade is based on an article by Theodore Delavigne in the Detroit Free Press, November 17, 1929; Mr. Macalla has checked its accuracy. Maynard tells of preparations for the Yorkshires' march from Murmansk to Archangel; Shackleton's visit to the city is reported in The American Sentinel. Ironside describes the British mutiny of February 26; also that of the French in March. The fullest account of the difficulty in Company M is given by Moore

& Mead. Senator Townsend's worries about North Russia are reported in a contemporary issue of *The Literary Digest*; La Guadia's reaction in the *New York Times*. The Coates volume gives details of the British effort to organize a "relief" force; Churchill also describes it. Ironside quotes the morale message sent by the War office. York, Moore & Mead, and Sharman recount the Soviet offensive in March on the Vaga. Mr. Mead and Mr. McPhail have added personal reminiscences. The speculation as to Soviet strategy with respect to the Allied force in North Russia is my own. Moore & Mead, Ironside, and material in the Archives supply the facts for the account of the battle at Bolshie Ozerki. Spring operations on the Vaga are described by Moore & Mead, Cudahy, and Sharman; supplementary details are drawn from the Archives. General Richardson's speech to the 339th is recorded in Moore & Mead; other details about Archangel in May are from Ironside and Strakhovsky (*Intervention*), and from Archives records. The quotation at the end of the chapter is from Moore & Mead.

NOTES: *Chapter 13*
Ironside and Sharman tell of the Russian mutiny on April 25. Miller's difficulties with Bolshevik citizens are covered by Strakhovsky (*Intervention*); Albertson supplies the comment comparing Miller's government to "the old regime." Ironside's optimistic plans for the summer are reported in *Foreign Relations, 1919*. The Sherwood-Kelly episode is worked out from Ironside and the Coates volume; Ironside does not identify the officer involved, but it clearly was Sherwood-Kelly. Soutar, Strakhovsky, and Ironside cover the July mutinies. Kolchak's fortunes are described by Coates, Stewart, Dupuy, *et al.* Ironside is the source for the account of summer military operations; results of these are also reported in *Foreign Relations*. The appeal from the citizens of Archangel to President Wilson is printed in the latter volume; Churchill mentions the visit of their committee to see him in London. Ironside gives a detailed story of his last twenty-four hours in Archangel; Strakhovsky supplies the comment of the Russian colonel after the British left, as well as a rather full account of the remaining months of anti-Bolshevik resistance.

NOTES: *Chapter 14*

What happened to Ironside "afterward" is learned from his own memoirs, various articles in periodicals, a few brief passages in Churchill's *Their Finest Hour* (Boston, 1949), and obituaries in the London *Times* and *New York Times*. Information about other figures in the North Russia story comes from such ordinary sources as *Who's Who* and *Current Biography*. Cudahy's experience as U.S. ambassador to Poland and later to Belgium can be gleaned from the appropriate issues of *Time*; also from 1940 and 1941 issues of *Life*. Information about Joel R. Moore and Harry H. Mead comes from Mr. Mead. Mr. Donald Shand supplied data on the Polar Bear Association. The story of the expedition to recover bodies in North Russia is based on interviews with participants, including Colonel Bettelheim, Mr. Michael Macalla, and Mr. Walter Dundon; also on material supplied by the office of the Quartermaster General, Department of the Army. Khruschev's remarks on the Allied invasion were reported by the *New York Times*, September 20, 1959. Mr. Kennan's comment on the nature of American action in North Russia is from his article in the January, 1959, *Atlantic*. Finally, Churchill's view on the strangling of Bolshevism is from a speech made in the House of Commons on May 11, 1953, drawn to my attention by Mr. Gerald Kloss of the Milwaukee *Journal*.

Bibliography

Albertson, Ralph. *Fighting Without a War*. New York, 1920.
The American Sentinel (newspaper). Archangel, December, 1918-May, 1919.
Bailey, Thomas A. *America Faces Russia*. Cornell University Press, 1950.
Browder, Robert. *The Origins of Soviet-American Diplomacy*. Princeton University Press, 1953.
Bunyan, James. *Intervention, Civil War, and Communism in Russia: Documents and Materials*. Baltimore, 1936.
A Chronicler (John Cudahy). *Archangel: The American War with Russia*. Chicago, 1924.
Churchill, Winston S. *The Aftermath: The World Crisis, 1918-1928*. New York, 1929.
Coates, W. P. and Zelda K. *Armed Intervention in Russia, 1918-1922*. London, 1935.
Coote, Colin R., ed. *A Churchill Reader*. Boston, 1954.
Costello, Harry J. *Why Did We Go to Russia?* Detroit, 1920.
Cumming, C. K., and Pettit, Walter W. *Russian-American Relations, March, 1917-March, 1920: Documents and Papers*.
Dupuy, R. Ernest. *Perish by the Sword*, Harrisburg, 1939.
Fischer, Louis. *The Soviets in World Affairs*. 2 vols. Princeton University Press, 1951.
Francis, David R. *Russia from the American Embassy*. New York, 1921.
Graves, William S. *America's Siberian Adventure, 1918-1920*. New York, 1931.
Great Britain, Army. *The Evacuation of North Russia, 1919*. London, 1920.
Great Britain, Navy. *A History of the White Sea Station, 1914-1919*. London, 1921.
Ironside, William Edmund (Lord Ironside). *Archangel, 1918-19*. London, 1953.

Kennan, George F. *Soviet-American Relations, 1917-1920: Vol. I, Russian Leaves the War.* Princeton University Press, 1956.

Kennan, George F. *Soviet-American Relations, 1917-1920: Vol. II, The Decision to Intervene.* Princeton University Press, 1958.

Liddell Hart, B. H., ed. *The Red Army.* New York, 1956.

Lloyd George, David. *Memoirs of the Peace Conference.* 2 vols. Yale University Press, 1939.

McEntee, Girard L. *Military History of the World War.* New York, 1937.

Maynard, C. *The Murmansk Venure.* London, 1928.

Moore, Joel R.; Mead, Harry H.; and Jahns, Lewis E. *The History of the American Expedition Fighting the Bolsheviki.* Detroit, 1920.

Moore, Joel R. *Company 'M,' 339th Infantry in North Russia, 1918-1919.* Jackson, Michigan, n.d.

National Archives of the United States (documents). Naval Branch World War I Branch.

Noulens, Joseph. *Mon Ambassade en Russie Sovietique, 1917-1919.* 2 vols. Paris, 1933.

Schuman, Frederick L. *American Policy Toward Russia Since 1917.* New York, 1928.

Sharman, C. H. L., ed. *N.R.E.F., 16th Brigade C.F.A. in North Russia, September 1918 to June 1919.* Toronto, n.d.

Soutar, Andrew. *With Ironside in North Russia.* London, 1940.

Steele, Dan. *Snow Trenches.* Chicago, 1931.

Stewart, George. *The White Armies of Russia.* New York, 1933.

Strakhovsky, Leonid I. *Intervention at Archangel.* Princeton University Press, 1944.

Strakhovsky, Leonid I. *The Origins of American Intervention in North Russia (1918).* Princeton University Press, 1937.

Terpenning, Walter A. *To Russia and Return.* Evansville, Indiana, n.d.

U.S. Department of State. *Papers Relating to the Foreign Relations of the United States: 1918, Russia.* 3 vols. Washington, D.C., 1931; 1932.

U.S. Department of State. *Papers Relating to the Foreign Relations of the United States: 1919, Russia.* Washington, D.C., 1937.

Unterberger, Betty Miller. *America's Siberian Expedition 1918-1920.* Duke University Press, 1956.

Warth, Robert D. *The Allies and the Russian Revolution.* Duke University Press, 1954.

Welter, G. *La Guerre Civile en Russie, 1918-1920.* Paris, 1936.

York, Dorothea. *The Romance of Company 'A.'* Detroit, 1923.

For sales, editorial information, subsidiary rights information or a
catalog, please write or phone or e-mail
IBOOKS
Manhanset House
Shelter Island Hts., New York 11965,
1-800-68-BRICK Tel: 212-427-7139

ibooksinc.com
email: bricktower@aol.com

www.Ingram.com

For sales in the UK and Europe please contact our distributor,
Gazelle Book Services
White Cross Mills
Lancaster, LA1 4XS,
UK Tel: (01524) 68765 Fax: (01524) 63232 email:
jacky@gazellebooks.co.uk

* 9 7 8 1 5 9 6 8 7 4 3 0 5 *